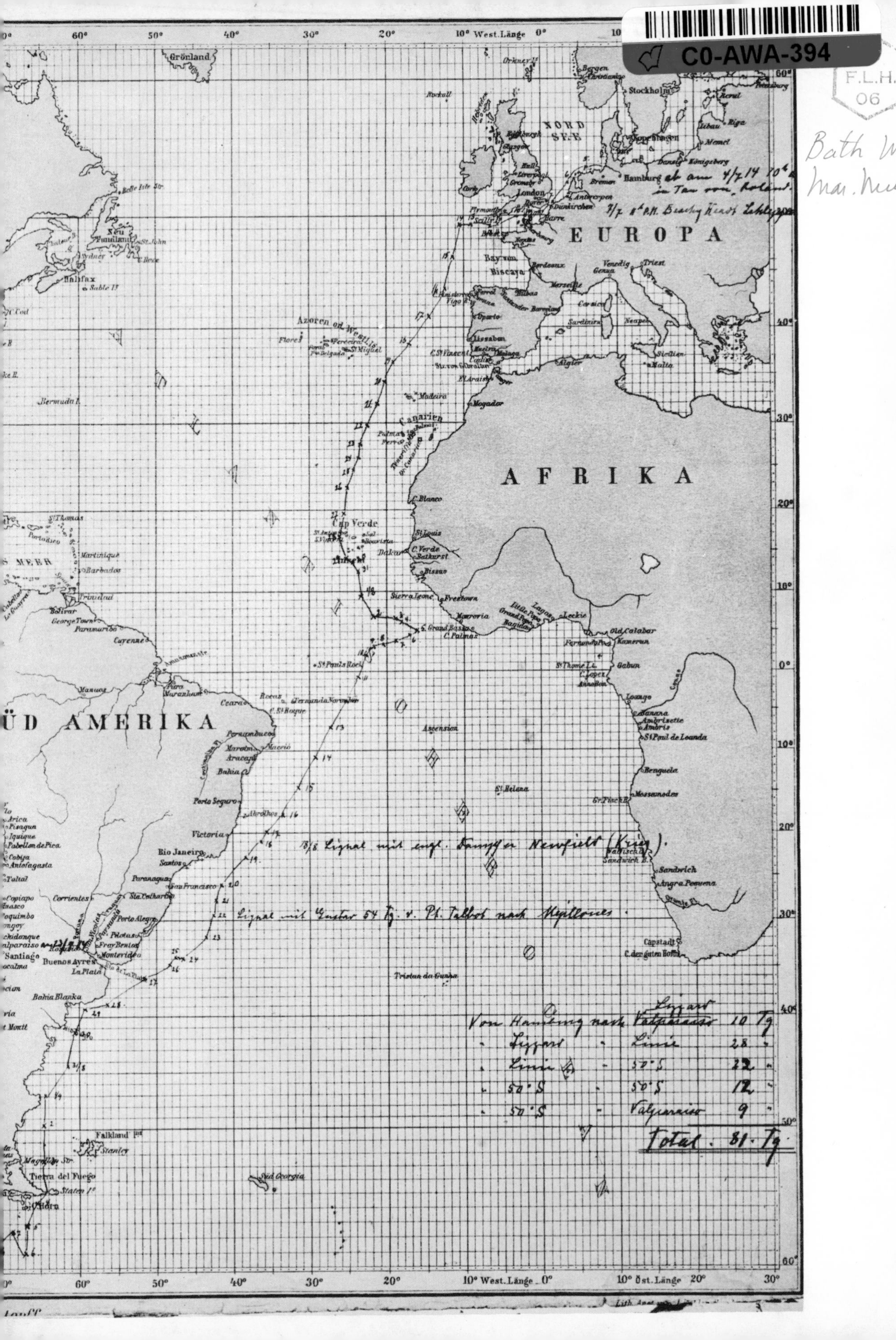
Grönland
NORD SEE
Stockholm
Hamburg
London
EUROPA
Bay von Biscaya
Azoren od. Westlie
Madeira
Canarien
AFRIKA
Cap Verde
Sierra Leone
St. Pauls Rock
Ascension
St. Helena
SÜD AMERIKA
Pernambuco
Bahia
Rio Janeiro
Buenos Ayres
Montevideo
Falkland Ins.
Tierra del Fuego
Süd Georgia
Tristan da Cunha
Capstadt
10° West. Länge 0°
10° Öst. Länge
18/8 Signal mit engl. Dampfer Newfield (Krieg).
Signal mit Gustav 54 Tg. v. Pt. Talbot nach Mejillones
Von Hamburg nach Lizzard 10 Tg.
Lizzard – Linie 28
Linie – 50° S 22
50° S – 50° S 12
50° S – Valparaiso 9
Total. 81 Tg.

F L

J. F. COLTON & CO.

HISTORICAL SERIES

1937

LAST OF THE SQUARE-RIGGED SHIPS

The Descriptions And Histories Of More Than 300 Of The World's Square-Rigged Sailing Vessels Surviving Into 1937 Including Those Now Afloat. (Seventy-four illustrations)

J. Ferrell COLTON

1954

WINDJAMMERS SIGNIFICANT

The Story Of Two Of The Finest Square-Rigged Sailing Vessels Ever Built. (One-hundred-eighty-eight illustrations and nineteen plans)

J. Ferrell COLTON

1957

F L : A CENTURY AND A QUARTER OF REEDEREI F. LAEISZ

Owners Of The "Flying P" Nitrate Clippers. (Eighty Illustrations)

Dr. H. C. Paul ROHRBACH
Captain J. Hermann PIENING
Captain A. E. (Fred) SCHMIDT

1958

CITIES THAT PASSED IN THE NIGHT

History Of Many Of The Ghost Towns Of The North American South-West. (Illustrated)

Philip JOHNSTON

(F. LAEISZ)

The Laeisz Memorial

FL

A CENTURY AND A QUARTER OF REEDEREI F. LAEISZ

(Owners Of The "Flying P" Nitrate Clippers)

By

Dr. H. C. Paul ROHRBACH
(Father-In-Law of Director Willi GANSSAUGE)

In Co-Operation With

Captain J. Hermann PIENING
(Marine Superintendent)

And

Captain A. E. (Fred) SCHMIDT
(Marine Historian)

Translated From The Hans Dulk German Edition By

Dr. Antoinette G. SMITH
(Editor, J. F. COLTON & CO.)

United States Of America Edition Edited By

J. Ferrell COLTON
(Director, J. F. COLTON & CO.)

An Account Of

The Founding And History Of Reederei F. Laeisz, A Pioneer German Mercantile Firm Which Has Been At The Forefront Of International Insurance, Export-Import, And Shipping Throughout The 19th And Much Of The 20th Centuries.

And

The Afrikanische Frucht Cie A. G.

Illustrated With 80 Photographs

J. F. COLTON & CO.
Flagstaff
1957

LITHOPRINTED IN THE UNITED STATES OF AMERICA BY
CUSHING - MALLOY, INC., ANN ARBOR, MICHIGAN, 1957

This, The United States Of America Edition Of "F L", Is Dedicated To:

The Men And Women Of

REEDEREI F. LAESIZ

1825 - 1956

FOREWORD

Throughout the World, the number of commercial houses bearing their original names and still controlled by the descendants of their founders after the passage of more than a century and a quarter is small indeed. Since it is axiomatic that the present is the product of the past and the future is the sum of both, it is self-evident that an account of such a firm, especially one that has played an important part in global commerce despite the vicissitudes of this period of the earth's history, should be of universal interest and value. At the least, such an account must provide an interesting commentary on the activities of the principals themselves. At the most, it should provide a more definite understanding of the underlying conditions that made it possible for an enterprise to function successfully, within the framework of its times, over so long a period.

Reederei F. Laeisz of Hamburg, Germany, is the subject of this book. Through the years, I have often touched on the periphery of this company's activities, had correspondence with certain of its principals, knew a number of its personnel, and sailed on several vessels once owned by them. I early recognized the important niche they occupied in World affairs and had planned to write their history myself.

It can be imagined, then, with what interest I read, in May of 1950, that Dr. H. C. Paul Rohrbach, father-in-law of the firm's Director Herr Willi Ganssauge; Captain J. Hermann Piening, its Marine Superintendent; and Captain A. E. (Fred) Schmidt, one of Germany's foremost marine historians, were collaborating on such a history. This was no disappointment to me, as might be expected, but, rather, a pleasant and unexpected surprise. Fred, with unnumbered articles and more than 8 books to his credit; Captain Piening, with more than 45 years service, mostly as officer and Master in F L vessels; and Dr. Rohrbach, student long acquainted with the inner workings, are far more equipped to undertake a project of this magnitude than is possible for an English-speaking North American based 5,000 miles from the home office.

"F L : The History Of A Shipping Firm" is the result of their work. Had they written their book prior to World War II, it would have been an even better production. It was, however, their task to piece together this story out of what records remained among the ashes and rubble of a Hamburg smashed by the terrible bombings of those unfortunate years. In consideration of this fact, the readers will agree, I am sure, that they have done a magnificent job.

It is difficult to know just how much detail to put into such a book, as it is written for those connected with the Firm, students of business, historians, and the lay public. This was a problem of the authors and has been a problem of those responsible for producing an English-language edition from Hans Dulk's fine German publication.

It so happened that I possessed a considerable amount of information and photographs, collected from all over the World, and not now available in Hamburg. This material, I felt, should be included in the work. A problem was, how to achieve this without, in any way, altering the text of the original authors. The solution proved to be a preface giving an outline of the House and including certain statistics useful to students of business and economy, footnotes enlarging upon and explaining certain facts, the addition of detail to existing schedules, inclusion of more schedules, and expansion of the appendix. This, I think, has been accomplished with a minimum of duplication of material already covered in the text. The paucity of photographic material now existing in Germany is evident in those illustrations that the authors were able to obtain for the German edition. Fortunately, since the publication of Hans Dulk's handsome work, Captain Piening was able to locate a number of useful photographs and, from among my extensive collection of pre-World Wars I and II pictures covering Laeisz activities, we were able to multiply several times the number of illustrations in the German edition. The inclusion of these should assist the reader in achieving a better idea of many matters spoken of in the text.

"F L : A Century And A Quarter Of Reederei F. Laeisz" is the United States of America edition of the tale of a business house conducted over a period of 131 years by 4 successive generations of 1 family. It is an account of its ups and downs, successes and failures, in the face of world competition, recurrent economic slumps, and wars. It is an account of an undertaking that, 3 times, has been close to disaster, but which, in the end, has survived to make a not inconsiderable contribution to present day economy. The 3 authors consulted many published and unpublished works and delved into numerous archives in their search for information. Publisher Hans Dulk of Hamburg, producer of so many excellent works, first brought this valuable history before the public. Together, we trust that you, the reader, will find the work of interest and value.

J. Ferrell COLTON
DIRECTOR
J. F. COLTON & CO.

30, June, 1956

PREFACE

The movements, under the managing ownership of Messrs. Zerssen & Co. of Hamburg, Germany, of the auxiliary steel 4-masted barques PAMIR and PASSAT during the past 18 months have been noted in the principal newspapers of the World largely because these 3,000 gross ton square-rigged sailing vessels are 2 of the 9 survivors of their rig afloat and are among the few commercial deep-water wind-propelled vessels in existence. To many readers, of varying nationalities throughout the Globe, their departures from and arrivals in European and Eastern South American ports have stirred long-quiescent memories of sailormen, such as Robert Hilgendorf, dead these 19 years; of the 3-island multi-masted sail carriers, often called "The Nitrate Clippers", which, in the mighty POTOSI and the giant PREUSSEN, brought wind-driven craft to the zenith of their development; and of the 131 year history of Reederei F. Laeisz, more familiarly known as "The Flying P Line", whose flag they flew.

In far away Northern Arizona, in the United States Of America, my thoughts turned back to "Flying P" sailers I had known. There, in retrospect, was De-Cloux's big PARMA at anchor in a barren roadstead in South Australia loading bagged wheat consigned to United Kingdom millers, by the windjammer tract, more than half the World away; the huge PASSAT, then Erikson's and laden scupper deep, running heavily under fore sail and 6 topsails before the roaring westerlies in the region of Cape Horn; her consort, PAMIR, a breath-taking vision of loveliness ghosting, under a cloud of canvas, into a mirror-like anchorage in Queenstown Bay; that sea-worn ocean tramp, barque PENANG from Finland, discharging dusty guano from the desolate Seychelles Islands in a cool New Zealand port: and the graceful POMMERN resting quietly among the pines, by her owner's house, in the still waters of the West Harbor hard by the northern town of Mariehamn. I thought of the West Coast of South America and nitrates, of the forested Baltic shore-line and its timber, of Indian Ocean islands and their acrid guano, of South Australia and golden grain, of New Caledonia and nickel ore, and of half a hundred ports of call that knew the 20th Century wind ship. Visions, too, came to me of friends who had sailed in and commanded these former Laeisz sailers in a day when they were younger and the red F L on white field houseflag had snapped proudly from their main trucks. There were Laeisz Captains: driving Robert Clauss who took PRIWALL from Hamburg to Port Victoria in 67 days in 1933; crack Robert Karl Miethe who sailed POTOSI over her last miles for his firm; J. Hermann Piening, man of many parts, who drove PADUA on passages that have not been equaled since World War I; bearded Hans J. Rohwer of PASSAT who had the misfortune to be run down by the steamer BRITISH GOVERNOR; and patient Johannes Thomas Wendler who, first, took that fine barque to sea. These vessels were the fittest of an economic age that bred great craft. Their requirements made a way of life that bred great men.

To Erich Ferdinand Laeisz, fourth head of the venerable Hamburg firm bearing his name; to the other partners; to Captain Piening, now Marine Superintendent; and to their staff, news of PAMIR'S and PASSAT'S wanderings forth and back across the Atlantics meant much more. These vessels had been designed by them in 1903 and 1909, built for them by Blohm & Voss in 1905 and 1911, owned by them from 1905 and 1911 to 1921, and, again, from 1924 and 1922 to 1931 and 1932. Moreover, PAMIR had been the 65th and PASSAT the 72nd of 83 sailing vessels owned by their firm in over 131 years of business, the 41st and 44th of 47 especially built for the company, and two of the 6 4-masted barques they had purchased and the 11 they had caused to be constructed.

The firm's appellation, Reederei F. Laeisz, is a name to conjure with. A pioneer German mercantile firm, whose office building, the Laeisz House, is located at No. 1 on the Trostbrücke, they have been leaders in Hamburg business and civic affairs and at the forefront of international insurance, export-import, and shipping throughout the 19th and much of the 20th Centuries. Consequent to the establishment of trade relations with South America in 1825, new trade routes were developed and spheres of business widened until the Company's operations encircled the Globe on a scale surpassed by few, if any, of the great houses of commerce anywhere. Likewise, they built up old trades and, for a time, the bulk of soda-nitrate leaving Chilean ports for European consumption was nearly a Laeisz monopoly. In addition to their own underwriting, they have assisted in the establishment of more than 8 insurance companies. Branch trading houses were established in excess of a dozen countries. They have been co-founders and/or partners in the founding of 2 fruit companies, at least 15 shipping concerns, and 2 whaling enterprises. To date, they have owned outright 88 vessels and had shares in 11 more. They were responsible, not only for the greatest sailing vessels, but employed the largest modern fleet of such vessels to exist. Until 1914 they employed sailing vessels exclusively, the last quarter of a century of this operation being a period in which most shipowners were switching to steam, and continued to employ them to 1946. Between 1902 and 1926, they brought man's use of the wind as a means of propulsion to its peak with the launch of the 3,000 gross ton steel 4-masted barques PANGANI, PETSCHILI, PAMIR, PEKING, PASSAT, PRIWALL, POLA, and PADUA. They successfully experimented with the two giantesses, the 5-masted barque POTOSI of 1895 and the 5-masted ship PREUSSEN of 1902 (the only one of her kind ever built). They instituted and carried on meteorological and management studies which, for the first time, brought reliability to sailing vessel operation. These factors, together with hand-picked crews commanded by the finest Masters available made an unbeatable combination. Of the 148 odd men who have commanded Laeisz flyers since 1839, the name of Robert Hilgendorf stands out. Nonetheless, there are many other outstanding commanders on the list, and the names of such as Robert Clauss, H. A. Denhardt, J. Frömcke, M. Grapow, Hauth, M. Jurgen, H. Jürss, Robert K. Miethe, Hinrich Nissen, Boye R. Petersen, J. Hermann Piening, and J. Steincke will be remembered long after the last man of sail is gone.

The firm was founded, grew, and flourished during one of the most unsettled periods of the World's history. It began in the days when the disunited states of the geographical area we now know as Germany were little interested in the half-explored World beyond their boundaries and what maritime international trade existed was carried on by the ancient seaports dotting the southern fringe of the Baltic Sea and the western river cities of Bremen on the Weser and Hamburg on the Elbe. The latter had been taking an increasing part in Atlantic trade as the 18th Century wore on, although exports from these communities consisted largely of agrarian products carried in vessels which flew the numerous flags of the Schmalkaldic League.

Recovery from dislocations and devastations of the 25 year period embracing the Napoleonic Wars was extremely slow, but, by 1825, industrial activity was on the increase and Germans were beginning to turn their attention to overseas trade and doing it with typical Teutonic thoroughness. German business houses were appearing along the east and west coasts of Africa, in China, in Japan, in Central America, on both sides of South America, and among the far flung islands of the South Seas. The founder, Herr Ferdinand B. Laeisz, was quick to pioneer, to venture in many unrelated lines, and to take advantage of the increased employment opening to German shipping in this period.

It is known that he had shares in various vessels before 1839, and it was, therefore, an entirely natural succession of events that led to his financing the construction of a vessel for his own account. In 1839, he went to Jacob Meyer in Lübeck who built for him the 220 gross ton brig CARL. Under Captain J. J. Visser, she laded 288 tons of general cargo, including a consignment of hemp rope and silk hats, at Lübeck for the Brazilian port of Pernambuco and followed this with a similar cargo, out around Cape Horn to Guayaquil in Ecuador. Flying the free-city Hamburg ensign from her spanker gaff and the, then, unfamiliar "F L" houseflag at the main truck, she sailed 7 years for this first Laeisz before being sold, in 1847, to A. J. Schön of Hamburg. Evidence of her original owner's shrewdness in regard to the quality and upkeep of vessels is the fact that she was re-sold to Gustav John Sörensen of Laurvig in March of 1869 and was still in that owner's possession in 1880 at the advanced age, for a wooden vessel, of 41 years.

The next 8 years, during which the firm was without a vessel of its own, were ones of political unrest in Germany and study, travel, and expansion on the part of the Principal. By 1856 it had become evident, as our own countrymen in New England well knew, that these were the days when well managed, competently manned, sound vessels could and did found fortunes. The World and its riches belonged to the enterprising opportunist with the ability and the versatility to make the best of what he found. So was purchased the 195 gross ton wood schooner SOPHIE & FRIEDERICKE, the only schooner ever to be owned by Laeisz, which had been built in Stettin in 1834. For the succeeding 90 years, the House of Laeisz was never without a vessel.

Upon this basis, was built the enterprise that not even the depression of 1857, the uncertainties of the 1864-1866 Preussen War, the 1870 Franco-Preussen War, or the crippling blows dealt by World Wars I and II and their aftermaths could stop. Soon the Laeisz schooner, its brigs, and its barques were dropping into odd ports from Habana to Buenos Aires, from Portland to Valparaiso, from Vladivostock to Singapore, from Suva to Sydney, from Bombay to Batavia, and from Mombasa to Sierra Leone.

Under the "F L" flag, as elsewhere, such vessels often carried their owner's merchandise to be traded on board or ashore as circumstances dictated. It was, at first, not so much the common practice to carry freights for others. Thus, often with a supercargo on board to do the actual trading, these traveling warehouses laded general cargoes outwards from Hamburg, picked up coastal cargoes along the way, and came homewards deep with the produce of half-a-dozen lands. Then, more so than now, much depended on the individual masters, and to the 35 men, ranging from F. Wenzel of SOPHIE & FRIEDERICKE to H. F. M. Schröder of the PYRMONT, Laeisz owed a great deal of his early success at sea.

The World-wide scope of Laeisz operations during the first three-quarters of a century of the firm's existence is clearly delineated in the names of COSTA RICA, INDIA, PACIFIC, PANAMA, PATRIA, PERU, PERSIA, and REPUBLIC. While bespeaking the areas in which the House had business connections, the sale of SCHILLER to purchasers in Batavia, Java, in 1859; the loss of REPUBLIC, under Captain N. Lottge, and PERU, under T. Truelsen, in the China Sea in 1865 and 1870 respectively; the losses of CAROLINA, Captain P. M. Thomsen,

PAVIAN, Captain H. F. M. Schröder, and HENRIETTE BEHN, Captain J. Piening,[1] on the West Coast of Mexico in 1881, 1883, and 1885; and the abandoning of PARSIFAL, under Captain Robert Hilgendorf, off Cape Horn in 1886, emphasize them. Laeisz vessels now sailed every major sea, Laeisz masters were rapidly acquiring a varied knowledge of meteorology and world trade, and the staff in Hamburg had achieved a degree of global economic knowledge surpassed by few.

To 1887, the year of the death of Founder Ferdinand Laeisz, the firm had been in the ship-owning business a total of 39 years. Their maritime operations had begun half-a-dozen years before the opening of the so-called extreme clipper era in 1845 which had had its inception in the United States and Britain over the growing demand for more rapid delivery of tea from China, had continued under the stimulation of the discovery of gold in California in 1848 and Australia in 1850, and had ended with the building of the last extreme clipper ship in 1859. Laeisz and his fellow countrymen, being occupied elsewhere, paid little heed to the mad rush in search of that elusive mineral which fascinated Americans and British of the time. In fact, his sale of CARL preceded the California strike by two years and he did not acquire another vessel until a year before this factor ceased to profit sailing vessel operators.

That, however, he was aware of and interested in the development of the extreme clipper as it became steadily larger and sharper under the twin pressures of competition and public opinion is indicated by a journey he undertook to the United States in 1852. Sailing from Liverpool, England, on the S. S. NIAGARA, he was in East Boston, Massachusetts, to witness the launch of Donald McKay's great extreme clipper, the wood 4-masted barque GREAT REPUBLIC, on 3, October, 1853. Having seen the largest merchant vessel ever constructed in the United States slide down the ways and talked with her designer, he had, then, returned to Bremen on the S. S. WASHINGTON. In fact this, coupled with studies of other American and British vessels, unquestionably influenced the design of the 4 brigs, 14 barques, and 1 ship which were especially built for him prior to 1882, the date which marked the end of construction of small carriers. Tradition and a few existing records indicate that from PUDEL of 1856 to PARNASS of 1878, all were fast and handy vessels for the time. It can be assumed, as it is borne out, that the 18 bought units from ADOLPH of 1854 to PAVIAN of 1864 were well chosen, likewise.

A century and a quarter ago, merchant sailing vessels of 400 to 500 gross tons were considered large, although vessels of much greater size were occasionaly built. By 1860, the bulk of first class deepwatermen coming down the ways was in excess of 1,000 tons. Thus, the relative size and rig of the pre-1882 fleet is noteworthy as it reflects the type and scope of the Company's trading operations. In common with other China packets, coffee traders, fruiters, and Indiamen, Laeisz craft remained relatively small as the mean of 479 gross tons demonstrates. PUDEL, on dimensions 141.1/28.7/16.6 typifies this early fleet. With a net tonnage of 441, she was capable of lifting 582 deadweight tons.

In the general period marked by the outbreak of the war between the North American states in 1861, came wide-spread political, technological, and industrial developments whose resulting commercial changes had far reaching effects on ocean commerce everywhere. United States domination of World trade under sail came to an abrupt end and was replaced by the rising star of British shipping. Composite construction for deepwater sailing vessels was already common-place and, by this date, more than 30% of Great Britain's ocean going tonnage was being built of iron. The substitution of steel for iron was still to come

[1]Cousin of Capt. J. Hermann Piening.

in the decade between 1870 and 1880. The inexorable increase of faster vessels, both sail and steam, coupled with new demands for services and goods made for changed opportunities.

Throughout the 1860's father Ferdinand and son Carl Heinrich, who had joined the firm in 1852, had been feeling out the copper-ore, guano, and soda-nitrate business as it existed along the Southwest coast of South America. Then, copper-ore was being moved in large quantities to South Wales in Britain in the holds of a considerable fleet of sturdy wooden sailing vessels, which under the British flag, had been rounding Cape Horn for years. A wealth of guano, in ever-decreasing quantities, was being loaded in the exposed roadsteads of the Chinchas and Lobos Islands in sailing vessels of every nationality. Nitrates from the great salt desert of Tarapaca in Chile were being shipped to the United Kingdom and Europe largely in British ships of sail. Yet, the earning of a freight from Peru or Chile was a protracted affair entailing thousands of miles of sailing, at least one doubling of "Cape Stiff", and months in open roadsteads exposed to the time-consuming ways of the local inhabitants, desert heat, insects, earthquakes, tidal waves, and the dreaded Norther. In short, it was a trade nobody wanted. Shipowners of all nationalities considered the West Coast trade fit only for second-class vessels and avoided the place altogether if they could.

Nevertheless, it was becoming obvious that all three of these commodities, the fertilizers, the ore, and the saltpeter, were becoming very necessary to the economy of the civilized World. Taking the long view, it appeared that the ore business was being adequately handled by the copper-ore men. On the other hand, it seemed unlikely that current generations of sea-birds could maintain the ancient deposits of droppings and, thus, the guano trade must end when the last sack was dug out. Nitrates were a different matter, however, Hamburg was the port of entry and the depot for storage and distribution of this chemical, not only to Germany itself, but, also, deep into Europe and much of Scandinavia. There were plenty of outward cargoes for German and native firms in Mexico, Central America, Ecuador, Peru, and Chile. Sensing that the carriage of this commodity could be made a lucrative thing for many years to come if the neglected trade were properly organized and the right class of tonnage employed, the Laeiszes purchased the 6 Stülcken-built Bahr barques in 1867. Ranging in size from 421 gross tons to 457 gross tons, these were MERCEDES, DON JULIO, CAROLINA, RICARDO, HENRIQUE TEODORE, and ROSA Y ISABEL. It fell to Captains C. A. H. Nissen, Ferd. Hoyer, P. M. Thomsen, V. B. Diederichsen, H. W. B. Nissen, and H. J. Diederichsen, formerly of PYRMONT, to make the initial passages. So began the saga of the "nitrate clippers".

From the very first entry into the nitrate trade in 1867, "P" Line vessels began to make a reputation for speed. Before Laeisz entered the trade, any passage from Europe to a Chilean port in less than 100 days was reckoned good and the 1,200 miles from South 50° Atlantic around the Horn to South 50° Pacific averaged some three weeks. Laeisz sailers were covering the 10,000 mile course in less than 80 days before 1880. Men like J. W. G. L. Wunderlich, C. J. Steinicke, and the Grapows were rounding the Horn in under 10 days.

When, at the age of 86, Ferdinand Laeisz lay upon his death-bed, he knew that he had founded well. The operations of the firm had the strength of diversification. From 1856 onwards, the ship-owning end had gone well and promised better. Twenty-seven vessels aggregating 16,501 gross tons had been especially built. Six of these were wooden brigs, 16 wooden barques, 4 iron barques, and 1 an iron ship. CARL, of 220 gross tons, had been the smallest and PROMPT, of

1,446, was the largest. Within the same period, the firm had purchased 20 other wind ships of a combined tonnage of 10,252. The single wooden schooner, 2 wood brigs, 11 wood barques, 5 iron barques, and iron ship averaged 512 gross tons apiece. The brig ADOLPH, 164 gross tons, was the smallest while PAVIAN at 1,162, was the largest. Twenty-one vessels had been sold out of service and 11 lost, by one means and another. Starting with 1 vessel in 1839, the fleet had grown to 17 in 1867, 1869, 1870, 1878, 1879, and 1880, and its mean units had equaled 12.5.

It is interesting to note that the wooden vessels constructed to order of the firm lasted an average of 13.7 years, the brig PACIFIC flying the flag for 6 years and the barque PATRIA for 21. Among the purchased wooden vessels, the brig ADOLPH and the barque PANAMA (1) lasted a minimum of 1 year while the barque ROSA Y ISABEL flew the flag for 17. Nonetheless, the average working lifetime for these vessels was only 6.8 years. Since their mean age was 5 years at time of purchase, however, it would appear that the quality of built vessels was comparable to that of those bought from other owners. The longevity of the new iron vessels averaged 20.8 years, the barques PIRAT at 19 and PROMPT at 21 being the minimum and maximum. The second-hand iron vessels already averaged 19.6 years at date of acquisition. They lasted 10.6 years, the barque PUCK being the shortest time with the firm at 5 years and the barque PROFESSOR, at 20 years, the longest.

Carl Heinrich Laeisz was 59 years old and had been a partner with his father for 35 years when the older man passed on in 1887. His son, Carl Ferdinand, had, also, been with the firm for some 10 years and, for that time, 3 powerful men controlled the helm of the ever-growing enterprise. For the next 14 years, under the guidance of the survivors, father and son, the business continued to prosper. Likewise, the tonnage replacement program begun in 1882 continued. Three sister barques came from the yards of Blohm & Voss in Hamburg: PAMELIA and PERGAMON in 1888 and POTSDAM in 1889. Steel 1,400 tonners, they sailed well, PAMELIA'S passage of 65 days from Dover to Valparaiso in 1902 under Captain J. Schmidt being a good example. In 1889, also, Blohm & Voss and J. C. Tecklenborg of Geestemünde each launched a steel full-rigger. Both the 1,808 ton PARCHIM and the 1,797 ton PALMYRA were consistent passage-makers, PARCHIM, under Captain F. Ahrens, coming home from Iquique to Scilly in 69 days while PALMYRA, under Captain A. Teschner, made her record run from Prawle Point to Valparaiso in 1895. PARCHIM, under J. Früdden, once ran from Nagasaki to Astoria in the remarkable time of 28 days.

A Blohm & Voss product not built for the firm, the iron barque PAPOSO, 1,062 gross tons, was acquired simultaneously with the launch of the steel ship PERA, 1,758 gross tons, from the Tecklenborg yard, in 1890. I have no records for the 1885-built PAPOSO, but the PERA was another 70-80 day pacer with occasional exceptional passages such as that of J. Frömcke's 66 day run from Lizard to Valparaiso in 1905.

PREUSSEN (1), which was renamed POSEN when the great 5-master came out, and PAMPA were the 1891 additions. The last steel full-rigged ships built especially for the Company, the 1,761 ton former and 1,777 ton latter, were Blohm & Voss and A. C. Neptun products. PREUSSEN (1) was a worthy equal of the finest of the Clyde or Mersey beauties, but PAMPA was somewhat crank. Their best known commanders were Boye R. Petersen who had POSEN from 1897 to 1901, R. K. Miethe and J. Jürss who were in PAMPA from 1906-1908 and 1912 to 1913. Under Petersen, POSEN sailed from Dover to Valparaiso in 63 days in the Spanish American War year of 1898. In 1893 and again in 1894, PAMPA, under J. Steinecke, ran from Dungeness to Valparaiso in 64 days.

It is a little surprising to me that Carl H. Laeisz hesitated so long to go into 4-masted barques. As long ago as 1875, Barclay, Curle, & Co. had launched the first big vessel of this rig, if the unorthodox GREAT REPUBLIC be excepted. Where increased length and tonnage capacity required a fourth mast after the advent of the TWEEDSDALE, an increasing number of owners had found this rig to be almost as fast as the 4-masted ship and without demanding so large a personnel to handle it.

It was not until 1892 that the first Laeisz 4-masters appeared and when they did it became clear that much thought and planning had gone into them. PLACILLA and PISAGUA, Tecklenborg products, exceeded by more than 1,000 gross tons anything else that had flown the "F L" houseflag and were twins of massive beauty. Departing from the tradition of the long open main deck, they were equipped with the Rickmers innovated midship bridges from which they were steered and in which all personnel was housed and they had fore-and-aft "Liverpool bridges" along their starboard sides which connected forecastle-head, bridge, and poop, permitting their personnel to pass their lengths without having to set foot on either fore or main decks. Cargo was loaded and discharged through four hatches and they were fitted with many aids to manual labor including steam winches for working anchors, sail shifting, and cargo; upper topsail and topgallant halyard winches at each square-rigged mast; and Jarvis brace-winches to handle the 3 sets of lower and topsail braces.

Each was built on dimensions of 314.5/44.7/26.1. However, PLACILLA grossed 2,845 tons while PISAGUA measured 7 tons more. In addition, there was a difference in net tonnage, PLACILLA'S being 2,681 and PISAGUA'S calculating at 2,652. Featuring the modern arrangement of all lower and topmasts in one piece and measuring alike and with pole jigger masts supporting standing spanker gaffs, they had interchangeable yards consisting of royals over double topgallants and topsails. All masts, yards, and standing rigging were of steel and steel wire.

Being cleverly designed and well built for the hardest of all trades participated in by sailing vessels, they could be safely driven and would neither be dismasted nor go under as had many a lesser craft. These were the prototypes of the built 4- and 5-masters that followed and, while there were differences, they were largely those of detail. It is a tribute to their designers, builders, and personnel that no Laeisz 4- or 5-master was ever lost at sea, except by collision.

Captain Robert Hilgendorf, the Laeiszes' most trusted master, late of the barques PARSIFAL, PIRAT, PERGAMMON, and PALMYRA, was entrusted with PLACILLA and this superb seaman proceeded to drive her from the English Channel to her port in Chile in just 58 days! J. Früdden, last off the PARCHIM and, before that, the PARNASS, was given the PISAGUA. He was 72 days from Dover to Valparaiso. From the West Coast homeward is a much longer route, by some 500 miles, but both Masters came it in 75 days. Hilgendorf was out again in 62 and home in 70. O. Schmidt left POTRIMPOS to take PISAGUA and he went out in 69 and came back in 80. So they sailed. Hilgendorf, Früdden, and Schmidt had demonstrated the superiority of the big 4-master in the nitrate trade.

In 1893, the steel 4-masted barque PITLOCHRY was purchased from her builders. In September, 1894, this 3,088 gross ton flyer was launched from the yard of A. Stephen & Sons of Dundee in Scotland. Again, Hilgendorf took her from the stocks, and he made one fast round to Chile in her before going over to POTOSI in 1895. G. Schlüter took her next and had her for 7 years. Seventy-six, 79, 77, and 65 days passage after passage showed what she could do.

It was Antonin Dominique Bordes Et Fils of Bordeau, the great French nitrate importer, and not the second generation Laeisz, as is often supposed, who had the enterprise and daring to build the first 5-masted square-rigged sailing vessel. This was the first FRANCE, constructed by D. & W. Henderson at Patrick, Glasgow, Scotland, and launched on the 2nd of September, 1890. Grossing 3,784 tons on dimensions 361.0/48.8/25.9, she could lift 6,200 tons deadweight. While she was building, Rickmers Reismühlen Reederei & Shiffbau, Act. Ges. of Bremerhaven, Germany, one of Laeisz's competitors in the Eastern trade, was planning another 5-master. This was the auxiliary steel 5-masted barque MARIA RICKMERS, 3,813 gross tons, which came from the yards of Russell & Co. at Port Glasgow in 1891. The German was 14 feet longer than FRANCE, but with .8 of a foot less beam and .9 of a foot less depth. Her engines and bunkers occupying some space, she could carry only 5,700 deadweight tons. Both these giants proved to be rather tender. MARIA RICKMERS has been missing since the 24th of July, 1892, while on her maiden voyage with a full cargo of rice from Saigon towards Europe. FRANCE was last seen in the middle of May, 1901, on her beam ends in the South Atlantic having been overwhelmed by a pampero.

Whether or not either of these vessels influenced the design of the Laeisz's next addition to their nitrate fleet, I do not know. None the less, J. C. Tecklenborg was commissioned to build a steel 5-masted barque for the firm in 1895. Grossing 4,026 tons on a net of 3,755, she measured 366.3 between perpendiculars, 49.7 in breadth, and 28.5 feet in depth and was able to lift well over 6,000 tons deadweight. The FRANCE had made an outward passage in 1892 of 74 days from Dunkirk. POTOSI, under the command of Robert Hilgendorf, took her departure from the Weser on 26, July, 1895; passed Ushant on 1, August; crossed the Equator 20 days later; crossed S50° in W64° on the 14th of September; rounded Cape St. John in the teeth of a westerly gale on the next day; and anchored in Iquique Roads on the 6th of October 73 days from Germany and 66 from the Channel. The perfection to which discharging and loading afterwards was brought by "P" Line organization had not yet been attained and POTOSI was 20 days unballasting and stowing 6,000 tons of saltpeter. Thus, she sailed from Iquique on the 26th of October, passed in sight of Diego Ramirez on the 21st day out, rounded Cape Horn on the same day, crossed the Line on the 49th day, passed the Lizard on the 68th day, took steam on the 73d day, and arrived in tow in Cuxhaven on the 11th of January, 1896, 77 days out. Her first voyage had proved that POTOSI was an all-around boat which sailed well on all points and was able to log over 16 knots in strong fair winds. Subsequently POTOSI made 9 more voyages under Captain Hilgendorf, 2 under Captain Schlüter, 8 under Captain Nissen, 4 under Captain Frömcke, and 4 under Captain Miethe. In 28 voyages, she never made a bad passage.

Robert Hilgendorf was bringing his huge charge into Iquique Roads to end the first half of his seventh voyage, 68 days from Beachy Head, when Reederei F. Laeisz acquired their next vessel. This was Gillison & Chadwick's 3,100 ton steel 4-masted barque DRUMROCK. A 3-islander, built by Ramage & Ferguson at Leith, Scotland, in 1891, she was the last of the famous DRUMS and the best of them. Unique for her time, she had unusually fine accommodations for her crew which even included a bathroom and complete hospital under the poop. Undoubtedly one of the finest steel sailing vessels ever built, she was a 3-skysail yarder. Captain T. S. Bailey had her from her launch and turned her over to Captain H. A. Dehnhardt when the British flag came down. Under Dehnhardt, Horn, and Oetzmann she made a number of the voyages of which, afterwards, the firm of Laeisz was proud.

Carl Ferdinand Laeisz passed away, at the age of 47, in 1900, and was followed the next year by his father, Carl Heinrich, who was 73. Herbert F. and Erich F. Laeisz, Carl Ferdinand's sons, being only 15 and 13 years of age, Paul Ganssauge, J. Reisse, and H. Struck, the Confidential Agents took over. When the elder Laeiszes had assumed full control of the firm in 1887, there had been the 3 wooden barques PARNASS, PARADOX, and PANDUR. the 7 iron barques PROFESSOR, PONCHO, PAQUITA, PIRAT, PESTALOZZI, PUCK, and PLUS; the steel barque POTRIMPOS. and 2 iron ships, POLYNESIA and PLUTO of an average size of 863 gross tons and totaling 11,221 tons. Eight of these had been designed and built for the firm and 5 had been purchased outside. Their average age was 13 years. In 1901 the red "F L" flew from the spanker gaffs of 26,205 tons of shipping consisting of 4 iron barques, 2 steel barques, 5 full-rigged ships, 2 4-masted steel barques, and 1 5-masted steel barque. Of a mean tonnage of 1,872, they averaged 11.8 years in age.

The caliber of the Confidential Agents, who now assumed full managerial responsibilities for Reederei F. Laeisz, is a credit to the character of Carl H. Laeisz who had chosen, trained, and promoted them. To them goes full credit for the round dozen good years that followed. From 1867 on, it had been the policy of management to establish a reputation for reliability, particularly in the nitrate trade. Shipper and receivers had to be confident that cargoes shipped in Laeisz square-riggers would go quickly, arrive intact and in good order, and, more or less, when expected. To accomplish this, they built first-class craft, manned them well, and systemized operations both at loading and terminal ports. With the increased competition following the opening of the 20th Century, it fell to these Agents to make a liner trade out of the West Coast of South America business if the company was to survive.

Whereas in the middle of the 19th century, the firm's vessels went all over the Globe, towards the end and, especially, after 1900 they went more and more on a scheduled service to the West Coast with general cargo out and nitrate back, interrupted only by voyages to South Australia for wheat and, not so often, to Japan. For many years the mainstay outward-bound cargo was cement in barrels, coke, and large parcels of lump sugar in boxes. Up to the first World War, the vessels very often took part cargoes of beer, hay, potatoes, etc. coastwise from Valparaiso to their respective nitrate ports and, by doing this, paid all expenses on the coast discharging cargo at Corral, Talcahuano, San Antonio, and Valparaiso and taking in ballast as soon as possible, all work done by the crews. Discharging, sailing, and loading a full cargo of saltpeter where stevedores for the actual stowing were employed was generally done in about 30 days. Nitrate had to be supplied "as fast as ship can take", which meant, for a 4-masted barque, about 800 to 1,000 tons daily.

All the masters had to sign instructions which began: "My ships can and will make rapid voyages". "P" liners would run into the crowded anchorages of the nitrate ports, shortening sail as they came, seamen rigging cargo gear and opening hatches, and with their winches turning over. Agents ashore would have loaded lighters ready at the appointed anchorage. As the great 4- or 5-master rounded head-to-wind under backed main canvas and her anchor ran out, the lighters would already be alongside and cargo-handling began at once as in the smartest steamer of today. They were days discharging and loading where other sailing vessels with their antiquated equipment and disorganized methods were sometimes months. At the end, it was not unusual to see "Flying P" Liners making sail as they moved through the roadsteads outward bound with the last lighter still alongside from which the final slings of cargo were being hoisted on board.

Soon after the turn of the Century, competition along the Chilean coast became acute. Antonin Dominique Bordes Et Fils of Bordeaux, France; F. A. Vinnen & Co. of Bremen, Germany; and the Hamburg firms of G. J. H. Siemers & Co., H. Fölsch & Co., Knöhr & Burchard, NFL, Rhederei Aktiens Ges. Von 1896; and others were operating magnificent sailers in the trade. The Bordes' DUNKERQUE, Vinnen's ALSTERDAM ex SOMALI, Siemers' HANS and KURT, Fölsch's WALKÜRE ex ALSTERBERG, Knöhr & Burchard's SCHURBEK, and Rhederei Aktien Ges.'s ORATAVA ex COMET were typical. Bordes, Siemers, and others had, likewise, built up their own organizations.

A partial answer to this growing challenge was the PREUSSEN (2), the only 5-masted sailing ship square-rigged on all 5 masts that was ever built. PREUSSEN displaced 11,150 tons, her registered gross tonnage being 5,081 on a net of 4,788. Her cargo capacity was reckoned at 8,000 tons. Four-hundred-seven and .8 feet between perpendiculars, 53.6 feet in breadth, and 27.1 feet in depth, this Tecklenborg masterpiece was planned by Carl H. and Carl F. Laeisz before their deaths and was launched for the firm in 1902.

In practice, the 4-masted ship had proved comparatively expensive to run, difficult to steer when under full canvas, and none too easy to work in comparison to the 4-masted barque of like size. Little or no loss of speed had been noted when a 4-masted ship was converted to a 4-masted barque and there were many such conversions before 1900. It is difficult to understand, therefore, why PREUSSEN was given ship rig at all or why the earlier 5-master was not the ship and the later the barque. It is not surprising, then, that PREUSSEN, on the whole, proved no faster than POTOSI.

Boye R. Petersen, formerly master of PESTALOZZI and POSEN, took her from the stocks. Leaving Geestemünde on 31, July, 1902, PREUSSEN was off Start Point, Devonshire, on the 4th of August and arrived in Iquique on the 8th of October, 69 days from Germany and 65 from the Start. Her turn-around in Chile was 16 days, she was off Scilly 79 days out, and arrived in Cuxhaven on the 88th day. Petersen had her for 11 voyages, including a charter for the Standard Oil Company during which he circumnavigated the World in 265 sailing days.

In 1909, Hinrich Nissen left POTOSI to take PREUSSEN for another 2 West Coast rounds. In all PREUSSEN sailed outwards to Chile 12 times, averaging 73 days from her ports of departure in Germany. Her best run was 65 days and her worst 84. She came home from Chile 13 times to average 77 days, the best of which was 65 and the worst 92. When it is born in mind that these passages are calculated from land to land instead of from English Channel landmarks to Chilean ports, one gets a clear picture of her performance as well as figures to use as a yardstick against which to measure the runs of other vessels participating in the trade.

Two other square-rigged sailing vessels larger than PREUSSEN were built. In 1906, 4 years after the building of PREUSSEN, Rickmers of Bremerhaven launched the last such craft constructed at their famous yard. R. C. RICKMERS was an auxiliary steel 5-masted barque of 5,548 gross tons, 441.0 feet in length, with a carrying capacity, including bunkers, of 8,000 tons. Her 1,000 h. p., coal-fired engines gave her a speed, under power alone, of 7 knots when loaded and 8 knots when in ballast and her huge spread of canvas made her a fine performer when wind driven. Her 1910 passage of 96 days from Newcastle-On-Tyne, England, to San Francisco, California, with coal; her 1911 passage of 57 days from Taltal, Chile, to Hamburg with nitrate; and her 1913 passage of 111 days (compared to PREUSSEN'S 112) from Philadelphia to Hioge, Japan, with case oil show that she was fully as fine a performer as PREUSSEN.

The largest such vessel ever built was the steel 5-masted barque FRANCE (2) launched from the yard of Ch. & Atel De La Gironde, Bordeaux, France, for Cie. Francaise De Marine Et De Commerce of Rouen, France, for the ore trade from New Caledonia. On dimensions of 418.8/55.8/24.9, she grossed 5,633 tons as against 5,010 net and could carry in excess of 8,000 deadweight tons. When she was launched on 9, November, 1911, she had twin screws driven by motors, but these were dispensed with in 1920. FRANCE was rigged bald-headed, that is without royals, and her passages do not appear to have been as good as those of POTOSI, PREUSSEN, and R. C. RICKMERS although 1 of 90 days from Wellington, New Zealand, to London, England, by way of Cape Horn, made after her engines were taken out, does not seem to have been so bad.

Between 1901 and 1912, Reederei F. Laeisz had the following 3,000 gross ton steel 4-masted barques built to their order. These were the racing twins PANGANI (3,054), built by Tecklenborg in 1902, and PETSCHILI (3,087), built by Blohm & Voss in 1903; the smaller PAMIR (3,020) from Blohm & Voss in 1905; and the sisters PASSAT (3,091) and PEKING (3,100) from the same yard in 1911.

Such passages as 63 and 64 days, under Captain J. Schmidt and 67, 66, 74, 72, 79, 73, and 70, made under command of F. Jünge from Lizard, England, to Valparaiso, Chile, underscore PANGANI'S sailing qualities. Her sister, PETSCHILI, under A. Teschner, ran out in 68 days twice, 74, and 79, and her record under C. M. Prützmann and F. Jünge was equally good.

The Blohm & Voss plans of PAMIR reveal that she was a little fuller-lined than her predecessors and a bit thick aft. Those of my friends who have commanded her (Robert K. Miethe and Robert Clauss for Laeisz and L. Lindvall, J. M. Mattsson, and Karl G. Sjögren for Firma Gustaf Erikson) report that she took some driving to make an average passage. The facts seem to bear this out. Her 10 Europe to Chile outward passages before World War I average 83 days or about 3 days more than normal for Laeisz 4-masted barques. Her best was 71 and her worst 95. Her 9 eastbound runs average 94 days or nearly 4 days longer. Her best was 66 and her worst 105. (These passages are all calculated from land to land.) C. M. Prützmann, R. K. Miethe, H. Horn, C. Becker, W. Ehlert, and J. Jürss had her, in turn, from 1905 to 1914 and every one of them was a driving master with an enviable reputation earned in other vessels.

The sister 4-masted barques PASSAT and PEKING, while the last but 3 built for the "P" Line were, probably, the finest of their rig built for the Company and were equalled only by G. J. H. Siemers & Co.'s HANS and KURT. POLA (3,104) and PRIWALL (3,105), though built from the same basic plans, were built during World War I and, therefore, suffered from certain war-necessitated economies. PADUA (3,064), the last of them all, was not finished to the same degree.

Captain John T. Wendler, who had served as a seaman on POTOSI from July, 1897, to January, 1898, under Robert Hilgendorf and whose last command has been the full-rigged ship PIRNA, came ashore at his owner's request in April, 1910, to overlook the building of the two sisters. After the two vessels were built, PEKING came under the command of Captain Nissen and Wendler was appointed master of PASSAT. On a draft of 22'9" forward and 23'5" aft, PASSAT sailed from Hamburg on the 24th of December, 1911. She passed Dungeness on the 29th, Rawle Point on the 2nd of January, 1912, and arrived in Valparaiso on the 14th of March, 80 days out. Her 4 outward passages before the first World War, all to Valparaiso, averaged $79\frac{1}{2}$ days, best being 73 and worst 80. She made 3 homeward runs and these averaged $90\frac{1}{2}$, with best at 86 and worst at 93.

PEKING, under Nissen, made the following passages, reckoned from the

Lizard to Valparaiso: 76, 70, and 74. Captain A. Oetzmann, just out of the full-rigged ship PINNAS, took her in 1914 and went out in 79 days from the Lizard. It is seen that both barques were quite capable of living up to, the, now long established, Laeisz tradition.

Between 1901 and 1912, the Confidential Agents purchased 3 full-rigged ships. These were the steel ARGO (2,131) from G. Amsinck of Hamburg which had been built in 1902 as BRYNYMORE by A. McMillan & Son of Dumbarton, Scotland; the steel OSORNO (1,789) from H. P. Schuldt of Hamburg which had been built in 1894 as BEETHOVEN by J. C. Tecklenborg of Geestemünde; and the steel FITZJAMES (1,946) from W. Montgomery & Co. of London which had been built in 1902 by William Hamilton & Co., of Port Glasgow. FITZJAMES cost $40,000.00 (Ⱡ 8,000). When bought in 1906, 1907, and 1909, they had been renamed PEIHO, PIRNA, and PINNAS. First-class vessels, their subsequent performances seemed quite up to Laeisz standards. Frömcke, Wist, and Eck sailed PEIHO from the Lizard to Valparaiso in 72, 74, 78, 74 days. PIRNA, under Wendler, Siemer, Wolf, Jürss, and Brockhöft ran up 74, 71, 75, 75, 73, and 65 for the same distance. PINNAS, mastered by Eck, Radfan, and Oetzmann were 78, 75, and 74 days out.

Within the same period of time, the steel barque PENANG (2,039), a Rickmers product as ALBERT RICKMERS, was purchased from that firm in 1911; the steel barque PELIKAN (2,103), built by Rijkee & Co. of Rotterdam as DIONE was purchased from Wachsmuth & Krogmann of Hamburg in 1912; and the steel barque PERIM (1,944), built by A. Roder & Co. of Port Glasgow as RADIANT for the Anglo-American Oil Co. of London changed from that to the "F L" flag in 1912 for the sum of $50,000.00 (Ⱡ 10,000). Built in 1905, 1905, and 1903, these were representative tonnage of the time and made such passages as J. H. Eck's 71 days in PENANG. The records carry the impression that PELIKAN and PERIM were not quite up to standard, although they had little time to prove themselves.

Finally, 4 steel 4-masted barques were purchased. These were the 2,413 gross ton POMMERN, built in 1903 by J. Reid & Co., as MNEME, from B. Wencke Sohn of Hamburg in 1907; the 3,090 gross ton PARMA, built in 1902 by A. Rodger & Co. as ARROW, from the Anglo-American Oil Co. in 1911; the 2,318 gross ton PONAPE, built in 1903 by Soc. Esercizio in Italy as REGINA ELENA, from Italian owners in 1911; and in 1913, a year later, the 2,102 gross ton PINGUIN, built in 1903 by the same firm as ERASMO, from E. Raffo Fue E. of Spezia, Italy. The big ARROW cost Laeisz $75,000.00 (Ⱡ 15,000). POMMERN, PARMA, and PONAPE had a chance to prove themselves. For instance, POMMERN, at different times under command of Captains M. Allwardt and J. Frömcke twice ran from the Lizard to Valparaiso in 65 days. Frömcke, in fact, had just been relieved from command of POTOSI when he was appointed to POMMERN in 1912. So accustomed to driving strong sailing vessels was he that he very nearly drove POMMERN under, as deep-laden with some 4,050 tons of heavy nitrates, she was running her Easting down in 1913. Already noted as a little queer, his mad driving washed half a watch of men overside. The mate relieved him of command, then, and locked him in his cabin. Driving the nitrate clippers with the words "My ships can and will make rapid voyages" ringing in your ears on the Cape Horn road was hard on men...

An annual average of 16 vessels had been managed by the Confidential Agents, 29 individual units having flown the flag. Of these, 10 were sold (Three to Finnish buyers, 2 to German purchasers, and 5 to Norwegian operators) and 3, PALMYRA, POSEN, and PREUSSEN (2) were lost.

At the ages of 26 and 24, Herbert F. and Erich F. Laeisz took up the reins of management in 1912. They now assumed full control of a fleet of 19 sailing vessels of an average individual size of 2,541 gross tons, all of which were engaged in the Chilean nitrate trade. The fleet with which they entered the year 1913 consisted of 3 barques, 4 ships, 11 4-masted barques, and 1 5-masted barque. This 49,218 ton fleet averaged 10 and a half years of age, the 21 year old PAMPA and PERSIMMON being the oldest and the 1 year old PASSAT and PEKING the youngest.

From the outset, it was evident that these fourth generation Laeiszes possessed the vigor of mind and body and the business acumen so characteristic of their male antecedents. Coincident with their assumption of directorial responsibility, they were faced with the problems posed to all operators of ocean sail tonnage by the impending opening of the Panama Canal and by the, already perceptible, growing threat of war. As the opening of the Suez Canal in 1869 had greatly shortened the length of journeys between North Atlantic ports and the Orient, bringing about new classes of shipping and establishing new trade routes, so would the presence of a canal midway between the continents of North and South America open new fields and close old ones to the maritime industry.

The first forward step was to order two steamers from J. C. Tecklenborg. It was the intention that these vessels be utilized to carry bananas for the Laeisz-affiliated company, the Afrikanische Frucht Co. of Hamburg, owners of large plantations in the Cameroons, a German West African protectorate. Planned and laid down in 1913, the specifications called for 3,600 ton refrigerated banana boats equipped with 3,200 h. p. steam triple expansion engines capable of a speed of 14 knots. These were to be the PUNGO, 3,602 gross and 1,898 net tons, built in 1914 and the PIONIER, 3,602 gross and 1,900 net tons, launched in 1915 under the eye of Captain John Wendler. In pursuance of these plans the 22 year old full-rigger PAMPA was sold to J. Tengstrom of Åbo, in Russian-Finland, and the 4-masted barque PERSIMMON let go to F. A. Vinnen & Co. of Bremen for a premium price for so old a vessel, both sales taking place in 1913. After the loss of PITLOCHRY, under Captain H. Horn, on the 28th of November, this left the firm with but 2 vessels, PIRNA and POTOSI, built prior to 1900.

The German Reich, under Chancellor Otto Von Bismarck, had become the most powerful state on the Continent. After 1890, under Emperor Wilhelm II, German policy became World policy. Many Germans, feeling hemmed in by an encircling alliance, had begun to think in terms of conquest. Illustrative of the fact that political rulers often make their plans without the consent of the people ruled, was the outbreak of World War I on the 4th of August, 1914.

It is quite evident that the intentions of the Emperor and the General Staff were not so much as suspected by the rank and file, otherwise Germany's by now, great maritime industry would not have proceeded so normally in the spring of 1914 nor made the commitments that it did. As it was, the bulk of the Laeisz fleet joined the seaward parade of German wind ships bound for Chilean ports in that spring, POTOSI being the last to sail on the 11th of July. Three, PAMIR, PERKEO, and PONAPE, like POTOSI, were at sea when the War began.

The firm's latest purchase was the first war victim. The huge PERKEO, a 3,765 gross ton steel 4-masted barque built by Russell & Co. at Port Glasgow in 1901 as BRILLIANT for the Anglo-American Oil Co., had been purchased from that concern in New York in July and Captain Nissen had gone over to bring her back. Passing inbound very close to Dover on the 6th of August to close a smart North Atlantic passage, she was seized by an English cruiser and brought into that port. Nissen had not known of the outbreak of war 2 days before.

At first, following Chile's declaration of neutrality in the European war, the Laeiszes, in common with other German shipowners, ordered their 9 vessels in Chilean ports to remain at anchor. The Chilean policy of neutrality was reaffirmed on the 11th of April, 1917, but on the 25th of April the same year diplomatic relations with Germany were broken off. Then, on the 4th of November, 1918, Chile seized the 84 interned German merchant vessels that were lying in her ports and roadsteads.

The war cost Reederei F. Laeisz the life of Herbert Ferdinand Laeisz, all but one of its vessels (PRIWALL), and a half dozen years of business. Erich F. Laeisz and the 96 year-old firm he headed could not be crushed out of existence by the simple method of confiscation. The firm had weathered too many crises in close to a century of doing business on a World-wide basis, they were far too experienced to have all their eggs in 1 basket, and their credit was still good almost anywhere. Thus, with PRIWALL, 3,105 gross tons, which was launched in 1919, and PARMA, which had been delivered to the General Steam Navigation Co. of London, England, in April, 1921, and was bought back in November of the same year, the famous "Flying P" Line was once more in being after an interval of only a few months.

In this way PASSAT, PEIHO, and PINNAS returned to their old flag in 1922, PEKING in 1924, and PAMIR in 1924. In 1924, also, a steel ship of 2,270 gross tons, built by Chant. & Atel. De St. Nazaire Penhoet of St. Nazaire, France as MARÉCHAL SUCHET was bought under the name of FAITH and renamed PELLWORM. Finally, in 1926, J. C. Tecklenborg launched the last sailing vessel to be built for the firm and, as it developed, the last deepwater commercial square-rigged sailing vessel built to this date and the last, but 3, 4-masted barques ever constructed.

This was PADUA. Measuring 320.5 feet in length, 46.1 feet in breadth, and 25.4 feet in depth she grossed 3,064 tons on a net of 2,678. On the 6th of August, 1926, PADUA sailed from Hamburg under command of Captain Schuberg. She was 87 days on the subsequent passage to Talcahuano, Chile. Considering that Talcahuano is some 240 miles south of Valparaiso and that much nearer Cape Horn, this passage does not seem so good. Neither does her homeward run of 94 days from Taltal to Delfzijl, Holland, seem to speak well of the barque. However, her passages improved with time. She was 82 days from Hamburg to Talcahuano and 87 from Iquique to Hamburg on her next voyage. Captain H. Piening then took her out from Hamburg to Talcahuano in 71 days and brought her home from Mejillones, far up the Chilean coast, to Terneuzen, Holland, 72 days out. This is, undoubtedly, the fastest voyage made by a sailing vessel in the Chilean trade since the 1914-1918 war.

Following the war, Tecklenborg produced two steamers to replace the lost PUNGO and PIONIER which had been requisitioned by the German Imperial Navy before they were even ready for sea. The turbine steamers POSEIDON and PLANET were launched in 1922. Wendler had the 5,823 ton black-painted POSEIDON for awhile in 1930 and I remember seeing her sister, PLANET in Shanghai, China, about 1937. She was a smart looking, well kept up freighter, but it seemed odd to see the "F L" flag flying from the main truck of a steamer.

Bremer Vulkan of Vegesack, Germany, built 2 steamers and 3 motor vessels for Laeisz's subsidiary company, the Afrikanische Frucht Cie., A. G., between 1930 and 1935. These grossed between 1,998 and 3,410 tons. Following these, Deutsche Werft, A. G., Bet Finkenwarder, Germany, constructed 4 more motor vessels of between 2,863 and 3,664 gross tons. Finally, Flender Werke Siems of

Lübeck built the 764 gross ton PORJUS in 1937 and Smit & Zoon of Westerbrock, Germany, launched the 557 gross ton PALOMA, both being motor vessels. The ones built between 1930 and 1935 were PUMA, PANTHER, PIONIER, PELIKAN, and PONTOS. From 1935 to 1941 the PYTHON, PALIME, POMONA, and PANTHER.

The ultimate effects of the opening of the Panama Canal on the 3d of April, 1914; of the vicious war that followed; and of their combined results became more and more apparent in the 5 years between 1921 and 1926. By the latter year, it had become certain that there was no longer a fortune to be made in the Chile-Europe saltpeter trade. First, the manufacture of synthetic nitrates, a process developed as a result of the demands of war, in European and North American factories, caused the freight on the natural Chilean product to slump badly. Second, again as a result of the war, the Chilean coastal trade was permanently lost to foreign vessels. This used to cover coastwise operating expenses and, as such, had been a material factor in maintaining a generous profit-margin where vessels had to discharge and load in different ports. Thirdly, the mainstay outward-bound cargoes of cement in barrels, bulk coke, and boxed lump sugar petered out. Chile had built cement factories and, consequently, slapped a heavy duty on imported cement while coke was used less and less. A shortage of war-time shipping had forced Chileans to grow their own beets and to construct sugar refineries, and that was that. So with one thing and another, the profits dwindled and the expenses grew, and, by 1931, the sailing vessels no longer paid their way.

By 1932, the fleet of splendid sailers had dwindled to 2. PEIHO, Captain P. Kleist, stranded near Cape San Diego in the Straits Of Le Maire between Tierra Del Fuego and Staten Island on the 16th of March, 1923. Six years later, PINNAS, Captain Lehmann, was dismasted and abandoned in a sinking condition off the pitch of the Horn. Neither was replaced.

For the first time, Laeisz vessels were laid up in quantity. In 1926, Captain A. Wist, an experienced mariner who had commanded PEIHO, PELIKAN, and PARMA before the War and sailed them from the Lizard to Valparaiso in as little as 71 days, met with crew trouble and failed to round the Horn to the westward on PELLWORM'S very first passage for Laeisz. According to the Company records, he lost his job as such and never got command under the "F L" flag again, for this was the first time a "Flying P" Liner was so beaten by this promontory. PELLWORM went to Syndikatsreederei of Hamburg and sailed no more.

In October, 1931, PARMA was sold for $15,000.00 (Ⱡ 7,000) to a syndicate headed by Captain Ruben DeCloux of Mariehamn, in the Åland Islands, and composed of Captains John Wenstromm and Alan J. Villiers, with others. Thereafter she sailed under the blue cross on white field of Finland. In November of the same year, Captain Gustaf Erikson of Mariehamn bought PAMIR for 42,000 German marks (Ⱡ 2,000) and the following year paid about $25,000.00 (Ⱡ 5,000) for PASSAT. Depression and time had so reduced their value from the $200,000.00 (Ⱡ 40,000) they had cost! PEKING, the last to be sold, went, in September, 1932, to the Shaftesbury Homes & Arethusa Training Ship Society and may be seen to this day anchored in the Medway stripped of much of her fine rigging.

Thirteen steamers and PADUA and PRIWALL sailed on between the wars. Robert Clauss and J. Jürss alternated in command of PADUA on the old familiar round for a time. Then, in 1938, Captain H. Richard Wendt, a young master, took her over for a run to Valparaiso; from there in $52\frac{1}{2}$ days to Port Lincoln, South Australia; and from Port Lincoln, with wheat at 25 shillings per ton, in $93\frac{1}{2}$ days to Queenstown, Ireland, for orders. Ordered, then, to Glasgow where she discharged, she returned to Hamburg in ballast and arrived on the 8th of August, 1939.

PRIWALL, likewise, continued in the nitrate run, Robert Clauss being in command from 1932 to 1934 when he was succeeded by Hauth. In 1938, PRIWALL, under Captain Hauth, set the all-time record for rounding Cape Horn to the westward. PRIWALL, deep laden with coke and manned by 73 men, for Hitler's Third Reich was subsidizing maritime officer candidates by then, left Hamburg on the 31st of August, passed Beachy Head on the 5th of September, crossed the Line on the 5th of October, passed Cape Horn on the 2nd of November, and arrived in Valparaiso on the 11th of November, 73 days out. So far as is known, this time of 5 days 14 hours for the passage Latitude S50°, South Atlantic, to Latitude S50°, South Pacific, beats any previous record by more than 1 full day. Now, it is likely that this record will stand forever.

On the outbreak of the Second World War on the 3d of September, 1939, PADUA was laid up in Hamburg, Germany, and PRIWALL in Valparaiso, Chile. PADUA, during and until the close of World War II, served as a training vessel for the merchant marine in the Baltic. In January, 1946, she was delivered to the Soviet Navy at Swinemünde. Later, she was re-named KRUSENBERG and refitted at Rostock to serve as a schoolship accommodating 400-600 men.

In June, 1941, the Third Reich purchased PRIWALL from Reederei F. Laeisz and made a present of her to the Chilean Navy in the hopes of keeping that nation's good will. She was fitted with a strong motor in San Francisco and sailed past the Golden Gate painted white and re-named LAUTARO. Four years later, her nitrate cargo was sabotaged off the Peruvian coast and she burned with the loss of 20 lives.

World War II, cost Laeisz his whole fleet. POSEIDON, Captain W. Nielsen, was recalled by the German Government from Buenos Aires on the 3d of October and was subsequently sunk by her own crew on the 22nd while being chased by 2 British auxiliary cruisers to the north of Iceland. PLANET, home with a cargo of maize from the Plate on the day the War broke out, was afterwards sunk in Narvik with a cargo of phosphate from Murmansk to shelter a valuable vessel against British torpedos. Although all superstructure was smashed by British shells, she was, later, salvaged and brought to Tromsö, Norway, to house Luftwaffe personnel. Given back to Laeisz in 1941, she was hit by air-plane bombs of the R A F while traveling down the Norwegian coast, with the loss of 4 firemen. Reaching Naskow, Danmark, she was re-built. PLANET, under command of Captain John Behrens, came to her end in the winter of 1944-1945 in the Bay of Swinemünde while serving as a navy transport. It took 3 magnetic mines to finish her.

The Afrikanische Frucht Co.'s PUMA, PELIKAN, PONTOS, PYTHON, PALIME, and PANTHER were all taken over by the German Navy. Elders & Fyffes, the British fruit firm, eventually acquired PELIKAN, PONTOS, and PANTHER. PIONIER was torpedoed on the 2nd of September, 1940, with the loss of 400 lives including the master, Th. Meyer. PYTHON, was held up by a British cruiser in the South Atlantic while supplying U-Boats and was scuttled by her own crew. PALIME ran into a minefield off Stavanger in Norway on the 6th of June, 1940, and was lost. POMONA, taken over by the British Ministry Of Transport and re-named EMPIRE MERCHANT, was sunk by a German U-Boat.

The small PORJUS and PALOMA, after many vicissitudes, survived the War, PORJUS coming under the flag of Johann Schuchmann of Kiel, Germany, and PALOMA being handed over to the Soviet on the 5th of April, 1946, at Rotterdam, Netherlands.

For the first time in 90 years the Company was without a vessel to carry the flag...

Today, these ex-Laeisz sailing vessels survive: PUCK, a rusting hulk in Miokko, Bismarck Archipelago; POMMERN, owned by the City Of Mariehamn as the result of the gift of the vessel by Mr. Edgar Erikson, an exhibition vessel in Mariehamn; PEKING, as ARETHUSA, as a stationary training vessel in the Medway, England; PADUA, as the Russian KRUSENBERG, training in the Baltic; PARMA, a hulk in Palestine; PAMIR and PASSAT cargo-cum-training vessels, presently in the Argentine grain trade. Five steamers, PELIKAN, PONTOS, PANTHER, PORJUS, and PALOMA exist, here and there, under other flags and in other trades than those for which they were designed.

It might well be supposed that World War II finished the career of Reederei F. Laeisz, at least as far as shipowning is concerned. This, however, is by no means the case. While presently engaged largely in export and insurance, the old standbys, 2 motor trawlers were built in the period 1947 to 1949. These, the PLISCH and PLUM, were sold to the eastern zone of Germany when prices for fish went down to nothing. By 1956, the keels had been laid for 9 modern refrigerated boats for the Afrikanische Frucht Co. These, the PEGASUS, PERSEUS, PROTEUS, PELION, PARNASS, PERIKLES, PIRAUS, PORTUNUS, and PARTHENON are now at sea.

The future? The future holds limitless opportunities for those who can recognize and grasp them. I do not doubt that the "F L" houseflag will exist in the 21st Century, even if it has to be painted on the side of an interplanatary space ship...

J. Ferrell COLTON

Long Ridge
Fort Valley Road
Flagstaff
ARIZONA
U.S.A.

TABLE OF CONTENTS

PART III

THE CHILEAN NITRATE TRADE

PART IV

FATES OF THE "FLYING P" LINERS

TABLE OF ILLUSTRATIONS

TABLE OF SCHEDULES

PART I

THE FIRST HUNDRED YEARS

PART I

THE FIRST HUNDRED YEARS

Chapter One: THE FOUNDER OF THE FIRM

INTRODUCTION

Introduction

The building up of the F. Laeisz firm of shipowners is the work of 3 men: the father, Ferdinand Laeisz; the son, Carl Heinrich Laeisz; and the grandson, Carl Ferdinand Laeisz... 3 generations, to whom was granted the good fortune of a long-enduring partnership in work leading from success to success.

FERDINAND LAEISZ

Ancestors of Ferdinand Laeisz

Ferdinand Laeisz was born in Hamburg on January 1, 1801, and hence in later life often jocosely termed "the first man of his century". The family originated in *Swabia*, whence a forebear came to Hamburg about the middle of the 18th Century. He worked as a carpenter in the building of the great St. Michael's church. In 1789, his son, John Hartwig Laeisz, married the daughter of Grewe, the senior member of Hamburg's Board of Glaziers. She was the mother of Ferdinand Laeisz, who was the sixth child among 10 brothers and sisters. John Hartwig was already a merchant with overseas connections, especially in England, whither he undertook many journeys. The family lived in good circumstances at first, but the annexation of Hamburg by Napoleon and the continental blockade undermined their prosperity. The French first came to Hamburg in 1806, and thereupon began hard times for the city and its inhabitants.

Memoirs

The memoirs left by Ferdinand Laeisz are so characteristic of the man and the times in which he worked his way up from small beginnings to a leading personage in Hamburg that a history of the firm cannot be better introduced than by a quotation from his "Lifetime Memories Of An Old Hamburger". It is astonishing to learn through what remarkable detours Ferdinand Laeisz became the founder of a firm of shipowners. Let us first hear from him on the subject of his boyish pranks and his years of wandering.

"When I was ten years old, I delivered for the landlord of the Cuxhaven tavern letters smuggled in by the skippers of Helgoland and Cuxhaven. These letters were furnished not with an address but merely with a number, for the French threatened such high treason with the death-penalty. Children, however, were exempt from punishment, and I still remember with what importance and secrecy old Herr Schubeck kept everything under lock and key in order to 'catch the youngster with the goods'. This often earned a good tip. Three Cuxhaven sailors who were caught forwarding English letters were arrested and were to be shot. It is said, however, that the beautiful sister of one of them helped them to flee during the night by throwing herself at the feet of the French commander.

"In the unruly condition of the French period, the wild oats of arrogant youth naturally ripened, and I was always well in front in the invention and practice of all possible mad pranks. In order to irritate a bad-tempered shoemaker of our neighborhood, who had on various occasions introduced us to a shoebuckle, we rolled a mighty snowball down his cellar steps and then banged on his windows. When he came out, the icy mass rolled onto his body, and he was further greeted with a hail of snowballs. A nearby teacher was accustomed to deal out more corporal punishment to his pupils than seemed to us necessary. In order to avenge our friends, I climbed into a tree in the court, and through the windows, open for summer, shot the tyrant in the head by means of a blow-gun with one clay bullet after another. Raging, he was about to punish his pupils, until the direction of the attack became clear to him. But I was already beyond the reach of his sphere of power and was greeted with shouts of triumph from within and without.

"At that time, no one knew anything of a regular police. Only the night-watch wandered through the streets. These men naturally had to be tormented, and so we drew ropes across the street, yelled "Uhl! Uhl!" and took to our heels until, to our great joy, the pursuing night-watch fell over the rope.

"Our chief affairs of state were naturally the battles between the young of different schools or parishes; my brothers and I were not absent. Especially lively were the fights on the great Grasbrock (grassy marsh), where we once put our opponents to full flight and drove them across the recently dredged up mire of the dike, over which a crust had formed through which they sank to their armpits. Another time, however, we were taken by surprise while in swimming and I saved myself only by swimming across the Elbe with my clothes tied onto head. For there was no fooling in these heated contests.

"From 1806 to 1811, I attended St. Michael's School, where the fundamentals of learning were supposed to be imparted to me. Many punishments were given for German speech, which may be the reason why even in later life I have never got along well with German grammar and orthography. In arithmetic, on the other hand, I led all my classmates. The arrogance which I displayed and the continual mad tricks which I practiced in school resulted in the teacher explaining to my parents that he could not put up with me any longer. This and the simultaneous precarious financial situation of my father put an end to my studies.

"In 1810, my father took onto his shoulders a business in colonial wares, which depended on purchases from smugglers. Smuggling was in full swing in the city, and all possible ingenuity applied to it. Men with Wellington boots, in which some 5-10 pounds of syrup had been poured, often brought through several hundredweights in a day and earned 3 marks for every hundred pounds. One tailor made coats with a pouch, which was filled with coffee. Milkmen put a good quantity of syrup into their buckets and poured milk over it; sand haulers filled the wagon half full of sugar with sand on top. The ingenuity of the smugglers grew with the danger. Dogs were fitted out and with a few pounds of coffee tied on their backs were chased through the gate. A coffin (in those days, burial within the city was still common) frequently held contraband instead of a corpse.

"But my father's business could not keep going under these conditions, and his circumstances became worse and worse. Only my mother kept her head high and did not despair of bringing the family through honorably. To free it from one pecuniary burden, I was employed by a distant relative who had a small business in the hog-market. Here I was usually appointed to the lowliest tasks: street sweeping, water carrying, etc., and for this I received small pay and plentiful blows, especially when the master came home drunk, which was not seldom.

"The dissolving of his business brought me back again to the home of my parents, who in the meantime had started a new venture, a little trade in candles, Holland ware, etc. My oldest sister married the mechanic, Libbertz, who came to the assistance of my parents in their distress. From this excellent man, distinguished for both skill and industry and successful in his undertakings — he was, for instance, the first man in Hamburg to install gas — I also learned many useful things. I was now sent back to school, and had to help my mother in the business.

"Soon things took a turn for the worse, as the war threatening all Europe drew ever nearer to our city. Within her walls, the first joyous sense of freedom over the defeat in Russia of the French tyrant found a mighty echo. In February, 1813, the embarkation of Prefect's guards, which consisted of the sons of the first families of Hamburg, took occasion to break out in a riot at the dikes. The young guard was disarmed by the people, and the French who accompanied them were chased out. The clothing of the mayor Abendroth, who was trying to restore order, was torn from his body, so that he was obliged to flee from the mishandling of the excited mob into our narrow street, from which he escaped through the houses to the Rödingsmarkt. Naturally, we were into everything. A French guardsman before the orphan asylum was disarmed by my brother John and fell a sacrifice to the people's rage. The wife of a French custom's officer saw this incident and reported my brother. The result was that the next day a detail of the Gendarmes appeared at our house to arrest him, and it would have been a question of his life if he had not been able to escape by the pulley line down to the canal... and from there away.

"A week later, the French departed from Hamburg, and the city remained without any established authority and without police. The civic guard was reorganized, and my father, who had formerly been an officer in it, sought out his uniform again. As the guard of some 20 men received him in front of our door and my father tried to draw his sword, it took the violent efforts of 3 men to get the rusty thing out of its sheath.

"On March 17, the first Cossacks arrived, and on March 18, the Russian General, Tettenborn, made his entrance into our city. The monstrous jubilation and the ecstacy with which this savior of the entire population was greeted will never be forgotten by those who were witnesses of the glorious day. My two older brothers, Anton and John, like hundreds of their age, offered themselves at once as volunteers in the war for freedom, and I lamented keenly that I was not yet grown up enough to join them. In the very first battle at Wilhelmsburg, in which the troops of the Allies had to give way before the superior force of the French, my oldest brother almost lost his life, being the only one of 12 men, in a boat that overturned, to save himself by swimming. My second brother served in the cavalry and had many opportunities to distinguish himself in the battles among the Mecklenbürgers. My brother-in-law, Libbertz, had taken the contract for the supply of cavalry swords (sabres), and I helped him night and day with the preparations.

"Next came the besieging of the city by the French, during which many shells struck in our neighborhood. The serving-girl who carried my little sister down the cellar stairs to safety was grazed on the arm by a shell splinter. I joined my neighbor, who was helping the artillery, and worked with him on the Grasbrock, bringing sods to repair the entrenchments torn by entering cannon balls. It was a task zealously undertaken by the youth, who were scarcely aware of the danger.

"Then came the terrible time, when the Allies withdrew and the French resumed their place in the town and took grim vengeance. In the haste of the retreat, my brother, who had held the watch on St. Michael's tower, was not relieved, and we found civilian clothes for him and two comrades, in which they luckily slipped through to Bergedorf and reached their troop again. My parents could not get together the contribution imposed upon them, which was tripled since they had sent two sons into the field, and they fled from the city, leaving their house and a good part of their possessions in the lurch. The most necessary of their belongings were packed in a barge and carried to Teufelsbrück, where we lived until the end of the war. In December, 1813, troops of the Allies returned to our neighborhood to lay siege to Hamburg, and we again took heart. But for a long time yet, the French held the city, and how terribly they behaved there and how many thousand helpless inhabitants — old men, women, children, and sick people — they drove out through the gates in the depth of winter to death and destruction, these are sad memories which belong to world history.

"During this time, those who had to suffer most under the dominion of the enemy seemed to keep most actively alive their love for the German fatherland; for out there among the people of Holstein, feelings were much divided, and Danish and French sympathies opposed Prussian and Hamburgian. When I, always active in the spreading of news, brought into the tavern in Flottbek the report of the glorious outcome of the battle of Leipzig, I was thrown out of the door. I had part in a good many incidents of that wartime life. A wherry laden with pepper was captured by a French coast guard and was to be sent to Hamburg; but the sailors threw the French overboard, ran into Teufelsbrück, hid their cargo in a copse, and began rejoicing over a glass of punch. They had been observed, however, and a detail of French soldiers was about to capture them. I had seen this, and hastened to warn the sailors and to lead them by devious ways through the Flottbek wood, followed by enemy bullets, into safety.

"On January 1, we saw how the town of Glückstadt, then in French possession, was bombarded by the English and Swedish, which after a few days resulted in its capitulation. In mid-January, the Crown Prince of Sweden held a great review of an army composed of Prussians, Swedish, Russians, English, and Germans, and moved with this variegated multitude across the hard-frozen Elbe toward France. Soon after, the Russian General, Bennigsen, approached with an army and took up headquarters in our neighborhood. Now almost daily we were witnesses of actions and skirmishes. In the night before the attack on Wilhelmsburg and Harburg, thousands of Russians bivouacked around us, and since the cold was grim, burned up a large part of the woods. At daybreak, the entire army moved across the ice; the first attack was on a redoubt on Finkenwärder, which was stormed by the Russians after the Lauenburg riflemen had shot down the gunners. Many of the Russians showed little enthusiasm for fighting; they threw out so many cartridges on the march that we gathered up whole sled-loads of them. All the houses in our neighborhood were filled with wounded, and I was often a witness to the amputation of the arms and legs of these unfortunates.

"When the ice broke up, a ferry containing some hundred Frenchmen, torn loose by floating ice, drove past us to Blankenese, where they had to surrender to the Russians. From this floating ice, I too was once in grave danger, when I slipped from a piece and was carried downstream until, after an hour's time, I was rescued, almost frozen. After the shipping was open again, a number of English gunboats came and anchored for a while before our doors, then went up to Altona and shot up the entrenchments at Grevenhof.

"At last, in May, after all Germany had long been rejoicing in freedom, Hamburg too was freed from the hated enemy, and we could go back to our old house in the city. My older brothers returned from the field to their civil occupations;

the oldest, in the book trade, later founded the still known and respected bookseller's firm of A. B. Laeisz; the other again became a clockmaker. My younger brother and I were sent to the St. Nicholas School. Under the circumstances of war, however, the youth had become so wild that it was hard to do anything with us. I fled from the narrow rooms at every opportunity, to make space for my excess of spirit in the open; swimming and skating were my special passions, through which I again got into great danger at various times. When I was at last through with school, my teacher bade me farewell with the assurance that I would become an utter good-for-nothing.

"It was at Easter, 1815, when I was 14½ years old, that I left school, and now I wanted very much to go to sea. But since the Hamburg shipping business had melted away during the war, it was difficult to find me a ship, until I was taken on board a Blankenese schooner, ELISABETH. But I went to sea on that vessel only once; then we had to put back because of damages, and my sea-faring was at an end, since my parents thereupon insisted that I should learn a handicraft. So I became apprentice to the bookbinder, Cornelius, and had to stick out a bad time there at work that accorded ill with my lively imagination, while I remained for years the youngest apprentice and during this time learned very little of the actual craft. Only at Christmas time, when the business went wild, was I drawn in and made to work till late in the night. For this, there was no other reward at Christmas than a few brown cakes. For the rest of the year, the fare was extraordinarily slender, so that the Mistress often complained that she could not even salvage the breadcrusts from the apprentices, an evidence of the hunger of the growing boys who needed nourishment. Added to that, hard treatment on the part of the Master, and more especially of the Mistress, with both of whom, moreover, I stood on a bad footing, and on whom I enjoyed playing pranks. The smoke-room under the roof gable exercised an altogether peculiar attraction. There hung many handsome hams and sausages. By means of a rope ladder over the gable, we got in through the dormer window, and regaled ourselves to our hearts' desire. Once the Mistress came up and into the room before I could accomplish my retreat. I crept into an empty chest and began to growl, because I was aware of her timidity. She fled downstairs frightened and with loud shrieking, and I over the roof and down through the back of the house to learn about the hunt for the supposed burglar.

"The name Ferdinand was too fine for an apprentice, and therefore I was called Henry. Since I had many errands to run, I could — naturally, without permission — get to my darling joy, the swimming hole. Once in the summer of 1818, near the Harbury ferry, I became aware of an eleven-year-old boy in the water who was drowning. Still half dressed, I threw myself in after him and succeeded in grabbing him, but in his fear of death, he clung to me so convulsively that we both almost went under. Luckily, I succeeded in getting my right arm free and thus in reaching the bank with my burden. The next day, the father of the boy came into our shop to offer his thanks, but as fate would have it, met the master. When questioned by him as to whether I had been swimming yesterday, I lied boldly, and so, instead of a medal for rescue, I received some sharp blows on the ear.

"Because of my unrestrained pranks, I should probably have been chased out long before if I had not known how to make myself useful to the establishment in another way. Noticing that the book-keeping was very slack, I kept for myself privately an account of goods delivered. When in January the inventories had to be made up, I showed that most of them were incorrect and demonstrated by my notes that there was around 600 more marks to get in. The reward at first promised me for this was however, soon forgotten, for when my apprenticeship was ended, I was let go without further ceremony.

"During my 4 years of apprenticeship, I had saved so much in tips that I was able to pay the cost of becoming a journeyman and to keep some over for the price of the journeying. In 1819, with 50 marks in my pocket, I started out in the spring on my travels as a bookbinder journeyman. I went first through Bremen and Hannover — for the most part on foot, naturally — to Kassel, where I found work. My first week's wages consisted of 18 good groschen. But here I had to make the sad discovery that the apprentice understood more of the work than I did, and I could only be happy in the opportunity to improve myself a little in my trade.

"In Kassel at that time, there still ruled the old elector, infamous and justly hated as a seller of souls, who had carried on a vigorous and shameless trade in the children of his own land to America.

"After a two-months stay, I continued my travels, visiting Frankfurt, Darmstadt, Mainz, Mannheim, Strassburg, Trêves, and Aachen, here and there working a while as occasion offered. This life of wandering gave me much joy, for I was eager to see something of the world and to learn to know other peoples. There were many difficulties to endure, however, and often poor quarters, especially in small places where many wanderers, dirty fellows among them, congregated. I soon learned to avoid such places and often made a hard day's march in order to reach a city. In the neighborhood of Mainz, we came to Dunkelwerden on the Rhine and found that the ferry boat had been left on the other side. On a quick decision, I swam the river with my clothing tied to my head, and, finding the ferry-man at the fair among the dancing guests, who were not a little surprised at the strange, foolhardy swimmer, got him out to take across my fellow-travelers.

"By the time I at last reached Koblenz, my money had melted away dangerously, and I had reason to be glad that I soon found a job. From my brother-in-law, I had an introduction to an officer of the garrison, whom he had rescued from the French in Hamburg in 1813. I was received by him in a most friendly way and invited to his table, a fine meal that contrasted sharply with the scant fare of the poor traveling journeyman. But to his question whether he could help me otherwise, I replied with a grateful refusal, as I did not wish to make any further demand on his generosity.

"In Koblenz, I spent 3 delightful months, thanks chiefly to the amiability of the pretty young wife of the master. Then I went to Bonn, where I soon found work. There I often had opportunity to take part in the conversation of theological and other students and to be present at many heated discussions over religious and theological themes. Thereby my meditation was awakened, and I formed for myself liberal opinions independent of tradition about many things that had been neglected in my upbringing. On the whole, I was working zealously at that time. Books were not merely my working materials, but their content also became of great interest to me. Often I read deep into the night and sought to become acquainted with the works of literature most praised at that period. I was most inspired by the noble and clear muse of Schiller, who pleased both my heart and mind. His most outstanding poems I soon knew by heart, and I have honored him all my life as, to me, the greatest genius of all time.

"In Bonn, on the beautiful Rhine, there arose in me a pure feeling of love for the pretty, spirited daughter of a baker, which might well have become serious, could I have made up my mind to go over to the Catholic faith. That, however, went against my nature, and so I took my leave and traveled farther, beyond Cologne and Elberfeld to Münster.

"In Münster, I went to work for a strict Catholic house and received no meat to eat during the entire 7 weeks of fasting, which naturally did not please me much. Also, the fanatical hatred of the Catholic majority toward the Protestants made my sojourn there uncongenial, and therefore I soon went on to Canabrück; but here too my master was an orthodox Catholic, who paraded around the streets in processions with a long church-taper.

"Now that I had worked almost 2 years as a journeyman, I felt myself to be sufficiently trained in the business to seek the high schools of bookbinding, Leipzig and Berlin. Therefore I wandered past Magdeburg to Leipzig, but could find little suitable work there and so went on farther to Dresden and Breslau. Finally, in the summer of 1821, I arrived in Berlin. Although here a great many bookbinder journeymen were seeking work, I soon succeeded in finding, in a business which employed perhaps 30 journeymen and had other manufacturing activities, a preferred position in which I earned as much as 5 to 8 dollars for a week's work. At the same time, I was also learning to make all kinds of fancy goods; and as just then silk hats were coming into fashion, we took up this branch of the business also, and I acquired a skill in it which was later to be of great use to me.

"Although I was now earning good money, I was not at the time in the habit of putting anything aside, since I paid out much for amusements and dressed after the Berlin fashion, which is to say, externally elegant with little attention to the linen, or as the Hamburger puts it, *Buten bunt, binnen schund!* (Fine without, filthy within!). I did not at that time consider it worth while to deny myself any expense from motives of thrift, for I did not believe in the possibilities of assembling riches by laying up groats and dollars, and I preferred to enjoy my life. However, my own intelligence was soon to cure me of this error.

"During my stay in Berlin, the marriage of the Crown Prince, later King Friedrich Wilhelm IV, was celebrated with great festivity, and I found myself in a dense crowd on the Schlossbrücke (Castle Bridge) when it broke under the strain and many lost their lives.

"My first activity with a business house in Berlin came to an end through an intrigue of the Master's. He was a dissolute fellow who wished to be separated from his wife, and he tried to involve me in a scandal. I did not fall into the trap, however, but took my leave and found a still better job with a competing firm. I had been working more than 2 years in Berlin when a letter from my mother called me back to Hamburg. She wanted my support in the business, which she was now running almost alone because of my father's growing weakness. As I was glad to get a further impression of the business places of the East Sea, I took my way by Rostock, Wismar, and Lübeck, and reached home on March 24, 1824, after a 5 year absence."

Hatter

We will now follow Ferdinand Laeisz further in his story of how, from a hatter, he came a ship-owner.

"Since the outlook for my parents' business was pretty poor, I immediately provided an activity of my own and began to make silk hats. As soon as I had a couple of dozen ready, I put an advertisement in the *Hamburg News*, and thereupon appeared a purchaser in the person of the hatmaker, Dittmer, who took the whole lot at 10 marks apiece, a price which left me a very sweet profit. Encouraged by this, I bound myself to Velbel of Berlin and went to work with all my might, so that in the course of the first year, I was idle hardly 10 Sundays and spared myself only the necessary sleep at night. I worked under such a strain principally because everyone believed that, as an article of a passing fashion, silk hats would soon be out, and also I could not find any helpers who understood the work. My mother and sister helped me to trim the hats and won thereby a handsome bit of money, such that my sister could later defray her dowry from it. Little by little, my skill became more widely known, and I aroused thereby the displeasure of the hatters' board, which tried to hinder me in my business, since it encroached on their privileges. Their complaint, handled chiefly by the Alderman Creutzburg, my future father-in-law, was, however, rejected by the Praetor.

"When my sister and true helper, Auguste, married the merchant, Nolte, this friend secured for me many connections in Berlin, to whom I sent larger consignments of hats at good profits. I endeavored now to increase the capacity of my business and took on several helpers, all of whom, however, I had first to teach. In the year 1825, I made the first attempt, through a friendly captain, to send a parcel of hats overseas to Buenos Aires, and had such good results that I soon got the idea that it would pay still better to have my own business in the overseas cities. Now I extended my activity over the entire hatter's trade, and became, on May 26, 1826, Master-Hatter of the Hamburg citizens.

Marriage

"Meanwhile, I had begun to think about setting up my own hearth. I became acquainted with the daughter of the senior member of the hatmakers, Creutzburg, and after a short acquaintance obtained her consent. To be sure, her strict parents, who had brought their daughter up to the trade, were not willing to have the maiden, who was not yet 20 years old, leave their home, and I had to woo for almost a year before arriving at marriage. At last, on June 4, 1826, the ceremony took place which bound me in long and happy wedlock with a true life-companion. We took a rented house in the Jungfernstieg (at that time not the elegant street it has since become) with a very spare establishment, for my bride's dowry was of the poorest. Of far more worth to me, however, was the industrious, thrifty nature and the tireless activity and skill of my wife, who soon became the best worker in the business. With the birth of our only son, on April 27, 1828, the happiness of our home was enduringly established.

Carl Laeisz. Born

"After I had earned enough money so that I could let myself in for farther-reaching enterprises, I made the first attempt to set up a business of my own overseas by sending a distant relative named Bonne, whom I considered to be a capable and trustworthy young man, with 3 helpers to Bahia, and established there a factory which both made hats and sold the hats I sent out together with a few other related articles."

The Firm Of Laeisz and Bonne

The agreement drawn up between Ferdinand Laeisz and Friedrich Bonne is preserved in the original in the archives of the firm. Its wording, so characteristic of the time and the personalities, may well follow here.

"Nr. 4194
B J. N. D.
v.12 Nov. 1828

"Be it known and understood by all concerned that on November 12 of the year one thousand eight hundred twenty-eight, between Mr. Ferdinand Laeisz on the one side and Mr. Friedrich Bonne on the other side, the following union is formed in order to establish in Bahia in Brazil a branch of the hat-factory existing here as the firm of F. Laeisz. For enduring record, this union is set in writing, signed by both contractors with their own hands, sealed atque notarii testimonio, and confirmed by witnesses.

1.

"The cosignatory Friedr. Bonne undertakes for four consecutive years the management of a branch of the hat-factory now in existence here under the name of F. Laeisz, said branch to be established in the above-named place as the firm of Laeisz and Bonne. Said four years are to begin on the day that the vessel on which the passage is to be made shall let down anchor in the roadstead of Bahia or of the harbor specified in #6, and are to reach their conclusion after a year's previous notice, which, however, neither party is permitted to give before the completion of the third year after the beginning of the contract, except in the extraordinary circumstances named in #13.

2.

"The cosignatory F. Bonne pledges himself during this time not to enter into any union of a contractual nature with any other individual to the disadvantage of one or more aspects of this present one without knowledge and consent of the cosignatory F. Laeisz; also, during the said four years not to step outside of this union even for unrelated honorable settlements, under the penalties prescribed in #15. On the other hand, the cosignatory F. Laeisz pledges himself not to enter into any other contract harmful either to the before-mentioned branch establishment in general or to his cosignatory in particular under any pretext whatever.

3.

"The cosignatory F. Laeisz also pledges himself to furnish enough raw and manufactured materials, implements, and all other objects and things pertaining to this factory conscientiously at the lowest price, and to act in such manner that the said factory there to be created shall be in position during this time to furnish good true wares of a quality in accord with the demands of the times and circumstances.

4.

"The expenses of the crossing, the freight of goods and effects, the insurance premiums, and all other costs and charges debited to this objective, are to be undertaken by the cosignatory, F. Laeisz; however, these same shall later be charged against the factory.

5.

"The bills of lading drawn for the factory equipment, as well as for all wares which at the first crossing are destined for the same, shall be set up with the stipulation that the goods must be delivered in Bahia, or in any other port in which the vessel shall enter and remain for some time, upon the producing of the like-worded copies. Of these bills of lading, the cosignatory, F. Bonne, shall receive the necessary copies in hand in order to make use of them under the circumstances defined in the following paragraph.

6.

"In any harbor in which the vessel shall lie to and remain for more than three weeks, the cosignatory, F. Bonne, is entitled and authorized to sell the finished products at any casually occurring opportunity without waiting for further order; also to establish the factory itself immediately at that place, and in that case the applicable articles of the contract shall have the identical power and value in the place chosen by the cosignatory, F. Bonne, that they would have had on direct arrival at Bahia.

7.

"If the vessel should anchor in any harbor from distress or other cause, and the passengers not be permitted to remain aboard there, but the same be obliged to provide for themselves, the cost of this provision, including abode, etc., as also the half of the stipend determined and defined in #11, reckoned for the time of remaining in that place, shall fall to the account of the factory, and the cosignatory, F. Bonne, to the extent that it cannot be laid to his personal expenditure, shall not be under any responsibility for it. Also, if by a blockade of the harbor or other uncontrollable hindrance, the establishment of the factory should be rendered impossible and thereafter efforts to enter another harbor be fruitless, the same is justified in returning without personal disadvantage, and in that case all the costs arising out of this undertaking, etc., would fall to the charge of the cosignatory, F. Laeisz, alone.

8.

"Upon a successful arrival in Bahia (please God), the co-director, F. Bonne, shall apply to the house recommended to him for clearing of wares and goods; but in case this cannot be, he shall attend to these affairs as well as possible himself and begin the work and business of the factory with all possible speed and precision.

9.

"Once established there, F. Bonne has full power to deal to the best of his ability with the disposal of the finished products as with the still unused materials, both within and without the country, and, by retail or wholesale, to ship the same anywhere to be sold through reliable firms, to cash the remittances therefor, to sell or ship out again any goods that may be returned, altogether to do as he sees fit as if this were his own possession, without, however, being responsible for possible losses, which it is his duty to do all in his power to avoid. Moreover, the same is justified, because of possible unforeseen unfavorable conditions arising, to move the factory to any other place, or to establish another branch in some other place. In such a case, however, he is bound, at the very first possible opportunity, to send word of these affairs to the cosignatory, F. Laeisz.

10.

"If no weighty local impediments arise, the cosignatory, F. Bonne, is to send back to the central management a yearly account on the business done to date, without, however, taking into account the returned goods, which, according to advice are to be taken care of by another local house, to which house, also after statement received, the cash collected is to be handed over on receipt.

11.

"As a fixed salary — outside of free victuals, lodging, light, heat, etc., so far as these things pertain to the factory — the cosignatory F. Bonne, is to receive six hundred Hamburg marks banco. Beyond that, if the yearly account shows a clear gain of more than thirty-three and one-third per cent per annum of the original starting capital after deducting all costs, ten per cent of the remaining net profits is assured him. In case of the hoped-for significant gain in the factory's business, the fixed salary of 600 marks banco shall also be reasonably increased each year; but, once the factory is established, this sum cannot be reduced under any circumstances during the contractual year, and thereafter only by a year's previous notice — without prejudice, however, to the provisions of #16.

12.

"Maintenance and board, according to the special contracts required for factory workers, fall, as a right, to the expense of the factory.

13.

"The dissolution of the business before the end of the contractual year can be brought about only by visible loss, in perilous circumstances of war, through complete destruction by fire, or by other events and misfortunes impossible to foresee and in such case is to proceed as later prescribed.

14.

"In the afore-mentioned cases, F. Bonne is justified in selling or transporting the objects on hand, their remnant, or whatever else it may be, wherever it may seem best to him. Against the danger of fire, the goods shall be insured in Hamburg or Bahia or in whatever other location of the factory, and in any possible mischance, the cosignatory, F. Bonne shall be reimbursed up to three hundred marks of the sum to be paid by the insurance. This shall also take place if he himself in the journey out or back, as provided for in the contract, should lose his effects by the risks of the sea, and the above-mentioned sum therefor is in either case to be collected on the insurable value of the factory belongings or of his private possessions.

15.

"For each of the first four years, the cosignatory F. Laeisz reserves two hundred marks banco out of the fixed salary, to be put on deposit with Mr. Johann Diederich Thormölen in Hamburg, which, upon any wilful breaking of this contract by the other party, would revert to said F. Laeisz. After the fourth year, however, this sum will stand at the absolute disposal of F. Bonne, and the latter will not be bound to offer further security. In return, Mr. F. Laeisz guarantees his cosignatory the carrying out of the stipulations of this contract before the co-signing witness, Mr. J. D. Kamm.

16.

"In case of illness resulting in unfitness for work, the expenses of board, physician, etc., will fall to the charge of the factory. The salary, however, will be figured only for the first two months of illness; in case of a longer duration, only the expenses specified above would be reimbursed by the factory.

17.

"After the time of the contract has run out, if F. Bonne should desire to return to Hamburg or any other place, the cost of the return journey shall be debited to the factory. Also if later, after a possible renewal of the contract, on due notice and satisfactory accounting, the cosignatory, F. Bonne, should take ship within three months for the return journey, the co-contractor, F. Laeisz, shall be bound to restore the expenses of this return trip. If by a blockade of the harbor or any other unavoidable effective hindrance, the embarkation should be put off against his will, then shall the cosignatory, F. Bonne be bound, in order to receive the compensation, to return on the first or second boat which sails for Hamburg or Bremen.

18.

"If during the contract-year, proposals are made by another house to the cosignatory, F. Bonne to enter that house after the close of the current year under more favorable conditions, the same shall transmit the information to the cosignatory, F. Laeisz in Hamburg, and it will be left to the choice of the latter whether he will grant these same advantages to the cosignatory, F. Bonne, or appoint another manager for the factory.

19.

"All duties, taxes, assessments, dues, war contributions, or other collections, under whatever name, levied on persons or things, fall to the account of the factory.

20.

"Should situations arise which the points herebefore established can not be construed as covering, both contractors shall accept responsibility for the solution of the unforeseen perplexity, which the one best able to handle it shall consider a duty.

21.

"If, during the herein-established space of time, the cosignatory living in that remote part of the world should be called by the Almighty to depart from this life, his well-earned property shall go to his heirs, or, if a will exists, that shall be exactly followed.

"Finally, both cosignatories establish this partnership with their signatures in their own handwriting with the annexed seal sub hypotheca bonorum.

"Made out in triplicate, of which one copy shall be deposited with Mr. Joh. Diedr. Thormöhlen. Hamburg utsupra.

"Joh. Diedr. Thormöhlen
witness to this contract — F. Laeisz

"Jac. Diedr. Kamm
witness to this contract — Friedr. Bonne"

From here on, we shall continue with the reproduction of the life memoirs of Ferdinand Laeisz:

"In spite of many blunders which we made in the beginning, the outcome was extraordinarily fortunate, and the firm Laeisz and Bonne yielded splendid results until the year 1838, when an early death snatched away my excellent partner.

Günter and Mundt

"The business then went into other hands and formed other associations. It flowers still today, however, under the successors Günter and Mundt, who have always remained in close association with my firm." (The firm that finally did business under the name of Westphalen and Company was heartlessly liquidated during the second World War. In 1928, on their centennial of uninterrupted existence, they were able to look back on a successful past.)

Westphalen and Co.

"In the following year, 1829, in common with a friendly Bremer firm, I set up a similar business in Caracas. However, I was not so fortunate with this, for, although the conditions and outlook were very good, the otherwise capable head of the business deceived us by gambling away our money and taking his own life. The difficulty of finding people who combined sufficient ability with strength of character and health was always the chief hindrance to my foreign undertakings. In 1830, I found a man equipped with all these qualities to a superior degree in I. S. Renner, who at my risk went out with 3 assistants to Valparaiso. He worked in Chile 2 years to begin with, then turned over the business to a certain Schultz, and himself sailed to Lima to found there a like establishment. Both houses, Laeisz and Schultz in Santiago and Laeisz and Renner in Lima, especially the latter, yielded rich results. To be sure, I was often in doubt for long periods of time about the outcome of my speculations, for the mail arrangements of those days were extremely slow and uncertain. When in 1831 an undertaking begun in Pernambuco went to pieces because of shameful neglect by the head of the business and cost me a large fortune in comparison with my current circumstances and I also had not received any remittance from Renner for a long time, I lost courage and wrote to him that I wanted to get out of the business and that he was to settle our accounts and remit. For answer, I received my balance in one lump in a 5,000 pound sterling bill of exchange, which I at first had difficulty in converting, since I was still not known on the Bourse. Renner took over the business then on his individual account, turned soon to greater mercantile enterprises, and died many years ago in Lima, a wealthy man. I always remained in correspondence with him, however, and as he enjoyed a considerable influence with the Peruvian government, he brought it about that I should be named consul for the Republic of Peru in Hamburg. In this position, I later gained an interesting insight into the mammoth guano enterprises of Hamburg houses.

Laeisz and Schultz

Laeisz and Renner

"I also sent an expedition to Habana, which, however, was not established at my cost, since my means were already heavily tied up. Two of the proprietors of this business, which I supplied with goods, successively won for themselves handsome fortunes; but the third was a swindler, through whom I again lost what I had made through his 2 predecessors. From our Bahia house, an able man F. W. Ziegenbein, went to Rio Grande De Sul, started a similar business there and soon brought it to wealth and honor. With him and his successors, I have had many years of pleasant and profitable association and friendly trade.

F. W. Ziegenbein

"My overseas and other foreign associations now took up so much of my time that I gave up my shop and in 1832 for 32,000 marks banco bought a house in Grimm, Number 32. The proceeds of my overseas sales were often paid to me in produce, especially in sugar and cotton, and so my business acquired ever more of a mercantile nature. Since I had neither the time nor the knowledge to occupy myself with the conversion of this goods into money, I had to leave this branch to other people, whereby I often came out very short. Here, as everywhere in the organization of the business, the first fundamental improvement took place when my son came into the business with me and because of his commercial ability, set up a more rational management.

"The strenuous activity of the first 20 years gave me little chance to step out into civic life. To be sure, I belonged to the city militia and, probably thanks to my warlike antecedents, advanced in it as far as lieutenant. But I found little comfort in this post of honor, since military discipline had never suited me, and I was pretty lax about the whole thing. The guardsmen placed under me could, therefore, do pretty much as they liked, to the great annoyance of my superiors. Once I drew on myself 48 hours of arrest because I had forgotten to inform the lieutenant who was to relieve me as main guard.

Beginning of Civic Activity

"Also I was once assistant at the Church of Nicholas, as was in those days expected of any well-situated man. However, I was even worse here than in the military, and all that I gained from this service was a few experiences which I could use later in the Corporation in the interest of a more intelligent administration of the church budget.

Early European Travel

"When my financial situation had become good enough so that I could permit myself a luxury, the old desire for travel awoke again, and I decided to make myself acquainted, one after another, with the various countries of Europe, hoping also thereby to accumulate useful information for my business and to make contacts. Because of the slowness in connections in those days, I could not yet dream of transatlantic journeys, since it was hard for me to get free even for the few weeks which a trip into neighboring lands required. In 1836, I visited England for the first time, in the company of a business friend, filled out my scant knowledge of the English speech a little, and admired the magnificent government, commercial, and industrial set-ups. A few years later, I went by steamboat to Antwerp and from there by way of Brussels to Paris, the splendors of which naturally greatly pleased me. In the opera house just then Meyerbeer's new opera, "The Huguenots," was being put on with great splendor and colossal success. Arrived in Paris, I wished first to betake myself to a business friend, whose address I had noted down as Rue du Temple. Here, then, I was set down at the right number by the cab driver, but found no one with the name I had given living in the street. There I was, unfamiliar with the language, late in the evening, in a great dilemma until I found someone who understood English and cleared up the misunderstanding by the fact that I had been directed to the fairly distant Old Street of the Temple (Rue Vielle du Temple).

"From Paris, I went by diligence to Rouen, from there down the Seine to Havre, and then across to Southampton. This time in England, I visited chiefly the enormously expanding industrial cities, above all, Manchester, and learned much of interest. In London at that time[1] the tunnel under the Thames, then in process of construction, was altogether a world wonder.

"In 1840, in the company of my friend Dubbers, a manufacturer of hats in Altona, I made a journey to Russia, and of course by steamer from Lübeck to St. Petersburg. On arriving, we had endless passport difficulties and because of that had to waste a whole day in a horrible den of a police station. The hotel in which we first took quarters distinguished itself by its uncleanliness. Upon washing, we discovered that there were no towels at hand, and since no serviceable soul was to be aroused, we used the curtains to dry ourselves, but discovered the following morning that we had made ourselves all black with them. A business friend then won our gratitude by directing us to better lodgings. In his hat factory, several hundred bondsmen were at work, among whom we observed many very skilful workmen whom we would gladly have had in Hamburg. These poor fellows were mostly hired out for a series of years by their owner, and if by then they had learned any skill, the price of hire was raised. Discipline was maintained with the lash, of which no sparing use was made, especially in punishment of drunkenness. These people let the chastisement take place without protest, since they were not used to anything else and obviously considered it in order.

"Always I had had a strong inclination toward enterprises with ships, and I

[1] [Marc Isombard Brunel, engineer, father of Isombard Kingdom Brunel, designer of the GREAT EASTERN - EDITOR]

had been strengthened in this by my sea-journeys. Therefore I gave orders[2] in Lübeck for a sailing vessel of 400 tons capacity to be built for me, which was baptized "Carl" and cost me 42,000 marks banco when put afloat. This venture in ownership was not an especially lucky one, and after 5 years I sold the vessel for 22,000 marks. Only after my son later stood by my side in business, did we take a vigorous interest in shipping, with better results, and made it little by little into a main branch of our business, which brought us not only good profit, but also much joy and many interesting experiences."

CARL, the first Laeisz vessel

In the life memoirs of Ferdinand Laeisz now follows a rather long description of the great Hamburg fire of 1842, which we will skip here although in this catastrophe also the writer signally proved his energy and foresight. His memoirs then continue:

"Soon after the fire, I bought the fire-damaged homestead, Neueberg No 14, for 58,000 marks from the fire-insurance office. I had a house built suitable for my purposes, which, however, because of the rise in cost of building materials due to the fire, came to 80,000 marks, higher than I had dreamed.

"In the same year, I sent my vessel, CARL,[3] to Guayaquil with a cargo for my friend, I. F. Grund, who was setting up an establishment there that has worked out to good results. On the other hand, another undertaking in Rio de Janeiro failed through the manager's lack of conscience. Also a business founded in 1847 in Manila miscarried at first and cost me a good deal of money; it flowered later, however, under the management of my friend, T. Albert, and his successor, Franz Secker, and still continues with honor today as the firm of Adolph Roensch.

I. F. Grund

T. Albert
Franz Secker
Adolf Roensch

"The lucky results of the Bremer South-Sea Fishery led me in common with my friends, Tientgens and Robertson, to bring into being a like undertaking in Hamburg. We got together a share-holding capital of 400,000 marks banco, bought one vessel and had another built for us, but were not favored by fortune. The choice of one captain proved to be a mistake, and in the carrying out of the fishery we suffered great losses through the intervening outbreak of the Danish War and the blockade of the Elbe, so that, after a few years, the company was liquidated.

Tietgens and Robertson

"In 1847, Adolphe Godeffroy, H. I. Merck and Co., and I founded the Hamburg-American Parcel-Delivery Stock Company, later abbreviated to the name HAPAG, (Hamburg-Amerikanische Paket-Fahrt Aktien-Gesellschaft), Which, to begin with, put 4 sailing vessels into passage to New York. This undertaking also had to suffer much from the war and other hardships; but the tireless Godeffroy was able, in spite of all hindrances, to steer the society to success. In 1854, the firms of Johannes Schuback and Sons and C. Woermann joined us, and the enterprise underwent a great expansion when we took the step of building 2 steamers, the first under a German flag.

Hamburg-American Line Founded

"The wild year of 1848 did not fail to have its effect on my enthusiastic longings for true freedom. As an old Democrat, who had been brought up in indignation over the arrogance of the privileged classes and the oppression of every independent movement, I greeted the springtime of the people with joy. But I soon recognized the senseless paths which the movement was taking and the unfitness of the leader. Therefore I joined the moderate "patriotic" party which

[2] [to Jacob Meyer - EDITOR]
[3] [Capt. J. J. Visser - EDITOR]

GEFION | *CHRISTIAN VIII*

was growing up in Hamburg, although I had belonged mostly to the property-owning citizenry. In our city, after a few riots and much foolish chatter, everything went relatively well. However, when around us in Germany the political waves rose high, I could get no rest until I could see something of the scenes of the great events. Therefore in March I went for a few days to Berlin and saw much of the folk-uprising and of the deplorable sights of those days. In 1849, I went with several friends to Schleswig, and shortly after the famous sea-fight in Eckernförde was on board the severely damaged Danish frigate, GEFION, which had had to strike her flag there before the weak shore batteries after her sister ship, CHRISTIAN VIII, had been set afire by the guns.

Partnership with son Carl | *Carl Ferdinand Born*

"One result of the political unrest was the great decrease in worth of landed property, especially outside of the city, and I took advantage of this opportunity to acquire, for the cheap price of 15,000 marks banco, the beautiful estate of the alderman Brandenburg in Elmsbüttel, of which I made a summer home, in which I have experienced great pleasure, and to which, because of the physical labor in the garden, I attribute my health in my old age. Also, we celebrated the happy day of our silver wedding at this country seat. My son had then just returned home after finishing his mercantile apprenticeship with the friendly house of E. C. Schramm and Co. in Bremen and from getting a glimpse of England and France. On the first of March, 1852, he came into my business as a partner, and from that day dates its more significant rise. In family life too, fortune was kind to us, for on the 10th of November of that same year, my son married the fifth daughter of the well-known and much-respected ship-broker, C. L. Knöhr, and brought us thereby not only an admirable daughter-in-law, but also a large family circle of honorable and lovable people, with whom we have always remained in intimate association and whom we have to thank for many evidences of friendship. My wishes were crowned on August 10, 1853, by the birth of a grandson, who received in baptism the name of Carl Ferdinand."

HAMMONIA | *BORUSSIA*

Following this, a large space in the memoirs is occupied with various journeys into Italy, Danmark, North America, Spain, England, France, and the Levant. During the Crimean War, both of the Hapag steamers, HAMMONIA and BORUSSIA, were chartered by the French government as transport ships to the Black Sea. On the Bosporus during a thunderstorm at night, Ferdinand Laeisz was almost drowned. He visited also shot-riddled Sebastopol, which had shortly before been vacated by the Russians. With the return from this journey, we pick up again the thread of the account.

Wilhelm Reimers | *PUDEL*

"After the close of the Eastern war, business in Hamburg, as everywhere else, took a sharp upward swing, which put us in a position to extend our undertakings farther. We contracted with the Hamburg dockyard of H. C. Stülcken for the building of a barque, in which our friend, Wilhelm Reimers, shared. To honor my daughter-in-law, the vessel was named PUDEL (Poodle), her nickname, taken from her curly hair, and it made the beginning of a long line of "P" boats which we ordered built, half on the Rhine, half on the Weser.

Beginning of Insurance Business

"Already for some time, I myself had been covering the ocean risks of a large part of my exports in all directions, and thereby gradually had taken on the business of also writing insurance on the risks of others. This branch of the business, we now expanded considerably and have since then, with varying luck but on the whole with success, carried on a private insurance business. I entered the Association of Hamburg

Assurers and have always devoted an active interest to the efforts directed by this association toward the understanding of the common weal; and, for the improvement of the position of our Bourse, I have taken part in the founding of various insurance associations.

"As a result of excessive speculation in many directions, however, the general feeling of happy confidence came to an end in terror when in the fall of 1857 the great crisis broke out. Those were days of grief and wretchedness in Hamburg, almost worse than those of the great fire, as every hour brought more Job's posts of large suspensions of payment. In the general misfortune, I had for the time so lost my head that it required my son's entire presence of mind to convince me that our position was undamaged and that nothing could happen to us, rather that it was our task, through sharing in the Guarantee Cash-discount Chest to help rebuild the sunken confidence. Gradually the clouds disappeared, and we could be happy to have come through with relatively small losses. Unfortunately, at this time the Brazilian steamship association in whose founding we had taken part, also went to pieces, and not until 13 years later, did we, in common with a few other firms who shared in the South-American trade, succeed in calling back to life under the leadership of our friend, August Bolton, a steamship alliance with those districts so important for Hamburg's trade.

August Bolton

"The steamship business in those days could not make much ('could not weave much silk'), since it was still operating at altogether too high a cost. Furthermore, the first German steamship route between Hamburg and England, in which I had a share, had an unfortunate outcome, and in October, 1858, came the terrible news of the burning on the high seas of our packet-steamer AUSTRIA with several hundred humans being, among whom I especially grieved over the brave Captain Heidtmann. Of course there was a collection taken for the survivors of the unfortunate ones, which produced a rich yield, and my zealous sharing in this friendly human undertaking brought it home to me that it is an honorable duty for well-to-do people to establish a permanent aid for their fellow men brought to need by undeserved misfortunes. Therefore I decided on a building of perhaps 50 rooms that would accommodate some 90 persons at no cost to them. At my request, the Senate and the Corporation, with honorable recognition, gave the ground for this gratis, and named the street in which the foundation, which was completed in 1861, is situated Laeisz Street.

S.S. AUSTRIA

"The Italian war of the year 1859 again brought great agitation into the business world, for the Prussian army was also mobilized and there was every appearance of all Europe soon being in flames again. Matters did not reach this point, to be sure, but the threatened blockade of the Elbe on this occasion, and even more in the following years as the relations with Danmark grew ever more acute, made us feel most painfully the lack of a German navy — a condition that has fortunately changed in the meantime.

"A fresher political current now again flowed through Germany and, even with us in Hamburg, led to a new system of government based on liberal foundations. Since then, I have taken an active part in the affairs of the Corporation — on which I have been re-appointed every time without noteworthy opposition — and have bound myself to the "left center" faction, which, according to my opinion, unites in itself the most intelligent independent forces. Here, I stood for the abolition of many worn-out institutions, such as the closing of the gates and a citizen militia, and on the other hand took part in the establishing of timely enterprises for the public good, like the

Begins Work on City Corporation

zoölogical garden, the building associations for workmen's houses, folk kitchens, folk baths, naval school, sailors' registry, society for the rescue of the ship-wrecked.

"In the years now following, the wave of political feeling again swelled high in Germany. First, the war against Danmark sharpened an old cutting edge that we of North Germany were most keenly aware of, and I could not help finding a satisfaction in the fact that on our beloved Sunday excursions to Nienstedt and Blankenese, we no longer had to pay highway toll in Danish coins. However, when the strife flared up between Prussia and Austria over the possession of Schleswig-Holstein and over the leadership in Germany, the feeling in Hamburg was much divided. To Austria, we were obligated by gratitude for her help in the great crisis, and the Austrian military, while in garrison here, had made themselves much loved. Prussia, on the other hand, with her militarism and her pedantic bureaucracy, was uncongenial to the people of Hamburg. Luckily, however, reason triumphed over emotion, and we joined the power of Prussia, more solidly based and striving for the united good of Germany. After Hamburg had become a member of the North German Bund, strife blazed up again over accession to a tariff union, and in this matter I worked always for the unconditional necessity of retaining our free harbor, in which belief I also took part in the foundation for the destruction of the Customs Union.

Union with Prussia

"The glorious year of 1870 at last realized the dream of so many generations by uniting the various German branches into one great and powerful realm. Whoever, like myself, had seen the fatherland in its deepest humiliation and during a long life had not ceased to hope for the attainment of the desired goal, knew doubly to prize the fortune that had permitted him to live into this great, glorious time."

So far, we have allowed the personality of Ferdinand Laeisz to speak to us out of his own life-memories. His vigor of life remained undiminished up to his old age. He was early awarded a membership in Lloyds of London, an honor which that oldest and most important insurance-and-classification-association of world-shipping has shared with very few non-Englishmen. From 1871, he was president, by seniority, of the Hamburg City Corporation, in the affairs of which he took the most active interest. In the summer of 1873, he went on a walking trip and a mountain-climbing expedition with his grandson. At 75, he was standing on the top rung of a ladder in his garden and picking apples when the ladder fell, but that did not hinder him from remaining true to his belief that physical exercise serves health. On June 4, 1875, he celebrated in Elmsbüttel the festival of his golden wedding and was rejoiced by a deputation of the Hamburg Corporation led by its President with a flattering address. The high point of his life was probably the celebration of his 80th birthday, on which greetings and ovations arrived in extraordinary numbers. As the highest token of distinction, he received a testimony from the Senate addressed to the "Worshipful Fellow Member, Worthy Senior President of the Corporation, staunch friend of men, whose open heart and open hand for all that is good and beautiful, for all that is useful and beneficent, has so often been tested and proved true."

Member of Lloyds

When Kaiser Wilhelm I visited Hamburg, Ferdinand Laeisz, as chairman of the Horticultural Society, conducted him through the flower show. When the Kaiser heard that his guide was the Senior President of the Corporation, he jestingly called him his colleague, and it was a heart-rejoicing sight to see the two robust old men with snow-white hair walking

Kaiser Wilhelm I

(F. LAEISZ)

Ferdinand B. LAEISZ
1801-1887

side by side, the Kaiser in friendly conversation with his some 4 years younger contemporary.

For 63 years, Ferdinand Laeisz was able to take an active part in the leadership of the firm he had founded, which for 8 years was represented simultaneously by 3 succeeding generations. Even in the fall of 1886, at the trial voyage of a steamer of the Woermann line, his tirelessness from early morning until late evening awoke the admiration of the participants. After a sickbed of scarcely 8 days, on February 7, 1887, an easy death ended the restless active life of this unusual man.

Death in 1887

We believed that we could not paint the character portrait of this man better than by letting him speak for himself in both great and small matters, for from an early age, there is evident in him at any moment the foreward-driving initiative, the readiness to take a risk, and the ability to turn toward a new goal when the time is ripe. Thus the bookbinder-apprentice becomes a hatmaker, the proprietor of a hat business becomes an exporter, who from the beginning instinctively understood the soul of the export business, the creation of solid overseas bases. Along with this, we must remember that Ferdinand Laeisz laid the foundation of the firm which later became the most famous shipping business of Germany, and that not in a time of German expansion, but in the 2 decades from 1826 to 1847, the founding year of the Hapag, during which the economic depression following the Napoleonic tyranny with its resulting impoverishment and feebleness in enterprise lay with its full weight on Germany. That the Hapag, which Ferdinand Laeisz had helped to found, decided after a few years, because of the profit to be gained from the charter, to rent out both its steamers to the French government as transports for the Crimean War, was also a sign of the times.

Trade in the Far East Begun

A few years later, the firm wished to undertake a trade to the Far East. But since there was no business understanding between Hamburg and Japan, the Laeisz vessel that had been appointed for trade to Japan and China had to sail at first under the flag of Holland. There was no German empire, not yet even a North German Bund, and Ferdinand Laeisz proposed to the Senate to establish a Hamburg consulate in the Japanese harbor of Nagasaki. Just before this, Japan had, unwillingly enough, opened her shores to foreign trade. Ferdinand Laeisz was the first German on the spot. Openly — indeed, with pleasure — he confessed that with the entrance of his son into the firm in 1852, for the first time, a well-regulated, commercially trained efficiency got the rudder in hand. With the personality of Carl Laeisz, with whom the firm was to win world renown, we shall henceforth have to deal. However, the business, in which he became partner, already showed the traits of a future organization of great magnitude.

Chapter Two: CARL HEINRICH LAEISZ AND CARL FERDINAND LAEISZ

CARL HEINRICH LAEISZ

Carl H. Laeisz

Carl Laeisz, the only son of the founder of the firm, as we have already learned from the memoirs of his father, became a partner in the firm in 1852, when he was 24 years old. In 1879, his son, Carl Ferdinand, born in 1853, became the third partner, along with his father and grandfather, so that from 1879 to 1887, the year of the death of the senior Ferdinand, 3 generations at once stood at the head of the shipping house, which had grown meanwhile to international importance. Both Carl and Carl Ferdinand Laeisz were taken away by death in the midst of life's activity, the one immediately after the other, the son even before the father. Carl Ferdinand Laeisz died in August 1900 at the age of 47; his father, Carl Laeisz, in March 1901. Whereas we have the lively auto-biographical notes of the founder, Ferdinand Laeisz, concerning the beginnings of the firm, the son and grandson have left nothing similar. Significant as the House of F. Laeisz became at the height of the activity of Carl and Carl Ferdinand and well-known as it already was in the realm of world business, it is equally difficult, with the scarcity of all material of the time which has any individual coloring, to give to a history of the firm more than a prosaically factual character. In the handwriting of Carl Laeisz, there exists in the Laeisz archives only 1 instruction to his captains, which we will communicate to you later. Even this is impersonally signed merely with the firm-name, "F. Laeisz". Carl Ferdinand, who for 3 years was President of the Hamburg Chamber of Commerce, often meets us in the protocols of this corporation; but unfortunately not one text of his Chamber of Commerce speeches, which always carried a strong influence, has been preserved, and only a very little of what he said in the old Hamburg Corporation, concerning "An Honorable Merchant". Thus in order to paint a picture of the personalities of these two men, we are referred to the mirrored reflection of their character and their accomplishments which is preserved in the tributes and speeches to their memory.

Therefore in this chapter we shall proceed at first, by means of the available archive materials plus a few outside testimonials, to trace the business development of the firm up to the death of Carl Laeisz, that is, to the beginning of this century, including the part played in other related enterprises, and then we shall try to fill out as far as possible from intimations the framework of the personal picture.

At the time when Carl Laeisz entered his father's business, hat-making had not been its main branch for a decade. The journey to Russia which Ferdinand Laeisz took in 1840 with his business colleague and friend, Dubbers, the hat-maker from Altona, was presumably still an outgrowth of the hat business in general and of the search for a new sales outlet; but after that, nothing more is recorded in connection with the hat firm. Only one small reminiscence of the period of the hat-factory seems to have long kept a place in the picture of the growing general export business: until the outbreak of the war of 1914, materials for the making of hats were shipped to a firm of Adolpho Schritzmeyer in Saint Paul, Brazil. Presumably this connection had come down from the time of the South American enterprises under Ferdinand Laeisz.

The year of 1839 acquired significance for the firm through still another

(Capt. ROBERT K. MIETHE)

Carl Heinrich LAEISZ
1828-1901

event, aside from that business journey; for Ferdinand Laeisz decided to take his first step into a field in which he was destined to act as a marshall but concerning the strategy of which he as yet had everything to learn. As we have already seen, he became a ship-owner, by giving orders for the building of a sailer. In this, perhaps the characteristics of the time played a part. It seems as if in Hamburg of that day it was simply necessary for a merchant of repute to own at least one vessel! That first vessel of the new shipping firm was built in the dockyards of J. Meyer in Lübeck, a brig of 96 commercial capacity, that is, about 220 regular net tonnage. A very modest vessel in the concept of our day, and yet somewhat above the average of those years. Ninety-one feet long and some 22 feet broad, the first ancestor of the proud fleet of the most successful sailers that ever plied the ocean made her début. CARL, Ferdinand named his vessel, to honor his son, of course. About her voyages, nothing is known. They seem to have been not especially encouraging for the building up of a shipping business, for in 1847, the CARL was sold to August Jos. Schön and C. H. Wilink, reportedly for a little more than half of the building cost, and 9 years were to go by before Ferdinand Laeisz should again decide to own ships.

What a far-sighted merchant! Let us think in what era we are standing. The world appeared to be crumbling. Gone are the stout, full-bellied vessels of the East India Company. The first clipper-ships are flying around the Cape of Good Hope after the precious tea-cargoes of the East. Others are fighting their way around Cape Horn, their steerage teeming with the swarm of emigrants magically lured on by the glitter of the goldfields of California. A new era dawns under the whip of a new slogan: Time Is Money! Shiproom is demanded. A few years before Laeisz built CARL, a vessel had sailed for the first time under the flag of Hamburg through the straits of Gibraltar on a journey into the Mediterranean. All eyes were looking out toward new horizons; the East and North Seas had become too narrow for the German merchant.

Ferdinand Laeisz's enterprising spirit now directed itself to the opening up of another source of raw material. The smoky rapeseed oil lamps in the catboats and peasant homes of North Germany demanded a better light. Train-oil (whale oil) and lanterns signified a mighty advance. Laeisz succeeded in interesting the wholesale train-oil firm, Tietgens and Robertson, in the formation of a South Sea whaling industry. Carl Woermann was also interested. Those were good names, which enjoyed confidence in Hamburg. Therefore, when the step was taken in July, 1843, for the founding of the "South Sea Fishery Company of Hamburg", more than 250,000 marks banco of the capital stock was immediately subscribed. F. Laeisz took 20 shares for each 1,000 marks banco.

South Sea Fishery Co.

The first meeting of the company took place August 3, 1844, and was opened by Ferdinand Laeisz. A few days later, in a second meeting, he was chosen a member of the 5-man board of directors. The firm of Tietgens and Robertson officiated as corresponding firm; in their hands also was the chairmanship of the board.

Ferdinand Laeisz soon showed himself to be one of the most active leaders of the new undertaking. Together with an experienced captain and a well-known shipbuilder, he chose the ships with which the whaling should be carried on. The first one, a barque, they found on the spot, and, like true sons of their hometown, they named her HAMBURG. Later, Ferdinand Laeisz journeyed to Bremerhaven with an expert adviser, and there acquired a full-rigged ship, which then received the name, ELBE. It is worthy of note that a few years later, Ferdinand Laeisz again went to Bremerhaven to buy a vessel there, the fourth in the fleet of the newly established Hamburg-American Package-Delivery Joint Stock Company (Hamburg-Amerikanische Packetfahrt Aktien-Gesellschaft, the HAPAG). This vessel also, after its purchase, was named ELBE.

The "South Sea Fishery Company", however, was not destined for a long life. The time was not propitious for this undertaking. The Danish war and the blockade of the Elbe in 1848 led to considerable losses. One of the two vessels was forced to lie for months in England with a full lading and complete crew, to wait for the end of the war. Then it developed that the captain of the HAMBURG was completely inexperienced in whale-fishing and moreover was neither reliable nor able to keep strict discipline on board his vessel.

Ferdinand Laeisz did his utmost to further the undertaking. Often he advanced money, even on short notice, and redeemed drafts that had been drawn on the company from foreign parts. Also, as underwriter, he took a share of the risk for the insurance of both vessels, of their equipment and of the catch, at normal premium rates. But, as already said, the conditions of the time shaped themselves unfavorably. Therefore, in the year 1848, the HAMBURG was sold to the firm of Biancone and Co., and in the following year, the ELBE to Joh. Marbs. The South Sea Fishery Co. dissolved with a loss of something like a quarter of its capital.

Whaling & Fishing Industry

The recognition of the importance of whaling to our political economy seems to have remained always alive in the house of Laeisz; for when, after a long time, the attempt was again made in Hamburg to call into being a German whale-fishery, when in 1902 the Whaling and Fishing Industry, joint stock company (Walfang-und Fischindustrie, A. G.), was established, the firm of Laeisz was a leading share-holder, along with the firm of Knöhr and Burchard.

Hamburg-Brazilian Steamship Co.

Apart from the unsuccessful undertaking of the fishing industry in the South Sea, the firm was doing a general export business in the period just after the entrance of Carl Laeisz as a partner. Here we should remember the testimony of Ferdinand Laeisz in his memoirs that a "fundamental-improvement" in the organization of the entire business took place when the son became a partner (1852) and, "thanks to his business capacity, established a more rational management". It was presumably also due to the co-operation of a fresh enterprising force that at the founding of the Hamburg-Brazilian-Steamship-Company, Ferdinand Laeisz became co-director and a member of the supervisory board. This company also did not succeed, and, in the year 1860, had to plead bankruptcy. One can only suppose that the liquidation is to be explained by a severe misfortune which in 1859 resulted from the German emigration to Brazil. Enrollments and work-contracts were signed in Germany which set forth all sorts of promises, but the newcomers, once arrived at the plantations, were made dependent by usurious advance-payments and treated ruthlessly as slaves. Since at that time there was no possibility for a German state to take effective diplomatic steps overseas, the Prussian minister of finance, von der Heydt, abruptly forbade emigration from Prussia to Brazil, and this rescript naturally had its influence also in non-Prussian Germany. Thereby the business of transporting emigrants to South America was as good as paralyzed.

Early Development of Hamburg Shipping

Hamburg's shipping business had in the meantime developed most promisingly. Whereas in 1854 she had altogether 203 sailers with about 17,000 commercial loading capacity and 2 diminutive steamers, 10 years later 445 sailers with about 50,000 commercial capacity besides 11 steamships flew from their masts the 3-towered flag. When, at the end of May, 1850, the HELENA SLOMAN, as the first Hamburg steamer,

(F. LAEISZ)

Frau Sophie Knöhr LAEISZ
1831-1912

(1) (NAUTICAL PHOTO AGENCY)

Wood Barque PATAGONIA, 491 Gross Tons
1873-1886
Last But 5 Of The Wooden Vessels

(2) (F. LAEISZ

Wood Barque PUDEL, 485 Gross Tons
1857-1870
Second Vessel Built For The Firm

started the voyage across the Atlantic, it was an event. Many of the old travelers shook their heads thoughtfully. The first iron sailing vessel of Hamburg, which was bought in 1851, also caused a great sensation and adverse criticism from the "old school". The harbor had hardly quieted down when the next sensation arrived. Godeffroy bought one of the largest vessels of the time, the clipper, SOVEREIGN OF THE SEAS, a real wonder of elegance and speed. When the excitement had reached the highest point, there came a bitter disillusionment: the 262 foot ship could not come up the Elbe; her draught was too deep! Not exactly glamorous publicity for Hamburg as a world-harbor! In recognition and as a result of this fact, Laeisz, father and son, began working intensively for a deepening of the harbor by carefully planned dredging.

SOPHIE & FRIEDRICKE. And ADOLPHE

The continual opening up of new settlements in the American West and in Australia brought with it a perceptible growth in the shipping business. And so to both the Laeiszes it now seemed time to venture anew the step into ship-owning. "The will — the knowledge — the ability" was the slogan of the elder. It seems that he had in the time of waiting gathered together a fund of knowledge concerning the nature of the shipowner's calling, so rich that he was soon to lead himself and his son in a rapid ascent into the first rank of Hamburg shipowners. They began in a small way, and in the year 1856 bought the schooner, SOPHIE AND FRIEDERICKE, a wooden vessel scarce 85 feet long and of 87 commercial load capacity. In the following year, they acquired the wooden brig, ADOLPHE, from the shipping firm of Godeffroy and Son. The circumstances of this undertaking gave them so much satisfaction that in the same year they gave orders at the Stülcken docks for the building of a barque of 194 commercial load. This vessel received the name of Carl's young wife, who at home, because of her curly hair, was always called "Poodle". In this vessel, Wilhelm Reimers of Hamburg had a half share.

PUDEL and SCHILLER

PUDEL remains memorable for one special reason. With this sailer, the Laeisz shipowners began their custom of giving to their vessels, with few exceptions, names that begin with "P", a peculiarity that later gave occasion to the general title, "P-Liner", to all the Laeisz vessels. For his next vessel, Laeisz acquired from the firm of John F. Möller a wooden brig of 85 commercial loads. She received the name, SCHILLER, presumably to honor his good Hamburg business friend. How large must one picture these vessels? Well, a commerzlast, the unit of ship-measurement of those days, is somewhere near the equivalent of 2¼ of our modern register tons (of 2.83 cbm.). PUDEL, with her 194 commerzlasten, was a vessel far beyond the average, which around 1860 was about 130 commercial loads. The largest vessel of the Hamburg fleet in 1860 was the ELECTRIC of Sloman's with 459 commercial loads, that is somewhat over 1,000 register tons. A sketch (Plate No. 21) may make clear the growth in the size of vessels in the last 4 decades of the foregoing century. It shows PUDEL, the stately vessel of 1857, next to PARSIVAL of 1882, and beyond, one of the heavy Laeisz 4-mast barques, the typical P-liners of the turn of the century, which with their 2,800 register tons net, were likewise noticeably over the average size of the sailers of their time. What a powerful advance in shipping within 4 decades is evident in this comparison!

Sophie Knöhr Laeisz

Carl Ferdinand Laeisz

Soon after being taken into the firm, Carl Laeisz married Sophie, one of the daughters of the shipbroker, Christian Ludwig Knöhr. She came from a prolific family, being the eighth child and the fifth daughter of her parents. Nevertheless, the son, Carl Ferdinand, born to the Carl Laeisz couple on August 10, 1853, was to remain the sole heir of the family and the house.

The years of the rising tide of German shipping had dawned. Undoubtedly the restless urge of the Germans toward a united fatherland, through its tensions of domestic politics, had counseled a prudent holding back in mercantile business. But then came the stream of emigration, setting in after 1848, that steadily required more shipping space. Overseas, the influx of fresh blood led to a wider flowering in places until then closed to world trade. New marketlands for the products of Europe began to open, new sources of raw stuff became active. Along the North Sea coast there soon arose a new courage for bold planning and made promising connections with harbor-spots whose names till then had hardly been heard on the Elbe and Weser. On regular schedules, great 3-masters now sailed under the Hamburg flag to California, to return by way of Hawaii laden with sugar. The young republics on the Plata and on the West coast of South America incited the beginning of new shipping connections. Here the century-old barriers, with which the Spanish colonial rule had zealously held foreign trade at bay, were falling. But still more encouraging had been the effect of the abrogation in England of Cromwell's navigation act: after 1849, the way was free for direct exchange of goods with the overseas colonies of England. Now, too, German vessels, sailing westward, carried in their steerage whole battalions of emigrants from continental and Irish ports, to the coasts of Canada and the U. S. A., and returned more and more frequently with cargoes of Canadian wood. The news of gold in Australian sand worked like magic. In the year 1852, 8 Hamburg vessels were made ready for the continent farthest from Europe; 2 years later, there were already 42. Even in the harbors of British India, the red flag with the three white towers appeared regularly.

And now a new kind of cargo took on increasing significance in the shipping business: materials of cast iron. Shiploads of bar and rod iron, of girders, sheet metal, rails, went out to the harbor-building in America and Australia for the construction of railways and workshops where earlier had been only the steppes and the primeval forests. Harvests came across to populous Europe, wheat from the virgin soil of the prairies. The spindles in a thousand English spinning mills were calling for mountains of cotton. Before long there came from the west coast the first vessels with cargoes of sodium nitrate (saltpeter), which had been brought over previously only in small quantities for the use of the powder factories. It had been discovered that this salt gave a new fruitfulness to the worn-out fields of the old world. In this stuff had been found a fertilizer of astonishing effect, and from year to year the demand for saltpeter increased, which was in so little time to gain such great importance for the as yet but slightly known firm of F. Laeisz.

Still they waited, Father and Son Laeisz, noting and studying the revolutions in the shipping business. For, while these were boom years for German shipping, they were, to an even higher degree, years of desultory progress and surprising innovations. Shipbuilders lost the inherited knowledge and norms. For years, sailors had been bringing word of marvels of newfangled sailing craft built in the Yankee shipyards. People could hardly believe until they themselves saw the first clipper ships. Many of the old school shook their heads, but other shipbuilders became thoughtful, and a few decided to study where there was something to learn, and sent their sons across the Atlantic to those harbors in which the miracle ships had been planned and built. And then it was not long before in the German yards also sailing vessels arose such as until now would not have been thought seaworthy. Their waterline flowed away in undreamed-of slimness, the bow rose in a graceful curve without the old-time spreading build-up. In place of the comfortable familiarity of the four-square hatch, appeared the new round hatch which the Americans had invented. In 1853, Ernest Dreyer on the Elbe built his first clipper, the IMPERIEUSE. The second building of this kind was a great success. With the full-rigged ship, CID, a Hamburg ship for the first time since the days of the Hanse, became the talk of the world of international shipping. Under Captain Thiesen's conduct, the CID made astonishingly quick voyages to all parts of the world. Not only the seamen and shipbuilders paid attention, but even more carefully were the merchants watching. Fast-sailing ships, whose time of arrival could almost be predicted – at this, whole new vistas opened up. Quick passages, quick turnover.... They began to take note of the names of vessels and of captains.

In those years also, the first energetic efforts were made to shorten the time spent in harbor by the sea-going vessels. It was very costly of time to repair and clean the bottom of a vessel by the venerable process of careening her. Therefore, since 1851, in Hamburg the work had been done on dry dock, a plan of the young Robert Sloman and of the Bremer master shipbuilder, Wencke. Here a vessel could again be made seaworthy in half the time formerly required.

There were heated arguments in the harbor and on the bourse over the most important question of the day: sail or steam – or both together? And here too it was the young Sloman who fought with determination for the modern shipbuilding material, iron. And who could have surmised how that mysterious discovery of telegraphy would affect overseas trade and shipping! Not until 1850 were the first experiments made with an underseas cable between Dover and Calais. So there was much to grasp and more to think over, and it was a question of being prepared for unexpected developments in ship-building, administration, and politics. Yes, even in politics! Things looked threatening in the Near East. And sure enough the Crimean War first brought the awaited clearing.

Hapag

All this and much more may have had a part in influencing the decision of the two Laeisz men to hold back. In work toward a purposed goal, the elder man had earned himself a position within the merchant and shipping circles that yielded nothing to that of any of the old established shipowning families. His counsel had weight; men sought his co-operation. When the Hamburg-American-Parcel-Post Joint Stock Association was formed. Laeisz was chosen, though at that time not yet a ship-owner, with Godeffroy and Merck, to the directorship of the new firm. And it was he who received the most votes!

Ferdinand Laeisz was not the man to put this position in jeopardy by overhasty action. There was no lack of examples of risky enterprises in his milieu. Whoever leafs through the history of the mercantile houses of Hamburg in the middle of the last century will come often on the names of firms who were like day-flies. It seems as if those decades produced a fruitful soil for speculative plans which knew only one goal, the making of money, instead of, what the propriety of the merchant should be, serving the interchange of the goods of this rich earth.

Gebr. Schiller & Co.

Entries in the shipping registry of the city of Hamburg and ship passports of those days show that Laeisz, Father and Son, had an interest in the steamship company of Gebr. Schiller and Co. Under September 3, 1855, is a statement concerning the "3-masted schooner screw steamer, POLLUX", which indicates this, and under September 5, 1856, one concerning the screw steamer, CASTOR. Besides the firm of Gebr. Schiller and Co. and that of Ferdinand and Carl Laeisz, the firms of R. F. Pearson and of Max Th. Hayn were also interested in this shipping company. Their vessels were employed on the course between Hamburg and London. Concerning the outcome of this enterprise, nothing is recorded.

And still Laeisz bought no vessels. It may be that the ear of the elder Laeisz, sharpened by work-enriched years, became aware of the slight cracking in the timbers of so many outwardly proud mercantile houses and banks. At the close of the year 1856, a warning signal sounded through all the venture-happy activity: the banks suddenly raised the discount rate considerably. The year of 1857 was casting its shadow before. Perhaps this is the place to give a brief look at the medium of payment in the commerce of Hamburg at that epoch. The fixed standard of the stock-market was the banco mark. It contained 16 shillings at 12 pfennigs each. One banco mark was equal to 1.264 marks current Hamburg and had a value of about 15 silver groschen of North German currency. Until 1856, the relation of the banco mark to the current mark stood at 100 to 79.4. You will not go far wrong by comparing the value of a banco mark to DM 1.50 at our present standard. At the beginning of 1857, speculation again rose to a climax of fevered enterprise. But in the second half of the same year, came the crash of markets, which, starting in America, flashed like lightning across England and France to Germany and Austria. Among the important commercial centers of the continent, then, Hamburg was to be hit the hardest.

The Depression of 1857

In the chaos of this greatest economic crisis of the century, Carl Laeisz's commercial understanding and organizational ability showed themselves for the first time in their full strength. In the midst of the immeasurable series of business crashes, which even many of the oldest, most important firms suffered, the firm of F. Laeisz remained with endurable losses only. Yet they did not content themselves with salvaging their own interests. Through Carl's urging, the firm took an outstanding part in the establishment of the Hamburg-Guarantee-Discount Chest, a community undertaking with the purpose of re-establishing the lost commercial credit. The impact of this chest in the days following the great crisis was of decisive importance for the rebuilding of Hamburg's business. In 1858, Ferdinand Laeisz withdrew from the board of directors of the Hapag without leaving us any information concerning his motive. One reason was certainly the wish to devote himself more intensively to the development of his own shipping business. For years, he had shown great interest in the opening of new harbors and coasts to German shipping, and had encouraged young merchants to settle overseas and thus to establish bases for the extension of our trade-relations. We have already seen how the making of silk hats and their export became for him the starting point for his own establishment across the sea. Now in those years a friend of Ferdinand Laeisz's who as a merchant employed the same counting house was Jakob Bollenhagen. This man especially cultivated connections with Batavia, whither in the year 1848 he sent two of his employees, Pandel and Stiehaus, apparently with the advice and support of Ferdinand Laeisz. In Batavia, the two now built up a firm under the name, Pandel and Stiehaus. We can well assume that this new establishment was successful; for before long, in the winter of 1852-53, Bollenhagen was induced to send a third one of his people to Batavia, his commercial traveler for Hamburg, Louis Kniffler, a native Düsseldorfer. After a few years this man had already become a partner of Pandel and Stiehaus, and, after their death, became owner of the firm together with L. W. Stäcker. Kniffler, for his part, early directed his gaze toward the possibility of trade with Japan, and it is not impossible that it was he who interested Ferdinand Laeisz in this. On the other hand, it is also quite conceivable that it was Laeisz who, in his far-seeing way, brought the young Kniffler's attention to the new market in the Far East.

Hamburg Guarantee Discount Chest

At that time, Japan was obstinately closed against European and American trade. Only the Dutch had succeeded, since 1639, in holding a trading base on the tiny island of Deschima in the bay of Nagasaki. In the city of Nagasaki itself, the sole foreign establishment to be found was a Chinese factory. This exclusion of aliens lasted for 300 years, until, in 1853, the American Commodore Perry appeared before Jeddo and demanded the opening of certain harbors. When this demonstration was repeated in 1854 with stronger war-forces, the Japanese government decided to open a few harbors to foreign shipping. England, Russia, Holland, and finally also Prussia achieved trade relations with Japan in the following years.

In the year 1861, the merchants of Hamburg made the attempt to have the representative of the Laeisz firm, Louis Kniffler, appointed as the Hanseatic consul in Japan. This was refused; and likewise a conference of the Hanseatic resident minister, Geffken, with a Japanese embassy in Berlin failed to take place. Now Ferdinand and Carl Laeisz decided to act independently. In 1863, they purchased the Swedish barque, CECILIA, which lay just then in Hamburg harbor. Through the clerk of the Prussian General Consulate in Hamburg, they had her registered in the form of a supposed purchase in Stettin, and, under the new name, LOUIS KNIFFLER, with the right to fly the Prussian flag, the vessel was able to undertake the passage to Japan. On the 18th of May, 1863, the "Hamburg Börsenhalle", the most powerful shipping news sheet in Hamburg, carried the following notice:

The LOUIS KNIFFLER

"As the first vessel to go directly from Germany to Japan, the beautiful Prussian bark, LOUIS KNIFFLER, Captain Seemann, yesterday left our harbor. We call attention to this the more gladly since this vessel, which is of 190 commerzlast, had on board not only a full but also a richly assorted cargo for that destination."

What no one before had accomplished, the persistent enterprising spirit of Ferdinand and Carl Laeisz had succeeded in, the opening of a direct line from Hamburg to Japan. They had shown themselves once again as genuine pioneers, though it is true that a regular trade between Hamburg and Japan did not develop until after the German and French war of 1870-71. The year 1862 is also significant in the history of the firm in that for the first time one of their vessels sailed to the South American harbor of Valparaiso. The concentration of the shipping business on the South American passage lasted for a series of years. Up to the beginning of the eightieth year, the Laeisz vessels were preponderately engaged in free voyaging, so-called tramp traveling, that is, with the transporting of wares according to opportunity and need, and also with the regular transport of their own goods to the overseas ports.

From the year 1866 on, all the Laeisz vessels with one exception received names beginning with the letter "P". They were all sailers, and the firm remained consistent to the belief in sails up to the first World War. The year 1867 brought the first decisive increase in their fleet by 6 sailers with a combined 2,700 net register tonnage through the purchase of 6 of the 7 vessels of the fleet of the Hamburg owner, J. T. Bahr. This firm especially cultivated contacts with Chile and Peru. Their agent in Valparaiso was the well-known firm, D. F. Weber. As evidenced by old papers of the Stülcken works in Hamburg, the wealthy Doña Carolina Garcia De La Huerta in Hamburg, through the intermediary, Mr. Julius Theodor Bahr, had given commission for a series of stately barques. In 1864, Dōna Carolina became the wife of the merchant, Heinrich Th. Möller, in Hamburg. The vessels built at her order, although they were actually owned by the Bahr firm, flew the Chilean flag during the German-Danish

SAILING VESSELS OWNED AND OPERATED
BY REEDEREI F. LAEISZ BETWEEN 1825 AND 1878

Serial No.	Official No.	Const. & Rig	Name	Dimensions	Com. Load Gross/ Net Tons	Built	Builder	Acquired	Acquired From	Fate
1	7	W.brg.	CARL	91.9x23.0x13.3	92/96 CL 220 206	1839	J. Meyer Lübeck, Germany	1839	Builder	1847: Sold A. J. Schön, Hamburg, Ger. Belonged to G.J. Sörensen 1880.
2	308	W.sr.	SOPHIE & FRIEDERICKE ex GLADIATOR	82.3x19.8x10.0	87 CL 195 ---	1844	--------, Stettin, Germany	1856	--------	1860: Sold Godeffroy, Hamburg, Ger. Sold to China.
3	290 RBCG	W.bq.	PUDEL	141.4x28.7x16.6	194 CL 485 441	1856	H.C.Stülcken, Hamburg, Ger.	1856	--------	1870, Feb.: Sold J.Hinrich Parlow, Pillau, Ger. In 1890's afloat as lighter.
4	2	W.brg.	ADOLPH	75.5x19.8x10.1	60/71 CL 164 133	1854	Reiherstieg Godeffroy Hamburg, Ger.	1857	--------	1862: Sold C. Reimers, Wewelsfleth, Germany. 1870 sold Norway
5	181	W.brg.	SCHILLER	85.5x19.9x10.0	85 CL 220 192	1855	Von Somm, Hamburg, Germany	1858	--------	1859: Sold in Batavia, Java
6	19	W.brg.	PACIFIC	105.0x23.0x13.3	94/100 CL 223 211	1860	Schau & Oltmanns, Geestemünde, Germany	1860	Builder	1866: Sold Knöhr & Burchardt, Hamburg, Germany. Registered from Brake in 1891.

7	92	W.bq.	INDIA	115.0x23.0x13.3	132 CL 330 ---	1860	Ide Oltmanns, Brake, Ger.	1860	Builder	1863: Stranded. Total loss.
8	(1 (1870:212 (RCTL	W.bq.	COSTA RICA	117.4x23.1x14.8	136 CL 338 311	1860	L.F.Paulsen, Brake, Ger.	1860	Builder	1870: Sold
9	81	W.bq.	REPUBLIC	91.9x19.9x13.1	115 CL 267 ---	1861	P. Sager, Vegesack, Germany	1861	Builder	1865. Nov.: Missing China Sea.
10	169	W.bq.	NEPTUN	121.5x30.3x13.4	195/220 CL 450 ---	1851	Wittenberg, Ueckermünde, Germany	1862	--------	1863: Sold
11	392	W.brg.	PERU	110.2x23.3x13.9	120/110 CL 255 ---	1862	Schau & Oltmanns, Geestemünde, Ger.	1862	Builder	1870. Jan.: Total loss in China Sea.
12	349	W.bq.	PANAMA (1) ex MARBS	134.5x26.4x17.1	178 CL --- 455	1852	J. Marbs, Hamburg, Germany	1862	--------	1868, Sold: H.P.Samuelsen, Dröback, Norway
13	2	W.bq.	PERSIA	131.2x24.4x16.3	176 CL 405 ---	1862	J. Oltmanns Wwe., Brake, Germany	1862	Builder	1878: Sold Gebroeders Wittering, Amsterdam, Netherlands. Rechristened ANNA & BERTHA
14		W. bq.	LOUIS KNIFFLER ex CECILIA	119.9x27.0x12.9	275/279 CL 433 ---	1860	Sundström, Gumboda, Sweden	1863	--------	1868: Sold foreign
15		W.bq.	PATRIA	131.1x28.5x16.4	182 CL 424 391	1863	J. Oltmanns Wwe., Brake, Germany	1863	Builder	1884: Sold G. Kindler, Rostock, Ger. 1900: Out of register

Serial No.	Official No.	Const. & Rig	Name	Dimensions	Com. Load Gross/ Net Tons	Built	Builder	Ac-quired	Ac-quired From	Fate
16	508	W.brg.	PRINCESS	108.0x26.6x12.2	106/116 CL 271 257	1863	D. Denker, Brake, Germany	1863	Builder	1874: Sold/1880, Nov.: Stranded off Skaw.
17	400	W.bq.	PERLE	139.9x26.4x16.0	190 CL 421 406	1864	E. Dreyer, Reiherstieg, Altona, Ger.	1864	Builder	1881: Sold J. Sharp, Shanghai, China
18	205	W.brg.	LOS HER-MANOS ex NORTH POINT	88.8x19.8x13.3	125 CL 298 ---	1855	-------- Williamsburg, N.Y., U.S.A.	1864	--------	1866: ?
19	22 RBMS	W.bq	PAPA	139.9x25.5x16.1	175 CL 420 392	1865	J. Oltmanns Wwe., Brake, Germany	1865	Builder	1882: Sold J.H. Havemann, Rudköbing, Den. 1890. Nov.: Wrecked off Orfordness
20	14 RBHD	W.bq.	PYRMONT	129.7x28.6x16.5	188 CL 413 365	1866	J. Oltmanns Wwe., Brake, Germany	1866	Builder	1882: Sold Oetling Gebruder, Hamburg, Ger. Swedish GEORGE to 1905.
21	437 RCNS	W.bq.	CAROLINA	131.9x27.2x15.2	189 CL 425 402	1864	H.C.Stülcken Hamburg, Germany	1867	J. T. Bahr Valpa-raiso, Chile	1881: Stranded Mazatlan, Mexico Total loss
22	42 RBTK	W.bq.	DON JULIO	137.9x26.4x18.0	203 CL 457 ---	1863	H.C.Stülcken, Hamburg, Germany	1867	J.T.Bahr Valparaiso, Chile	1870, Nov. 30; seized by French Ended as Nor-wegian FRITHJOF NANSEN

23	501 RCGW	W.bq.	HENRIQUE TEODORO	133.4x29.6x17.2	201 CL 452 408	1865	H.C.Stülcken, Hamburg, Germany	1867	J.T.Bahr Valparaiso, Chile	1882: Sold Fr. Winding, Rudkjöbing, Sweden and renamed AAGE. 1888 Burnt in River Plate.
24	212 RBGL	W.bq.	MERCEDES	125.7x26.4x15.1	163 CL 367 354	1862	H.C.Stülcken, Hamburg, Germany	1867	J.T.Bahr Valparaiso, Chile	1881: Sold L.S. Christensen, Nibe, Denmark. 1889: Lost.
25	408 RBHW	W.bq	RICARDO	120.3x30.1x15.5	187 CL 421 402	1864	H.C.Stülcken, Hamburg, Germany	1867	J.T.Bahr Valparaiso, Chile	1870. Mar.: Sold Vorwerk Gebr. & Co., Hamburg, Ger., and renamed CHRISTIANE. 1901; Stranded Sheilds.
26	502 RBGK	W.bq.	ROSA Y ISABEL	138.0x28.9x17.0	197 CL 443 407	1865	H.C.Stülcken, Hamburg, Germany	1867	J.T.Bahr Valparaiso, Chile	1884: Sold Aug. Burchard, Rostock, Ger. 1887: Condemned and sold at Saint Thomas
27	3 RCWS	W.bq.	PANAMA (2)	124.6x29.5x16.5	204 CL 465 411	1869	J.Oltmanns Wwe., Brake, Ger.	1869	Builder	1887: Sold A.H.Arnold, Brake, Ger.
28	548 RCGB	W.bq.	PROFESSOR ex FLOTT- BECK	143.0x27.6x17.2	239 CL 536 512	1865	Reiherstieg, Hamburg, Germany	1869	--------	1889, May 2: Sold J.H.Christiansen, Nordby, Fano, Den. 1898: Stranded New Caledonia.
29	416 RDNT	W.bq.	PACHA ex ISABELITA	118.7x28.1x16.7	200 C.L 450 432	1866	J. Marbs, Hamburg, Germany	1872	--------	1877: Sold to Spanish owners.

Serial No.	Official No.	Const. & Rig	Name	Dimensions	Com. Load Gross/ Net Tons	Built	Builder	Ac-quired	Ac-quired From	Fate
30	RDNS	W.bq.	PATAGONIA	139.4x29.7x16.9	220 CL 491 ---	1873	J.Oltmanns Wwe., Brake, Germany	1873	Builder	1886: Sold P. Margaronis, Syria.
31	RDWT	I.s.	POLYNESIA	195.0x33.0x20.4	--- 1070 985	1874	Reiherstieg, Hamburg, Germany	1874	Builder	1890, Apr. 24; stranded East-bourne, Eng. May: Sold to wreckers.
32	RDLF	W.bq.	HENRIETTE BEHN	174.4x33.6x20.2	288 CL 644 590	1872	J.P.Dircks Oevelgönne, Germany	1875	A.Behn	1885, Nov.: stranded Mazatlan, Mexico Total loss
33	RFNV	W.bq.	PALADIN	136.2x29.5x17.6	--- 547 ---	1877	Schau & Oltmanns, Geestemünde, Germany	1877	Builder	1883: Wrecked W. Coast of Mexico
34	RFLB	W.bq.	PANDUR	151.5x32.5x18.8	--- 610 532	1877	Schau & Oltmanns, Geestemünde, Germany	1877	Builder	1889: Sold F. Harboe, Skelskör, Den. 1907: Abandoned N. Atlantic
35	RFLS	W.bq.	PARADOX	168.9x31.9x18.9	--- 716 683	1876	J.P.Dircks Oevelgönne, Germany	1877	Builder	1889: Sold I.T. Chiggini, Spezia, Italy. As AFRICANA no longer in register after 1917.
36	RFNL	W.bq.	PARNASS	165.3x31.1x18.9	--- 646 608	1878	Schau & Oltmanns, Geestemünde, Germany	1878	Builder	1890: Sold J.C.M.Block, Hamburg, Ger. 1916, Nov.: Sunk by U-boat.

war of 1864, and all carried Spanish names. These were the vessels that now came into the possession of the house of Laeisz. It paid a good price and took over with the vessels favorable transportation contracts. By this time, the Laeisz fleet consisted of 9 sailers with a combined capacity of around 3,400 NRT. Under German conditions of that time, this already amounted to a stately ship-owning business. The list of the sailing vessels in possession of the firm up to the building year of 1878, the last in which a Laeisz vessel built of wood is dated, is as follows:

In comparison with today, the size of vessels in this list was modest. To be sure, larger wooden vessels could have been built, but no shipping firm had need of such, and even in England the tonnage of the wooden vessels until somewhat past the middle of the century averaged under 1,000 NRT. It is not possible to paint an exact picture of the shipping business of the Laeisz firm until the eightieth year, since no records of it have been preserved. One may, however, infer from the firm's growing participation in new shipping enterprises in Hamburg that increasing gains were being made. In November, 1871, the father, Ferdinand Laeisz, at the founding of the Hamburg-South-American Steamship Association, accepted a seat on the board of directors: the son, Carl, received the chairmanship, which he held until his death. In January, 1872, the "Transatlantic Steamship Association", usually known for short as the Adler Line, was founded. In this, too, the firm of Laeisz occupied a seat on the advisory board. In 1875, the Adler Line, after a short rivalry with Hapag, was taken over by the latter. This fusion is not to be considered as a failure of the undertaking.

Hamburg-South-American Steamship Association

Transatlantic Steamship Association

The victorious outcome of the war with France, the establishment of the German Empire, and the influx of capital through the French war indemnity, which elsewhere in Germany led to the unhappy "speculation years", brought about in Hamburg a powerful and solid upsurge of the spirit of enterprise. In 1872, was born the German steamship company, "Cosmos", with a capital of 5 million marks, for service to the west coast of America. From 1877 to 1886, "Cosmos" paid an average annual dividend of 9.5%. The Laeisz firm was chief shareholder in the Cosmos Line. Carl Ferdinand Laeisz, who had just come into the firm in 1879, already sat on the board of directors of the Cosmos. In 1889, the Kirsten Line, which in the previous years had put up a strong rivalry with the Cosmos, was taken over in entirety. The firm of F. Laeisz also had a part in the German-Australian Steamship Company; Carl Ferdinand was for many years a member of its board of directors. On the other hand, the founding of the Hamburg-Calcutta Line with Carl Laeisz as its chairman, was a mistake. The prospering of this business was hindered by difficulties with steamship building, and in 1896 the shares had to be taken up in the ratio of 4:1. The following year, Hapag took over the Line's stock of vessels. India was still too thoroughly the domain of English trade. The Steamship Owners Hansa worked out more successfully. Founded in 1881, with a capital of 2.5 million marks, it was a tramp line without set routes. It was a creation of Ferdinand Laeisz and August Bolten of Hamburg. The chairmanship on the advisory board was held by the Laeisz firm. Bringing the Hansa to bloom was a particular service of Carl Ferdinand Laeisz. In 1892, it came to an advantageous understanding with the Hapag, which for the full amount of the then active capital, 5 million marks, bought the company's steamers of a combined capacity of 24,000 tons.

"Cosmos Line"

German-Australian Steamship Co.

Hamburg-Calcutta Line

Steamship Owners Hansa

German Nautical Union

Besides this astonishing activity in the business realm, Ferdinand Laeisz grew to be an acknowledged authority in a technical sphere of seafaring. On the 18th of February, 1869, he opened the first general assembly of the German Nautical Union. This was a corporate body of representatives of all business groups and offices interested in seafaring, with an authoritative influence on the development of German commercial shipping. In the order of the day of that first assembly were also discussed the functions of the "sea-courts", as our admiralty courts were then called, and the revision of ocean charts. Here we must remember that in those years German charts of the North Sea region had just begun to be made. It was further reported that Ferdinand Laeisz pledged himself that consideration should be given to a good outfitting of ocean-going vessels with charts and nautical instruments. Thereby also cheaper insurance premiums should be secured. The first day's discussion ended with a debate on the pilotage situation in Hamburg, in which Ferdinand Laeisz again took a leading part.

On the second day of the assembly, Ferdinand came out for another forward step in seafaring. The deficient state of telegraphy along the coasts of the North Sea furnished him occasion for some noteworthy suggestions. Among other things, he proposed that all lighthouses should be connected with the telegraph network so that help could be brought more quickly than before to stranded vessels. And thus his tireless spirit, while he worked at developing his own field of production, also constantly served the advancement of the common good.

Insurance

Along with this comprehensive sharing in the seafaring and economic life of Hamburg, the firm, through its own fleet of sailing vessels and through its financial interest in a series of newly founded steamship lines, continued to expand another branch of its activity: the insurance business. Very early, on January 2, 1847, under Ferdinand Laeisz, it became a member of the "Association of Hamburg Insurance Underwriters", in which it still holds the membership number — "1". Fifteen years after the entrance of Ferdinand into this association, his son, Carl, acquired membership, and another 15 years after that, the grandson, Carl Ferdinand. All 3 of the partners, with varying fortunes but for the most part with successful results, engaged in the practice of private insurance business and rivaled many companies in the number and extent of the risks assumed. What a compass their business had gained by the middle of the last century, one example may illustrate. The Hamburg firm, Tietgens and Robertson, placed with F. Laeisz in the space of 58 months no less than 727,000 marks banco out of a total insurance of 3,083,000 marks. For the most part, this was insurance on body and appurtenances of vessels in the trade with California, Australia, the Indies, the west coast of Central and South America, China, and the Mediterranean lands. Every interest which can be valued in money is insurable on an ocean journey. Besides the risk a passage brings with it for the vessel and its equipment, naturally the cargo can be insured (cargo insurance). Further, the freight payments, the passage money, and even the presupposed gain on the goods which make up the vessel's cargo. From this alone, one can see that a successful activity as insurance broker presupposes a high degree of commercial insight, a fundamental knowledge of the world market, and courage based on experience, guided by shrewdness. The premiums for the insurance of the "casco", that is, of the vessel itself, were astonishingly high in the middle of the last century. In the years 1853-54 for a passage from Hamburg to Melbourne via Pacific ports, they amounted to 6 per cent per year. Five years later, for the same passage, they rose as high as 7.5 per cent. If the year passed without damages, the broker returned $\frac{1}{2}$ per cent in acknowledgment. It is safe to assume that even in those years, F. Laeisz must have had at least 500,000 marks banco invested in the insurance business; more, therefore, than in the shipowning part of the business up to the end of the sixth year.

It lay in the nature of the insurance business that with the great and numerous risks, a significant number of insurance companies should become active. The firm of F. Laeisz, for its part, had an interest in a whole series of insurance companies. The General Nautical Insurance Association was founded in 1891, and Carl Laeisz was on its board of directors. It belonged to the most distinguished of the Hamburg insurance exchanges. Through the devastating storms of the winter of 1894-5, they suffered heavy losses. In the Northwest German Insurance Company, founded in October, 1895, Carl Laeisz was a major shareholder; Carl Ferdinand was likewise heavily involved in the joint insurance and re-insurance company, "Cosmos", founded in June of 1896. Also occasional losses through dishonest manipulations of authorized agents came to light. F. Laeisz had a further share in the direction of the Insurance Association of 1863, in the Globe Assurance Company, in the Insurance Company Alemania, and the Assurance Company Teutonia. Furthermore, Carl Laeisz worked until his death as corporation counsel of the Hanseatic Nautical Insurance Company, and of the General Nautical Insurance Company. The combined insurance business of the three Laeisz men, grandfather, father, and son, was thus considerable.

General Nautical Insurance Assoc.

Northwest German Insurance Co.

"Cosmos" Joint Co.

Other Companies

The structure of these separate insurance enterprises may be shown briefly by one example. In January of 1864, the Assurance Company, Teutonia, was established for 10 years. How cautiously these companies operated is apparent by their hedging in the risk per vessel by strict stipulations in their statutes. In an exceptional case, the highest sum for a sailing vessel was 15,000 marks banco, for a steamship 20,000 marks.

The board of directors of the association consisted of the firms of J. C. Godeffroy and Son, F. Laeisz, A. J. Schön and Co., later Conrad Warnecke, and Wachsmuth and Krogmann. The authorized agent was J. H. Dorrinck. The following emoluments were paid: to the directors an honorarium, a kind of royalty; to the agent 6,000 marks banco plus 5 per cent of the dividends and an honorarium. The capital of the company amounted to 150 shares to every 3,000 marks banco — that is, 450,000 marks banco. These shares were valued at 60 to 200 marks banco. The yearly returns varied between 6 and 10 million marks banco at premiums averaging from 1.3 to 2.0 per cent. The statutory charge incurred in 1874 was paid up by 1891.

The activity of the 3 Laeiszes in the nautical insurance market finds eloquent testimony in the work which the director of the Hanseatic Sea — and General — Insurance Company of Hamburg, Mr. Fr. Plass, with the co-operation of Mr. F. R. Ehlers, published in 1901 under the title, "History Of Assurance And Of The Hanseatic Nautical Insurance Market Of Hamburg". This book, scarcely known beyond the narrowest department circles, Plass dedicated to the memory of Carl Laeisz, who died while the work was in print. The foreword pays tribute to the distinguished services rendered also by the grandfather and the son, and then continues:

"The pillars of the firm to the present time were born wholesale merchants, who, besides their own gain, kept their sights constantly on the common good. When serious problems arose, they came forward of their own free will and went to work with energy. This is not the place to enumerate the instances of self-sacrificing help that they offered to the common welfare; but it is to be remembered here that as Hamburg wholesale merchants, they were also genuine patriots and republicans true to their convictions, worthy of those men who during the course of the century worked as pathmakers for Hamburg's world trade and Hamburg's well-being.

Hamburg Assurance Exchange

"The Hamburg Assurance Exchange, to which they belonged, not only as prominent private insurance brokers, but also in a controlling capacity as directors of many local companies, owes extraordinary successes to their initiative and practical penetration. Their counsel and their energetic help in hard times have often been tested. There can hardly have been ever another firm which through so many decades could have exercised so beneficent an influence on the development of nautical insurance as that of the F. Laeisz firm through its 3 far-sighted owners. When we put on the title page of our history of assurance the portraits of the 3 Laeisz gentlemen, we believe we are giving expression to the general gratitude of all Hamburg nautical insurance underwriters."

Following the clear and objective presentation by Plass, one can thus see beyond any doubt in the 3 Laeisz men the leading personalities of the Hamburg nautical exchange and this for the extent of the most flourishing decades of our shipping activity. A deep-sea passage in the grand style is unthinkable without insurance against the unavoidable risks. Consequently, the helpful influence of the 3 Laeisz men reached deep into the field of our political economy through endlessly ramifying channels and far beyond those boundaries which, to the eye of an outsider, would seem to circumscribe the work of a merchant and shipowner.

For a long time, as we have seen, the insurance business remained, next to the export trade, the chief field of activity of the firm. In the course of time, beside these 2 divisions, the ship-owning business moved very gradually up into the foreground. But even then, when at about the turn of the century, the importance of the individual underwriter was noticeably receding because of the intrusion of great capital, the firm of F. Laeisz retained its firmly established place on the insurance exchange.

On January 2, 1897, the Hamburg Association Of Insurance Underwriters celebrated for the first time the golden jubilee of a member: It was Ferdinand Laeisz, who had belonged to the Association for fifty years. In the same year, the Association was celebrating the centennial jubilee of its existence.

Erection of Laeiszhof in 1857

In the circles of nautical underwriters, the wish had long been felt to bring together as far as possible the counting houses of all members into one place. As early as 1868, the question had been broached of assembling them into one building. It was the firm of Laeisz which took up this idea. In the year 1897, the firm erected near the Trostbrücke the imposing building in which many of the most important underwriters of that time established their offices, and so the Laeiszhof soon became the focal point of Hamburg's nautical insurance business. With this side-light on the insurance activity of the firm F. Laeisz, we will close this part of the subject.

Within the ship-owning business, it was the trade with Chile that in the outer world established the fame and honor of the firm. It may have been the purchase of the Bahr vessels, of which mention has been made above, that gave the decisive impulse to the building up of this connection. At first, the passage around Cape Horn seems to have been carried on as a sort of tramp business; that is, only occasionally. However, this did not last long. As early as 1878, it

SAILING VESSELS OWNED AND OPERATED
BY REEDEREI F. LAEISZ BETWEEN 1878 AND 1921

Serial No.	Official No.	Const. & Rig	Name	Dimensions	Gross/ Net Tons	Built	Builder	Ac-quired	Ac-quired From	Fate
37	RGBC	I.s.	PLUTO ex AMINTA	213.9x35.1x22.8	1,159 1,133	1862	Jones, Quiggen & Co., Liverpool, Eng.	1881	Moore, & Co., Liverpool, Eng.	1891: Sold, after collision, to W. Maack, Rostock, Germany. 1892, Aug.: Missing
38	RFVW	I.bq.	PONCHO ex WEYMOUTH	187.0x32.2x21.0	841 819	1858	J. Reid & Co., Port Glasgow, Scotland	1881	Temperleys, Carter, & Drake, London, Eng.	1892: Sold J. H. Wagnar, Hamburg, Ger. 1898, Feb.: Foundered.
39	RGCV	I.bq.	PAQUITA ex IRMA ex MAGGIE LESLIE	163.7x27.1x16.1	484 460	1862	A. Leslie & Co., Newcastle-on Tyne, Eng.	1881	Hamburg owners	1888: Sold W. Maack, Rostock, Germany. 1903: Wrecked.
40	RGHP	I.bq.	PAVIAN ex s. TIVERTON	214.3x34.7x22.9	---- 1,162	1864-	Millwall, London, Eng.	1882	W.Coupland Liverpool, England	1883: Missing
41	RGUP	I.bq.	PARSIFAL	210.3x34.0x22.9	1,075 1,050	1882	Blohm & Voss, Hamburg, Ger.	1882	Builder	1886: Foundered off Cape Horn.
42		I.bq.	PUCK ex PEEP O'DAY	154.0x27.5x17.6	494 474	1863	Marshall Bros. Newcastle-on-Tyne, Eng.	1883	J.H.Holdsworth, London, Eng.	1888: Sold J.P. Clausen, Nordby, Fano, Denmark. Later hulk at Miokko, B.A.
43		I.bq.	PIRAT	212.6x34.4x20.0	1,059 991	1883	Blohm & Voss, Hamburg, Ger.	1883	Builder	1902: Sold H. Bramslow, Hamburg, Ger. 1911, Jan.: Condemned at Cardiff.

Serial No.	Official No.	Const. & Rig	Name	Dimensions	Gross/ Net Tons	Built	Builder	Acquired	Acquired From	Fate
44		I.bq.	PESTALOZZI	210.6x34.4x19.9	1,065 1,039	1884	Blohm & Voss, Hamburg, Ger.	1884	Builder	1904: Sold O. Christensen, Arendal, Norway. Scrapped 1937.
45		I.bq.	PLUS	225.5x36.0x20.6	1,268 1,160	1885	Blohm & Voss, Hamburg, Ger.	1885	Builder	1908: Sold L. Schubeler, Frederikstad, Norway. 1933 stranded Mariehamn, Åland, Finland.
46		S.bq.	PROMPT	238.8x38.1x20.5	1,446 1,354	1887	Blohm & Voss, Hamburg, Ger.	1887	Builder	1908: Sold H. Lundquist, Mariehamn, Åland, Finland. 1935: Scrapped.
47		S.bq.	POTRIMPOS	227.7x35.9x20.7	1,273 1,245	1887	Blohm & Voss, Hamburg, Ger.	1887	Builder	1896: Dec.: Stranded Ilwaco, Columbia River, Wash., U.S.A.
48	RHJL	S.bq.	PAMELIA	244.5x38.1x20.8	1,438 1,364	1888	Blohm & Voss, Hamburg, Ger.	1888	Builder	1910: Sold A.T. Simonsen, Christiania, Norway. 1927: Scrapped.
49	RHLK	S.bq.	PERGAMON	244.4x38.1x20.7	1,447 1,411	1888	Blohm & Voss, Hamburg, Ger.	1888	Builder	1891, May: Missing.
50	RHMJ	S.bq.	POTSDAM	244.4x38.1x20.7	1,463 1,405	1889	Blohm & Voss, Hamburg, Ger.	1889	Builder	1891, Jan. 18: Stranded, Valparaiso, Chile. Total loss.

51	RHQL	S.s.	PARCHIM	259.3x39.4x23.0	1,808 1,714	1889	J.C.Tecklen-borg, Geeste-münde, Ger.	1889	Builder	1912: Sold H. Lundquist, Mariehamn, Åland, Finland. 1925: Scrapped.
52	RHQF	S.s.	PALMYRA	261.2x38.5x22.6	1,797 1,721	1889	Blohm & Voss, Hamburg, Ger.	1889	Builder	1908, July 2, Stranded Welling-ton Island, S.W. coast of Chile.
53		I.bq.	PAPOSO	211.4x34.3x20.0	1,062 1,038	1885	Blohm & Voss, Hamburg, Ger.	1890	--------	1904: Sold C.L. Endresen, Christiansund, Norway. 1918: Abandoned.
54	RHWC	S.s.	PERA	256.6x39.6x22.3	1,758 1,661	1890	J.C.Tecklen-borg, Geeste-münde, Ger.	1890	Builder	1910: Sold M. Lundquist, Mariehamn, Åland, Finland. 1917: Sunk by U-boat.
55	RJHS	S.s.	POSEN ex PREUSSEN	261.5x40.2x22.3	1,761 1,670	1891	Blohm & Voss, Hamburg, Ger.	1891	Builder	1909, Oct. 14, Burnt in the S. Atlantic. Total loss.
56	RJHN	S.s	PAMPA	259.5x38.1x20.8	1,777 1,676	1891	A.C.Neptun, Rostock, Ger.	1891	Builder	1913: Sold J. Tengström, Åbo, Finland. 1922: Scrapped.
57	RJLM	S.4m.bq	PLACILLA	314.5x44.7x26.1	2,845 2,681	1892	J.C.Tecklen-borg, Geeste-münde, Ger.	1892	Builder	1901: Sold Reederei A/G V. 1896, Hamburg, Ger. 1905: Stranded Haisbro Sands.

Serial No.	Official No.	Const. & Rig	Name	Dimensions	Gross/ Net Tons	Built	Builder	Ac-quired	Ac-quired From	Fate
58	RJPT	S.4m.bq.	PISAGUA	314.8x44.7x26.1	2,852 2,652	1892	J.C.Tecklen-borg, Geeste-münde, Ger.	1892	Builder	1912: Sold S.L. Christensen, Sandefjord, Norway after Channel colli-sion. 1913, Jan.: Stranded S. Shet-lands.
59	RKCM	S.4m.bq.	PITLOCHRY	319.5x45.2x26.5	3,088 2,904	1894	A. Stephan & Sons, Dundee, Scotland	1894	Builder	1913, Nov. 28: Sunk by S.S. BOULAMA in Channel.
60	RKGB	S.5m.bq	POTOSI	366.3x49.7x28.5	4,026 3,755	1895	J.C.Tecklen-borg, Geeste-münde, Ger.	1895	Builder	1920: Sold F.A. Vinnen & Co., Bremen, Ger. 1925: Burned.
61	RLHV	S.4m.bq.	PERSIMMON ex DRUMROCK	329.2x45.4x25.7	3,100 2,827	1891	Ramage & Ferguson, Leith, Scotland	1899	Gillison & Chadwich, Liverpool, England.	1913, April: Sold F.A. Vinnen, Bremen, Ger. 1927, Jan.: As DRUM-ROCK stranded in Tukush Bay, B.C.
62	RMPT	S.5m.s.	PREUSSEN	407.8x53.6x27.1	5,081 4,765	1902	J.C.Tecklen-borg, Geeste-münde, Ger.	1902	Builder	1910, Nov. 7: after collision with S.S.BRIGHTON, stranded on S. Foreland and became total loss.
63	RMTB	S.4m.bq.	PANGANI	322.2x47.0x26.2	3,054 2,822	1902	J.C.Tecklen-borg, Geeste-münde, Ger.	1902	Builder	1913, Jan. 28: Sunk in Channel after collision with S.S.PHRYNE.

64	RMVJ	S.4m.bq.	PETSCHILI	321.7x47.0x26.2	3,087 2,855	1903	Blohm & Voss Hamburg, Ger.	1903	Builder	1919, July 12: Stranded, Valparaiso, Chile. Total loss.
65	RNVE	S.4m.bq.	PAMIR	316.0x46.0x26.2	3,020 2,777	1905	Blohm & Voss Hamburg, Ger.	1905	Builder	1921: Allocated Italian Gov.
66	RNHB	S.s.	PEIHO ex ARGO ex BRYNYMORE	275.0x41.5x24.2	2,131 1,980	1902	A.McMillan & Son, Dumbarton, Scotland	1906	G.Amsinck Hamburg, Ger.	1919: Allocated British Gov.
67	QFWJ	S.s.	PIRNA ex OSORNO ex BEETHOVEN	255.4x39.4x23.1	1,789 1,687	1894	J.C.Tecklenborg, Geestemünde, Ger.	1907	H.P.Schuldt, Hamburg, Ger.	1916: Sold Schiffahrts Ges. Lignum G.M.B.H., Hamburg, Germany and renamed LIGNUM. 1920: Scrapped.
68	RNCK	S.4m.bq.	POMMERN ex MNEME	302.0x43.2x24.7	2,413 2,266	1903	J.Reid & Co. Ltd., Glasgow, Scotland	1907	B.Wencke Sohn Hamburg, Ger.	1921: Allocated Greek Gov.
69	RQT	S.s.	PINNAS ex FITZJAMES	267.1x40.1x23.6	1,946 1,790	1902	W.Hamilton & Co., Port Glasgow, Scotland	1909	W. Montgomery, London, Eng.	1919: Allocated French Gov.
70	QJBD	S.bq.	PENANG ex ALBERT RICKMERS	265.6x40.1x24.7	2,039 1,830	1905	Rickmers Reismuhlen Reederei & Schiffbau, A.G. Geestemünde, Ger.	1911	Builder	1917, Oct.: Sold J.H.Backmann, Bremen, Ger. 1940: Sunk by U-boat.
71	RQTD	S.4m.bq.	PEKING	322.1x47.1x26.5	3,100 2,883	1911	Blohm & Voss Hamburg, Ger.	1911	Builder	1921: Allocated Italian Gov.
72	RSCL	S.4m.bq.	PASSAT	322.0x47.2x26.5	3,091 2,882	1911	Blohm & Voss, Hamburg, Ger.	1911	Builder	1921: Allocated French Gov.

Serial No.	Official No.	Const. & Rig	Name	Dimensions	Gross/ Net Tons	Built	Builder	Ac-quired	Ac-quired From	Fate
73	RSHK	S.4m.bq.	PARMA ex ARROW	327.7x46.5x26.2	3,090 2,971	1902	A.Rodger & Co. Port Glasgow, Scotland	1911	Anglo-American Oil Co., London, Eng.	1919: Allocated British Gov.
74	RONT	S.4m.bq.	PONAPE ex REGINA ELENA	297.2x45.2x23.2	2,318 2,177	1903	Soc.Esercizio Baccini, Riva Trigosa, Italy	1911	Italian owners	1914: Captured by H.M.S. MAJESTIC. 1936: Scrapped.
75	RNMD	S.bq.	PELIKAN ex DIONE	271.0x40.0x23.0	2,103 1,935	1905	Rikjee & Co., Rotterdam, Netherlands	1912	Wachsmuth & Krogmann Hamburg, Ger.	1921: Allocated British Gov. 1925: Hulked and then scrapped.
76	RSPD	S.4m.bq.	PINQUIN ex ERASMO	288.9x41.5x22.0	2,102 1,935	1903	Soc.Esercizio Baccini, Riva Trigosa, Italy	1912	E.Raffo Fu.E., Spezia, Italy	1917: Sold C.J. Klingenberg & Co., Bremen, Ger. 1925: As JACOBSEN broken up.
77	RSGP	S.bq.	PERIM ex RADIANT	264.9x40.1x23.6	1,944 1,845	1903	A.Rodger & Co. Port Glasgow, Scotland	1912	Anglo-American Oil Co., London, Eng.	1917, Mar. 3: Sold H.Kayser & Sohn G.M.B.H., Hamburg, Ger. 1925: Scrapped.
78		S.4m.bq.	PERKEO ex BRILLIANT	352.3x49.1x28.2	3,765 3,609	1901	Russell & Co., Port Glasgow, Scotland	1914	Anglo-American Oil Co., London, Eng.	1914, Aug. 8: Captured by H.M.S.Cruiser off Dover, Eng. 1916: as BELL sunk by U-boat.

(1) (NAUTICAL PHOTO AGENCY)

Iron Barque PLUS, 1,268 Gross Tons
1885-1908
Second Iron Vessel Built For The Firm

(2) (NAUTICAL PHOTO AGENCY)

Steel Barque PAMELIA, 1,438 Gross Tons
1888-1910
Third Steel Vessel Built For The Firm

PLATE 6

(1) (NAUTICAL PHOTO AGENCY)

Steel 4-Masted Barque PITLOCHRY, 3,088 Gross Tons
1894-1913

(2) (NAUTICAL PHOTO AGENCY)

Steel 4-Masted Barque PERSIMMON ex DRUMROCK, 3,100 Gross Tons
1899-1913

(1) (NAUTICAL PHOTO AGENCY)

Steel 4-Masted Barque PETSCHILI, 3,087 Gross Tons
1903-1919

(2) (Capt. Robert K. MIETHE)

Steel 4-Masted Barque PETSCHILI
After Grounding 4:00 a.m. 12, July, 1919

PLATE 8

(PHOTO NEWS, LTI

Steel 4-Masted Barque PAMIR, 3,020 Gross Tons
1905-1921 And 1924-1931
Off New Zealand In 1941

(1) (Frank W. THOBER)

Steel Barque PENANG ex ALBERT RICKMERS, 2,039 Gross Tons
1911-1917

(2) (NAUTICAL PHOTO AGENCY)

Steel 4-Masted Barque POMMERN ex MNEME, 2,413 Gross Tons
1907-1921

(1) (Capt. J. Ferrell COLTON)

Steel 4-Masted Barque PASSAT
Off Cape Horn In 1936

(2) (Capt. J. Ferrell COLTON)

Steel 4-Masted Barque PASSAT, 3,091 Gross Tons
From A Painting Done By Hamburg Artist Johs. Holst In December,
1955, For Capt. J. Ferrell Colton, And
Brought To The Americas On The M. V. PERSEUS

was possible to organize a regular Laeisz line to Chile, once a month from Hamburg and every other month from Antwerp. Gradually the concentration on these passages developed, which in the 80 years of the management of the ship-owning firm maintained ascendency in accordance with the growth of the use of sodium nitrate in Europe, and especially in Germany. Its increase grew out of the great success of artificial fertilization following the principles demonstrated some decades before by Justus Von Liebig. Chilean saltpeter is one of the most powerful mineral fertilizing agents, and through its use alone, it was possible to raise the productivity of agricultural land to its present capacity, which is far over that of yesterday.

The growth of the Laeisz fleet up to the first World War is immediately bound up with the increase of the saltpeter trade after the midpoint of the 80 years, as the following table shows. The tonnage figures are partly in gross, partly in net registered tons, but in a sailing vessel the difference between gross and net tonnage is insignificant. By net tonnage is understood the space on the vessel exclusively reserved for the use of cargo and passengers. In the year 1870, the firm had 16 vessels with a combined net tonnage of 6,700. By 1875, the number of vessels had been reduced to 14; the combined tonnage, however, increased to around 7,100 net. From then on, the combined tonnage grew rapidly. It ran:

1880: 17 sailers with 8,641 tons net
1885: 16 sailers with 10,945 tons gross
1890: 15 sailers with 18,245 tons gross
1895: 15 sailers with 26,494 tons gross
1900: 16 sailers with 30,229 tons net
1905: 15 sailers with 35,064 tons net
1910: 16 sailers with 39,485 tons net

In 1887, the year in which the senior Ferdinand Laeisz died, his son, Carl, looking toward an increasing trade in sodium nitrate, began comprehensive building up of the Laeisz fleet. From this time on, it expanded into the famous "Flying P Line". The use of wood sailing vessels was by then already given up; in their place, the ships of the firm were iron.

Flying P Line

The first iron ships of the firm, with the exception of PROFESSOR and POLYNESIA, were bought in England. PROFESSOR, which was built at the Reiherstieg yards in Hamburg, was originally named FLOTTBEK. Three others, PIRAT, PESTALOZZI, and PAPOSO, were bought complete; all the others were built at the specified shipyards on order from the firm and according to their plans. Both Carl and Carl Ferdinand Laeisz had an unfailing eye for vessels. When opportunity offered to buy a proved sailer, the firm had no hesitation about buying in England, France, Italy, Holland. Up to the powerful 5-masted, full-rigged ship, PREUSSEN, with her 5,081 gross tonnage, and POTOSI, with 4,026 gross tonnage, the size of the vessels increased; it became evident, however, that the size-range between 2,000 and 3,000 tons was the most advantageous, and thereafter no vessels of greater tonnage were put into service. Sailers which had served for a number of years, usually about 20, were offered for sale. The firm lost quite a few vessels; but concerning that, we may quote the judgment of an expert, W. Laas, formerly professor in the technical high school in Berlin, in his book of 1908, *The Future of Great Sailing Vessels:*

"From the records of the greatest ship-owning firm in Germany, we may notice the change from wood to iron and steel ships, then the steadily increasing size, since 1891 the substitution of 4-and 5-masted vessels for the old barques and full-rigged ships. As especially gratifying, we may stress first the fact that since 1865 the firm has had all its vessels built in Germany with only two exceptions" (valid for the year in which the book appeared) "and second the extraordinarily small number of losses. Whereas the statistics bureau, Veritas, reports elsewhere about 3% a year loss of sailing vessels, the percentage" (with Laeisz) "amounts to only .9% since 1891, the firm has not lost one of its great 4-and 5-masters. It is certain that the small number of losses is a result of the first fact; although England still produces great sailing vessels cheaper than Germany, yet it is beyond doubt that in Germany at the yards named" (Blohm & Voss and Tecklenborg) "the vessels, particularly their bodies, are better built. The firm spares no expense always to get the best vessels, and the best captains and crews as well, and thereby proof is given that the modern great sailing vessels can be as secure as the steamships, when building, maintenance, and management are of the first class. The expense spent on these is equalized by the small number of damages and losses, by the longer life of the vessels, faster passages, and lower premium rates. In general, Germany has been spared the heavy casualty lists which England and France have experienced."

The use of the new building materials, iron and steel, not only for the hull, but also for masts and tackle, created new conditions. The Laeisz fleet went over entirely to metal construction. In Captain Fred Schmidt's book, *Schiffe und Schicksale,* (Ships and Fortunes), one section is devoted to the Laeisz vessels. There it is pointed out that the growing need of European husbandry for sodium nitrate was continually bringing new sailing vessels to the west coast of South America. For such mass cargoes, sailer-freight was cheaper than steamer-freight:

"Ferdinand Laeisz early recognized the opportunities for development in this trade. In the years following the French war, he built up in rapid succession an important fleet. Through purchase and building, he had provided by 1888 over 12 barques, which established the fame of Hamburg's shipping."

English seamen were the first to derive from the letter "P" with which the names of the Laeisz vessels began, the designation, "Flying P Liner". It soon became a name of honor in international shipping for the vessels under the white counting house flag with the red F L. With the regularity of packet steamers many of these great handsome vessels ploughed up and down the Atlantic. The captains that controlled them were familiar with the most secret moods of the weather on their routes. With these commanders, seafaring became a science. On these heavy-weather vessels, the masts rose all of metal to the masthead. Metal yards stretched out the sails to a smoothness never before believed possible. Where other vessels carried hemp and manila cordage, here steel wire had come to be used. And they made good use too of their metal tackle: when other vessels were making fast their upper topsails, these went rushing by with both top-gallant sails at the head. The rapid passages of the P-liners and their astonishing regularity were no result of chance. Laeisz knew why he wanted his sailers built just so and not otherwise. He procured for his commanders instruments with which they could accomplish the seemingly impossible amid the space and loneliness of the endless sea. What would have been presumptuous for weaker, less well provided veseels, for them was routine, hazard-accustomed navigation. It was no wonder that the name Laeisz, like a magnet, soon drew to itself many of those seamen who had in them the stuff and inclination for performances of an unusual sort. They found in their vessel's owner and in the nature of the Laeisz shipping activities full anticipation for performances above the average. That is best shown by the instructions which Carl Laeisz compiled for his captains, and which may well follow verbatim:

"My vessels can and shall make fast passages. From this follows that everything which is needful aboard, such as rigging, sails, cordage, etc., must be fully in top condition, and anything lacking or damaged at the return to Hamburg must be replaced or mended. Also the instructions of the inventory — and harbor — books are to be closely regarded. Likewise everything on board must correspond to the prescriptions of the Mariners' Association. I can absolutely not consent that objects of equipment or provisions should be purchased in foreign lands (with the exception of fresh meat, potatoes, eggs, fresh vegetables, water). The captain is answerable for leaving Hamburg completely outfitted. Next to skill in navigation, I value thrift, attention to possible improvement in management, and first-rate preservation of the ship and inventory. Absolute sobriety during service, I consider so self-evident a requirement of my captains that I hardly need to mention that a single instance in which a captain should appear drunk would render him irrevocably impossible for me. Also I require that the captain shall report to me any officers whom he shall once find drunk or asleep on watch, for which they shall be dismissed and not again restored to my service. From the foreign port of destination, the captain is to notify me by letter how well satisfied he is with his officers and crew, also again by word of mouth as soon as he returns to Hamburg. Likewise by letter from foreign ports and personally in Hamburg, he is to inform me of any noteworthy lack or damage on the vessel, in the equipment and in the provisions, as well as of any important events.

"The entire personnel, from the second officer down, must be examined by a physician in Hamburg, and only healthy persons may be accepted.

"Ship's boys are accepted only when I myself have accepted them. I take only sons of seamen who have grown up by the water; such boys, the captain may recommend to me.

"If, during the passage, men should desert or leave and new men be hired, I must be informed of the respective names and dates. Against desertion, the captain is always to petition the public prosecutor for a sentence.

"When the personnel serves overtime, the captain, in order to avoid later differences, must record this with them in writing weekly or before leaving harbor.

"In view of the present social-democratic tendencies among crews, the captain has to employ great foresight in the treatment of the men and especially to insist that the officers act reasonably herein. Discipline on board must under all circumstances be strictly kept, but this is better done tactfully and peaceably than with raw force. Insubordination and punishments must always be written into the log, read to those concerned, and signed by witnesses, so that on return further measures may be taken.

"For the ventilation of the hold, too much care can not be taken; whenever the weather at all permits, all admittances and ventilators are to be kept open.

"Vessels spoken on the way are to be entered in the log and communicated to me on a separate sheet immediately on arrival at a port.

"When abroad, it should be noted in the log how much is unloaded and taken on every day, and how many workers were employed ashore at the vessel's cost. Payment on the West Coast of demurrage caused by the launches holding over cargo is as far as possible to be avoided.

"The captain has to take care that the sealing is in the best condition and in every way sufficient, since with poor sealing, bilge water can very easily injure the cargo.

"In case my vessels take a cargo from Valparaiso or elsewhere abroad for a coast port, the captain is to send me a manifest.

"During the stay of the vessel in Hamburg harbor, I allow each captain 15 marks a week for expenses. With all accounts, vouchers should accompany the larger entries; also, on the reverse side of the account, the vessel's draught on leaving the harbor is always to be noted.

"In payment of all bills, the captain is to see that I benefit by every possible rebate and discount. All perquisites, gratuities, etc., are to be presented to me. I should consider it unjustifiable for the captain to receive payment or gratuity from anyone but me. That he take the best care of the cargo lies moreover in my interest, and, as a result, in his interest.

"In case of damage at sea, I am to be fully informed by telegraph, and as far as possible, my instructions are to be awaited. In cases of injury, it should be made clear to agents that they are not to compute their commissions on the value of the ship or cargo, or whatever else may be legal or customary in that place, but solely on the cost of the outlay. That is to be definitely arranged before the captain makes an assignment to anyone. Strict caution should be used against other good friends and advisors, especially ship-chandlers. 'Surveyors' are to be called in only when there is question of judging the condition of the cargo or the tide. The vessel is nobody's business, since it is uninsured. I appreciate that in many cases it can become very difficult for the captain of an incoming injured vessel to withstand the united pressures of insurance men, agents, inspectors, especially when backed by the consul; my captains therefore should never forget that I, as an uninsured owner, still have an important, and I should think, the first word to say. If this is put before the consul in appropriate courteous form, then my captains will unquestionably be in a different situation from other captains, and in accordance with this, will also have a say and be able to avoid unnecessary, superfluous, and costly inspections — or at least to postpone them until he has received my answer to the detailed telegraphic report which will have been made to me.

"All reports of injuries and other disagreeable happenings, which are not for the eyes of everyone, the captain is to make to me in separate letters marked 'private'. Concerning sealed freights and other such weighty dispositions, the captain, as my trusted agent, is to preserve silence toward everyone.

"Insurance on personal effects for captains, and under their responsibility also for the officers and crew, I will procure at their wish, if the amount of insurance desired is given me — always before the beginning of the passage — and the premium paid. Captains can also take out a certain amount of permanent insurance, good until cancellation.

Hamburg, June 1892"

Laeisz

Through these instructions speaks the whole business vigor of the owner, Carl Laeisz. The firm could well be proud of its vessels, its captains, and their crews; and the crews were proud of their shipowner. Basil Lubbock, that Englishman so enthusiastic over navigation by sail, says in the foreword to his book, *Nitrate Clippers,* that, like most of his countrymen, he had grown up in the belief that English seamen were without rivals and that English vessels were better planned, better built, and better manned than those of any other nation. But then he continues:

"Indeed, I fear that at the present time we have little right to claim superiority either in seamanship, maritime science or ship construction over nations which our seafaring grandfathers were wont to allude to somewhat rudely as Dutchmen and Dagoes . . .

"My readers will, I feel sure, agree that these "P" Line and A. D. Bordes' nitrate ships deserve to be remembered in the history of the sea along with our own clippers and carriers, for finer, better run ships could not have been found in our British Sailing Marine, even at the height of its glory."

The firm A. D. Bordes was a French shipping firm. In the comparison of them with the Laeisz Line, we may note that the French enjoyed a great advantage both in the building and management of sailing vessels through the government premiums by which the sailing business was sustained. Professor Laas gives circumstantial data in his before-mentioned book; but today there is no longer much point in repeating those details under the fundamentally changed circumstances. On the other hand, it is still interesting to mention that Professor Laas began the second part of his book with the acknowledgment: "It was Mr. F. Laeisz who led the easy-going saltpeter trade into the right way. He got his captains to make races between vessels; he got his agents to so incite the dockers on the West Coast that his vessels unfailingly were unloaded and loaded in a quarter of the time required for any other firm or nation. Mr. Laeisz also owed a great part of his success in the saltpeter trade to the excellent organization of tenders which he built up in the nitrate ports."

These specialties of the Laeisz management explain how the German shipping firm could keep up with the French sailing vessels in spite of the government premium system from which the French profited. Not least was the ability to get along with the often difficult manpower of the West Coast, unaccustomed to hard labor. That, too, was a specialty of the Laeisz captains and officers. In the comprehension of foreign countries, it was not so much the two personalities, Carl and Carl Ferdinand Laeisz, who stood behind the red FL on the white merchant flag, as it was the world-renowned Firm throned in Hamburg and publicized as "Herr Laeisz". For the completion of the picture, it is needful that in this part of the history, in which it gained an international reputation, we should again cast a glance at its share in other Hamburg enterprises.

Woermann Line

In 1886, when the Chile trade of the Laeisz vessels was already in full swing, there took place a transformation of the shipping service of C. Woermann, which then comprised 6 steamships with a combined gross tonnage of about 7,500 into a special association, "African Steamship Navigation Company" (Woermann Line) with a capital of 3 million marks. In this, the firm of F. Laeisz also had an interest. Carl Laeisz himself sat on the board of directors. In 1895, followed the transformation into the "Woermann Line G.m.b.H.",[1] with further participation by F. Laeisz.

German-Australian Steamship-Navigation Association

In 1888, the firm took part in the founding of a steamship line from Hamburg to Australia, which forthwith was amalgamated with the Australian Line created in the same day by Robert M. Sloman, Jr. and the German Bank. From this union of the 2 enterprises, arose the "German-Australian Steamship-Navigation Association", with capital shares of 4 million marks.

United Towing and Freight-Boat Co.

Meanwhile, the efforts of many years by the two Laeisz men and other shipowners to put through the citizens' council the regulation of the navigable water of the Elbe and the deepening of the river had at

[1][G.M.B.H.: Limited Liability - EDITOR]

last succeeded. For a port of the rank of Hamburg, it was an untenable situation that the larger vessels must lighten their loads as far out as Krautsand and Brunshausen in order to reach the harbor. Out there lay continually a whole flotilla of ocean-going vessels, and on both sides of them, like ducklings around the mother ducks, a large number of tenders into which a part of the cargo must be transferred. The passage of these lighters to the city was likewise a troublesome labor, especially when sharp ebb-tides ran with the east and south winds. To better this bad condition, 18 Hamburg merchants, Carl Laeisz among them, had formed the "United Towing and Freight-Boat Company" with its seat in Hamburg. The aim of this undertaking was at first the conduct of the lighters from the ocean vessels on the lower Elbe to the city by steam tugs of the required power. Later, however, came more and more cargoes destined for the smaller ports of the North and East sea-coasts. Naturally, the ocean-going vessels could not reach these harbors, and even for the larger steamships it was impossible to bring their cargoes to their final goal. Thus it now became the task of the steam-tugs to seek out these little coastal towns with the full lighters in tow. Soon the Towing Company also put small freight boats into service which could carry with their own power the portions of the cargoes from overseas destined for the little coast ports.

When the progressive regulation and deepening of the Elbe channel made unnecessary the lightening of the ocean cargoes below the city, the greater part of the fleet of lighters were used as tramp-transports to these ports of the North and East Seas. Then in 1890 the Association opened the first regular line of coast service between Hamburg and Bremen. In place of the tugboats, small freight steamers found employment in increasing numbers.

Very soon the steam tugs of the Association were put into a new service, one which, if it is carried out in the right spirit, can acquire a high moral value: the salvaging of vessels in distress at sea. This demands an unusual amount of nautical experience on board ship and carries at the same time an extraordinary risk for the shipowner. Even before the war of 1914-18, the salvage tugs of the Towing Company had succeeded in many a fine rescue, which had established the reputation of the company as a dependable undertaking for rescue work. After the war, the firm was re-named "Towing, Shipowning, and Salvaging Share-Company". It became an enterprise of world-renown, whose great salvage vessels during the winter months lay ready at many stations on both Atlantic coasts for immediate use, while in the summer they carried out towing passages of remarkable difficulty. Thus they conveyed a number of giant floating docks and dredgers to East Asia. But that which drew the eyes of the entire professional world again and again to the German vessels was acts like the bringing in of the British steamship, NEATH ABBEY, by the motorship rescuer, HERMES, in the hurricane of November 1928, and of the English MAGDALA, which the powerful SEEFALKE found helpless in the Atlantic and brought to safety. SEEFALKE earned a certain fame along the coast, partly because she was for years the largest salvage steamer in the world, but more yet through her daring rescue trips, like the bringing in of the SULTAN STAR, in which the rescue tug, MAX BERENDT, also had a prominent part. A particularly famous page in the history of the "Towers", however, will always be the action of the HEROS. In a severe storm, in the face of the wild surf against the crags of the Channel islands, she saved the 79-man crew of the school-ship, POMMERN, and brought them to land uninjured up to the last boy. The fervent gratitude of many sailor-parents is perhaps the finest reward of the "Towers" and their men. In the meantime, the Towers had gone into other hands.

(Capt. Robert K. MIETHE)

Carl Ferdinand LAEISZ
1853-1900

PLATE 12

(1) (F. LAEISZ)

The Laeisz House
No. 1 Trostbrücke, Hamburg, Germany, As It Was In 1901

(2) (F. LAEISZ)

LAEISZ & CO.: Petalchuco, Guatemala
1911

When in 1888 the Turkish government gave to the German Bank the concession for the building of the Anatole railroad — Kaiser Wilhelm had then undertaken his first journey into the Orient —, good prospects began to open to the German trade in Asia Minor, Syria, and Persia. Thereupon, in 1889 followed the establishment of the German-Levant Line, in which also Carl Laeisz had a prominent share. He was a member of the Board. At first, the undertaking had to put up quite a struggle, but later, in the years 1896-1900, it paid 4% to 10% dividends. Carl Laeisz was active also in the founding in 1890 of the German-East-Africa Line, undertaken at the suggestion of the Imperial Government, and again was chosen on the Board.

German-Levant Line

German-East-Africa Line

This list of enterprises in which the firm took part, either as leader or with important influence, and therewith its partaking in other business activities not immediately connected with the shipping business, such as the Hamburg Union Bank, is testimony to what a place in the economic life of Hamburg the foundation of Ferdinand Laeisz, who had begun his business activity in a hat shop, had grown in 2 generations. The great working power displayed by the firm, it certainly owed not least to the fact that it was directed for almost a decade by the representatives of 3 generations, all 3 impressive personalities. Carl Ferdinand Laeisz was from his entrance into the firm an especially active and progressive force. Under his leadership and his father's, the insurance business also flowered mightily.

CARL FERDINAND LAEISZ

Carl Ferdinand Laeisz was a shipowner in the grand style. That was evident not only in his constructive management of the building of sailing vessels and in the business success of the line which he directed together with his father, but also in the warmth of his heart for the personnel on the vessels. For after the absorption of the steamship-firm, Hansa into the Hapag had brought a lightening of his many-sided range of duties, he devoted a great part of his energy to the building up and development of the Mariners' Association. In July, 1887, along the lines of Bismarck's social legislation, the foundations were laid for the Accident Insurance for Sailors and Others Concerned with Shipping. It was the forerunner of the Imperial Insurance ordinance of July, 1911. This law made necessary an alliance of all owners, the establishment of which followed on December 5, 1887. And no one seemed better fitted to undertake the leadership of this association of owners than Carl Ferdinand Laeisz. To the satisfaction of the entire profession, he was chosen as director of the Mariners' Association, which office he wielded with the greatest success until his death. His successor was the shipowner, Richard C. Krogmann, the father of the man later mayor of the Hanse city of Hamburg.

Carl Ferdinand Laeisz and the Mariners' Association

True to that enlightening proverb, "To avoid misfortune is better than to heal the unfortunate", the avoidance of accident has always been one of the principal tasks of the Mariners' Association. Carl Ferdinand Laeisz personally formulated the first statement of the accident-avoidance precepts and later worked them out further. Along the same line of provision for the welfare of his employees falls the setting up of his own employment bureau. Thereby Carl Ferdinand relieved his crews from many arbitrary acts and defraudings by the then very influential so-called shipping-masters. Though the name of Carl Ferdinand may be lost in the background of his work, yet even in this fact the portrait of his character remains true as of one to whom the work alone counted for anything. The president of the Naval Architects knew what he said when he spoke of the splendid contribution which Hamburg and Bremen had made to the affairs of shipping through their ship-building. Fundamentally, however, only the ship-owner or the professional shipmaster can fully evaluate what the Laeisz sailers brought to pass.

Death of Carl Ferdinand

The last great accomplishment of the fleet of sailers which they had created, neither Carl nor Carl Ferdinand Laeisz lived to see. When Carl Ferdinand was snatched from the firm by a sudden severe illness, the entire heavy burden of the undertaking fell upon his 72-year-old father. He too was struck down soon after the death of his son by a disease for which there was no hope of cure. To maintain the business for his two young grandsons, Herbert F. Laeisz and Erich F. Laeisz, sons of Carl Ferdinand, born in 1886 and 1888, he appointed, in October 1900, Messrs. Paul Ganssauge, J. Reisse, and H. Struck as authorized agents; he took care, however, to do the planning himself to the last detail. As he felt his end drawing near, like a model business man, he took all further measures for the continuance of his work, said farewell briefly to the leaders of the companies on whose boards he belonged, and announced his resignation from his positions of trust because of illness. To make secure for his grandsons the great piece of work wrought by 3 generations was his last important task. On March 22, 1901, his life came to an end.

Death of Carl H. Laeisz

Chapter Three: MEMOIRS AND SPEECHES

Carl Ferdinand, Authority on Shipping

In everything that concerned shipping, Carl Ferdinand was a recognized authority, and acknowledged as such even in the International Association Of Naval Architects. His relations with England were as active as they were valuable. At the sessions of the "Naval Architects" in Glasgow on March 30, 1898, Carl Ferdinand was welcomed as an honor-guest by the President of the Association, Sir William White, together with the Lord Provost of Glasgow. The address made to him and his reply are worth being repeated, in English as they were spoken. Sir William White said:

"... Then as to Mr. Laeisz — what can we say of Mr. Laeisz? What can we say of that splendid gift, which has come to the institution from Hamburg and Bremen, which we saw today? This I will say — I have conferred with Mr. Laeisz as to what I should say about him. He has given me no help whatever. I asked him to aid me to make some jokes — not at all, not one, not even a suggestion. He has the power of making jokes in many languages, and all equally well, and I will ask him to relieve the dullness of my speech by giving us at least one joke in one of the three or four languages he commands. I give you the toast of 'The Guests', coupling with it the name of the Lord Provost of Glasgow and Mr. Laeisz." To this, Carl Ferdinand answered:

ADDRESS TO THE INTERNATIONAL ASSOCIATION OF NAVAL ARCHITECTS

Glasgow Address

"My Lord, Sir William White, and Gentlemen:
In returning very sincere thanks for the very kind words, which you, Sir William White, have just dedicated to the guests, and which you all, Gentlemen, have been good enough to so heartily approve of, I cannot but repeat, what we expressed in our Address to the President and Council of the Institution; that is, that your guests of last summer can never adequately acknowledge the cordiality of the splendid reception you gave them. The magnificent sight of this great country could not have been seen to better advantage, than under your auspices, and every one of your guests derived a vast amount of information on scientific, technical, maritime, and commercial subjects from those days, which were so admirably divided between interesting work and delightful relaxation — (hear, hear!). British hospitality has ever stood in high fame, but nothing can surpass the cordiality extended to us. The natural beauties of your coasts are justly celebrated, but few see them as we saw them, since you provided for the most glorious Queen's weather — (Laughter) — even for sunshine in regions where, I have heard it said, it never stops raining but it snows (renewed laughter). But that is calumny. The crowning lustre was thrown upon our meeting on that memorable day at Windsor Castle — (hear, hear!) when Her Majesty the Queen the august Sovereign, who is not only beloved by the hundreds of millions of her own subjects, but admired and revered by all other nations — (applause) — conferred a most gracious compliment upon the members of the Congress, and at the same time testified to the high esteem in which the profession of the naval architect and the engineer is held in this country. One result of the Congress, in my opinion, is, that you have proved once more, that you are not only foremost in shipbuilding, but that you also vie with other nations in

matters in which they profess to excel. Our French friends, I think, will admit, that nothing could surpass the examples of the culinary art, which you have placed before us – (laughter) – and Austrians and Italians, who were, as you know, born musicians, must confess that a finer concert cannot be imagined than the one it was our privilege to hear in the Queen's Hall – (hear, hear!). To revert to naval architecture: I trust, you will not grudge our endeavours to keep abreast of you -- (hear, hear!) -- especially when you remember that in point of members, we are still keeping far behind, both as regards men-of-war and the merchant navy. Although we find it stated in the Presidential Address, with which your lordship favoured us this morning, that Germany had last year turned out the largest and fastest ocean greyhound, and the biggest carrier, I am afraid that next year's report will already find that you have turned the tables – (hear, hear!). Thus, if you have for once ceded a place in the front rank, if you have for once waived rules, you will continue to rule the waves. – (Laughter and applause.)"

The witty English pun at the close (wave = die Welle, to waive = aufgeben) is untranslatable, but shows to what a degree the speaker was familiar with the English tongue.

In the following, let us share something of the material – unfortunately so scant and hard to come by – concerning the personal characteristics of Carl Heinrich and Carl Ferdinand Laeisz. Carl H. Laeisz, known on the water front only by the Low German "Korl", was one of the most powerful, roughest figures of Hamburg. A Hamburg voice pictures him with the words: "He looked like a Holland skipper, large, heavy, broad-shouldered, with a ruddy healthy face, framed by the English cheek whiskers of old tradition. At home, in the counting house, or on his vessels, the gruff old ship owner spoke only Low German. Whoever wouldn't or couldn't *snaken* (joke) with him, he had little use for. He made few exceptions for people who came from outside. His rudeness was proverbial. Once when he was deep in conversation on the bourse, someone called his attention to a bank-director who was waiting nearby for a chance to speak with him. Korl only growled, 'That is a pushing fellow; the ass can wait'."

In the memorial speech which the President of the Hamburg Citizens made at the grave of Carl Laeisz, he said: "How often, when we have praised his accomplishment in shipping, not only in his own business but also in the reliable advice which he never withheld when called upon, has Carl Laeisz answered us in his jesting way: 'Yes, but that is the only thing I have learned'. The saying which guided his action was: 'To will, to know, to be able'."

There are in Hamburg 2 paintings which in spite of their facetious character, are expressive of the 2 men, father and son, who then stood at the head of the firm. The one pictures Carl Laeisz as, throned at his office desk, he snubs a dismayed shareholder with the words: "The aim of the company is the furtherance of shipping, not the counting of dividends!" In the other painting, Carl and Carl Ferdinand are represented in the costume of the Middle Ages, busied in an alchemist's kitchen trying to cultivate the Discount bacillus! Whoever has studied the history of the firm will understand the deeper meaning of these jests.

Union of Hamburg Shipowners

What esteem his experience as a shipowner enjoyed in the world of shipping is best shown by the fact that until his death he belonged to the executive committee for the Union of Hamburg Shipowners.

We find a bit of Hamburg humor dedicated to the personality of Carl Laeisz in a facetious birthday address by his colleague in the shipowning business, John Meyer:

JOHN MEYER'S FACETIOUS BIRTHDAY ADDRESS

"Elysium, April 27, 1891.

"My good Corl:

Your old true Goddess Fortune cannot let this day go by on which so-and-so many years ago, she stuck the first sugar plum up your snout, which was then not nearly so large as it is today — without expressing to you her satisfaction that you have become such a vigorous and fine person. My old friend of long standing, Mercury, he of the goat's beard and the dung fork, whom I recently met accidentally up there at the corner of Valhalla Street in Elysium, informs me that he is also especially well satisfied with you and that he actually has the intention of having you made a senator. But I have strenuously advised him against that. I say to him, 'Mercury, my boy, don't do anything stupid. My Corl is a fine father of a family and much beloved of rich and poor. What do we want more? The high authorities already have got him into the devil of a stew, which I cannot blame my Corl for, since even I, as a goddess, find it hellish hard to get along with the committees, and what shall Paul do among the Gentiles?'— With special interest I have followed you from up here, my Corl, out on the voyage to the Orient with the AUGUSTA VICTORIA, and if there does seem to be a hellish lot of red wine and brandy trouble in the conduct of your life, I will not lecture you on your red-letter day, only assure you that if you will be more careful of yourself with that infamous broth and go on for all time having the warm heart and open hand with your fellow men who have gotten into predicaments, I will continue to hold my old blue umbrella over your handsome white head so that no storms may descend on you, only so much sunshine as is needful to make you and yours remain fortunate and contented through countless years.

Your old Goddess Fortune
(née Johanna Meyer)

P.S. If Mercury brings up your advancement again, I'll paste him one in the paunch and knock him down a couple of pairs of steps. My good Corl, don't let yourself be browbeaten."

HAMBURG STOCK EXCHANGE TESTIMONIAL

A few days after the death of Carl Laeisz, a testimonial to him appeared in the *Hamburg Stock Exchange,* the sustained seriousness of which forms a contrast to this jesting address of his friend that nevertheless lets the moral and economic force of the man shine through so clearly. The memorial of the great Hamburg news sheet begins with a testimonial by his father, Ferdinand Laeisz, who in his memoirs bore witness that the entire presence of mind of the son had been needed to make it clear to him that the firm was still uninjured during the year of the great business crisis of 1857. It was at that time that Carl Laeisz put through their participation in the "Hamburg Guarantee-Discount-Chest" for the assistance of endangered but credit-worthy firms. The reminder of this transaction is followed by these sentences:

"After this classic testimonial to the talent of the son here proclaimed by the father, it is indeed not to be wondered at that Carl Laeisz should be the one to make the respected but still only moderately celebrated firm of F. Laeisz a world-wide business of the first rank. The merchants of Hamburg have not only never hesitated to acknowledge the significance of Carl Laeisz as a wholesale merchant, but have always considered themselves highly honored thereby. His counsel and his participation have been sought by and given to countless commercial undertakings, and after the firm of F. Laeisz had also taken on the ship owning business and had sent out a fleet of its own onto the oceans of the world, which has since developed into the greatest ship owning business of Hamburg, there has hardly been a shipping enterprise begun in Hamburg with which Carl Laeisz was not associated. His many-sided practical knowledge gained in the shipping trade, his shrewd insight, his enterprising ambition were put at the service of countless shipping undertakings, and it was his love of work and his joy in work that moved him to take a leading part in almost all of our great ship owning associations.

"But not only in the realm of shipping did this co-operative activity of the deceased find play. Just as he belonged to the board of directors of the Union Bank in Hamburg, so he had a place on the directing boards of numerous insurance enterprises in our town, and many of these insurance companies owe their beginnings mainly to his initiative. In the field of insurance, Carl Laeisz was an authority, and his opinions as well as his judgments were in most cases decisive. To our enterprise too, this shareholding association, the *New Stock Exchange*, the deceased devoted his labors for a long series of years in a leading position on the board.

"To all frequenters of the Hamburg Exchange, Carl Laeisz was a familiar and highly honored sight. His bonhommie had become even proverbial, which hid behind an occasionally sharp sounding habit of speech a heart full of sympathy and helpfulness. 'Old Laeisz', as he was called in his last years, was everywhere joyfully greeted, and in answer to questions on business matters, he knew how to hit the nail on the head point-blank and in a few concise words. His departure from the business circles of our parental city will be felt most painfully; everyone with whom he came into contact will miss his revered personality... All the merchants of Hamburg, yes, almost our entire commonalty, share in the grief of his sorely afflicted survivors. With Carl Laeisz, one of the finest citizens of our parent city, one of the best patriots of Germany has departed this life. The significance of the man who has now been called home shone so clearly in his actions that His Majesty, Kaiser Wilhelm, kept himself informed regularly concerning the state of health of this honored man; and the brother of the Kaiser, His Royal Highness Prince Henry, only a few days ago on a visit to our city, called at the Laeisz house on Neuen Jungfernstieg in order to give personal expression to his wishes for a speedy recovery. Unfortunately Providence decreed otherwise. In spite of all good wishes, the illness ended not in recovery, but in death, and again Hamburg has to lament the loss of one of her best men."

BUILDING OF THE HAMBURG MUSIC HALL

Music Hall

In Carl's will was found a clause in which he made over to the Hamburg State a considerable sum toward the building of the music hall. Many had not suspected in the robust, blunt man any particular inclination toward the fine arts. His intimate friends, however, knew that in that heroic frame was rooted a deep reverence for everything beautiful. Later, his widow raised the sum by an impressive contribution from her own means, and therefore made possible on the Carl-Muck Place a far more extensive, more beautiful music hall than had been originally planned.

A far more complicated personality than his father Carl, was the son, Carl Ferdinand. His speech before the Ship-Builders conference in Glasgow in March 1898, as he stood on the summit of his life and activity, showed us a man of the great world, in the center of the international commercial and economic life of his time, who also understood how to conduct himself on alien soil with a sovereign and elegant amiability. The men of the older generation in Hamburg who lived to see him President of the Chamber of Commerce could tell of his manner which carried all before it and was always in command of the exigencies of the situation, and to which an occasional sharp sarcasm was no stranger. So it can hardly surprise us that this man, as a member of the Hamburg Citizens Association, was also in the law-giving body of the Hanseatic state.

An entirely different aspect of his personality meets us in the quotations which he had copied onto the first page of his New Testament, perhaps under the growing presentiment of approaching departure. At all events, a Hamburg shipowner and wholesale merchant who drew his philosophy of life from Goethe and Byron, from Dante, Wilhelm Von Humboldt, and the English romantic poet Wordsworth, was an unusual personality. All these passages have in them something deeply moving:

And thus the heart will break, yet brokenly live on,
Even as a broken mirror, which the glass
In every fragment multiplies; and makes
A thousand images of one that was,
The same, and still the more, the more it breaks,
And thus the heart will do which not forsakes,
Living in shattered guise, and still, and cold,
And bloodless, with its sleepless sorrow aches,
Yet withers on till all without is old,
Showing no visible sign, for such things are untold.
Byron

The purest joy that one can take in a beloved person is that of seeing that he brings joy to others. Goethe

There is one thing which remains ever present in the soul, of which one does not cease to think merely because he is thinking of something else, over which the other thought rolls away like a brook in its bed. In these thoughts lies the true inner happiness; they do not let one become really unhappy.
Wilhelm Von Humboldt

There is no greater sorrow than to remember happy times in wretchedness.
Dante

And often, glad no more,
We wear a face of joy, because
We have been glad of yore.
Wordsworth

How far out beyond his own narrow field of interest as an owner of sailing vessels, Carl Ferdinand's thoughts went, 2 examples may show: In September, 1892, under his influence, the Hamburg Chamber of Commerce went on record for the planning of a German experiment station for research into the resistance of a vessel in the water to onward motion, not only for sailing vessels, but especially for fast passenger steamers, and, in general, for vessels to which unusual tasks were assigned. It was expressly stated that in the opinion of the Chamber of Commerce, such an experiment station would be of high value for

Advisory Council on Emigration

the taking over by German shipyards of the building of warships for foreign lands. In 1892, the Hamburg Chamber of Commerce was taking part in a conference for the drawing up of a national law for emigration. The proposed law did not reach a decision and was again, with some changes, laid before the Federal Council of 1896. The Hamburg Chamber of Commerce subscribed to the judgment of the authorities of the Reich in the matter of emigration, with exception of the stand taken on indirect emigration; that is, emigration through non-German ports. Many emigrants preferred to make the ocean passage in English vessels, and used German vessels only for the passage to an English emigration port. The Chamber of Commerce insisted on not forbidding indirect emigration, at least for foreigners, but on conceding it in the interest of Hamburg shipping. The Advisory Council on Emigration provided for in the decree was introduced in 1897 and formed the following year. To this, too, Carl Ferdinand Laeisz belonged, ex officio as the president at that time of the Hamburg Chamber of Commerce. His vessels were not emigration vessels, but his range of interest and his participation reached out to all systematized planning.

Speeches on Marine Bills

In the two years, 1897 and 1900, the German government brought up in the Reichstag marine bills which looked toward an enlargement of the war-fleet. On December 7, 1897, the Hamburg Chamber of Commerce called a conference of the members of "An Honorable Merchant" in order to decide on a resolution that had been presented by the Chamber emphasizing the necessity of the navy-decree. An effective speech by the chairman of the Chamber, Carl Ferdinand Laeisz, led to an almost unanimous acceptance of the resolution in question. More memorable yet in German marine history are the words which Carl Ferdinand addressed to the audience in the meeting of the Hamburg citizens' committee of the German Navy League on February 12, 1900, on the occasion of the second marine bill.

GERMAN NAVY LEAGUE ADDRESS

"I have been assigned the honorable task of clarifying the navy bill from the standpoint of commercial interests, a difficult task in an assembly of Hamburg citizens, most of whom understand as well as I, and many of them better than I, what is for the good of commerce! Let me try, nevertheless, to clear up a few points of view in particular. We have just heard how from of old it has been the belief of Hamburg and how Hamburg's history has proved that sea-power is the best, and in the long run the indispensable, support of sea-commerce, not only of shipping but of the entire overseas trade, and therefore of the German commerce which goes through Germany's principal port of both entrance and exit, Hamburg.

"It must have an adverse effect when one continues to hear the opinion expressed now and then that the Hanseatic merchant was entirely contented with the state of things in the days when no German Empire protected him abroad, that he knew very well then how to carry on his business without having rules behind him everywhere. If that were even halfway true, we Hamburgians would indeed have to long for the return of the time of the old German Confederation. (Amusement.) I should, however, like to see the Hamburg man who would express such an opinion! (Shouts of 'There isn't any!')

"Yes, our fathers managed as well as possible, and probably much better than we should have done. But history is silent about the difficulties they met, how many disappointed hopes and failing endeavors are to be credited to the weakness of Germany.

"For years, it was the French fleet that protected Hamburg's trade in the South Seas. Under the flag of Holland, the first German merchants established themselves in Japan; under the English flag, the first in China; and everywhere the naval powers have lent their support willingly to the industrious Hanseatic merchant.

"One large portion of our German vessels sailed under the Danish flag, another part under the flag of the kingdom of Hanover, which England considered a sort of dependency.

"Do you believe that a power could yet be found today which would seriously guard the German merchant? (Cries of 'No!') God be thanked, we have seldom need of that today, and it is to be hoped not at all tomorrow.

"Our fathers, too, well understood the power of a strong German fleet. When, in the year 1848, the German Fatherland seemed about to be made over into a powerful united state, it was in the first place Hamburg merchants who, while in Frankfurt people were arguing over paper paragraphs, gave practical proof of their patriotism by contributing a notable – yes, for their limited circumstances of those days, an astonishingly large sum – for the creation of a German fleet.

"Now let no one come to me with the familiar argument: 'If commerce has so great an interest in the fleet, let it pay a substantial part of the cost'. That is a delightful speculation concerning the money-bags of the Hanseatic merchant, of whom one frequently hears inland the most unmeasured ideas. Certainly it is not only the few merchants on the seaboard that are interested in commerce, not even only the merchants everywhere; but everyone who produces, everyone who works for consumption, every middleman between production and consumption, everyone who is concerned with the protection or development of civilization, therefore the entire nation. To saddle the cost of the fleet on ocean commerce alone would be the same as to saddle the border districts with the cost of the army, since they are most threatened by unfriendly neighbors. Naturally no one thinks of doing that. On the other hand, the border districts do acquire a marked advantage from the numerous garrisons. The border dwellers would certainly politely decline such an extra burden and perhaps seek their dwelling in sunnier pastures. It is easier yet to banish trade. Man cleaves to the soil, but he cannot outlaw change, and every increase of hardship inclines him more to other pathways. Not on this occasion alone do we need to draw attention to the threatening competition of the rival western ports so fortunately situated geographically that they must not be strengthened still more by the actions of Germany.

"That our present war-fleet is completely insufficient even in times of peace, I do not need to prove here. How often has it been impossible for the Imperial Marine service, because of lack of material, to send even one vessel to foreign places where it was much needed! I had better say as little as possible, since it is too disgraceful, about the wretched old hulk in which Prince Henry was towed out to China, or about the nutshells with which we are supposed to impress foreign peoples side by side with the ironclad vessels of England and France. It was sheer luck that, a few years ago, the German squadron, ordered from Eastern Asia to Chile, appeared before Valparaiso at the right time to render invaluable service to the Germans in that place in the confusion of war. With two corvettes, the German navy, thanks to the skill and tact of our marine officers, protected and defended the German interests during the Brazilian war in so brilliant a way that the English complained to their government over their lack of protection although they had a much stronger fleet in the harbor of Rio. German training ships had to protect our interests in the harbors of Haiti and Venezuela. That everything went so well, we may thank the splendid personnel with which our fleet is manned. (Lively cheers.) To such men, however, we must give the best vessels. It is still a real question whether an English second-class cruiser would have dared treat our mailboats as it did recently, had a German warship of the same rank been on the spot. (Agreement on all sides.)

"If anyone objects that in all these conditions, nothing has changed essentially in the two years since the last naval decree, I am of the opinion that above all, the recognition of the need of a strong fleet has changed. And that this recognition has come to the German people principally from above, from the Kaiser, still more that we have a Kaiser who in understanding, in wisdom, in loyalty to duty, in conscientiousness, and in love for the Fatherland, is above all monarchs in world-history, that is a piece of good fortune for which we cannot sufficiently thank Providence! (Stormy, long-lasting applause.)

"However, there have also been many important changes in the last few years. Unexpectedly great is the growth of German industry, the increase in our export trade, the enlargement of our shipping, the well-being and advancement of our population, the desire for enterprise based on these things. Do we not have an excellent example of this right here in Hamburg in the development of our Hamburg-American Line? Who would have dared to prophesy this development a few years ago?

"In just the last two years, Germany has acquired a series of new colonies, with which again far-reaching enterprises are connected, which may perhaps not bring profit to the persons undertaking them, but which are, at all events, richly nourishing German industry. And not only in the German colonies, but everywhere abroad, near and far, are arising German enterprises for which the power and courage were naturally lacking before the founding of the German Empire.

"Although we have kept our eyes principally directed at foreign lands, yet I believe that the protection of the home shores is not therefore the less important, is even entirely unavoidable if we would ward off such calamities as we endured in 1848-51, 1864, and 1870. A blockade of our ports, or even an attack on our coastal towns, would today work far more havoc because of the immensely increased values which are exposed to the danger. Therefore a strong iron-clad fleet is a necessity to us. If it should still seem weak compared with the English fleet, it should be considered that English naval strength is scattered extraordinarily far, and that we may hope to equal in superior quality what we lack in quantity. (Bravo!) The other powers do not cease to support a strong army although they have not yet grown to the size of the German army. Who would have thought a few years ago that in our merchantmen we should in point of quality surpass England? Today we have, afloat and building, 9 twin-screw steamships against 7 of the English, and ours are the fastest. (Bravo!)

"That in sea-warfare, quality is of first importance, there are many examples in history to show. Philip II's invincible Armada was beaten by an English fleet much smaller in number, but more flexible and more easily maneuvered. Six years after the battle of Trafalgar, the then small and young American union won remarkable victories over that supposedly so mighty sea-power, England.

"However, I am certainly not thinking of war with England, and I surely hope that from such a misfortune our two peoples will be forever preserved (Bravo!); but to maintain peace, we must appear to any possible enemy as an opponent worthy of respect, so that he will not feel the desire to quarrel with us. We cannot shut our eyes to the significant increase of the French and especially of the American navies, and we dare not ignore the fact that in both these countries a strong Chauvinism prevails.

"Our fleet will be costly, that is true, but we do not want it 'cheap and poor'. (Bravo!) It is a sort of Naval Warfare Reserve Fund, like the millions in the Julius tower at Spandau. Every soundly managed business must keep a reserve fund for times of need. The money spent on the fleet will remain for the most part in our country, and will nourish numerous existences. Our ship-building, in which we of Hamburg take a special interest and a special joy, is still capable of greater development. It will be mightily furthered through naval building, and the shipyards in particular will have an unremittingly steady occupation independent of commercial opportunities, which is so necessary. Through this, they will be put in a position not merely to satisfy the needs of the German commercial fleet, but also to compete in increasing measure abroad. Every vessel built in a German yard, be it warship or merchant ship, is a strong recommendation for German business industry and productive efficiency and is an aid to countless other interests.

"But if there should still remain here and there in Germany any doubt of the usefulness and need of a strong navy, let us inquire of our fellow-countrymen across the sea, whose insight into what is essential in business and commerce has been sharpened to the nth degree. They are the warmest and most zealous advocates of a strong fleet. An example of this came to me just today:

"The Germans of Beni in Bolivia, a small colony which is as far as possible from the coast, have given expression to their enthusiasm over the plan for a fleet by sending a sum of almost 14,000 marks through the Imperial consulate in Riberalta. (Bravo!)

"Surely, we of Hamburg also know how to prize a strong fleet and to evaluate and disprove those lies which would accuse us of having no heart for it. – We are proud that Mother Germania stands so strong and ready for service by land, but doubly proud if now she also looks out seaward with courage, and shows there the same strength and determination. To this I cry with a full heart as a true child of Hamburg:

'Hurrah, min Mudder kann swemm'n!'
(Hurrah, my Mother can swim!)"

PART II

THE HOUSE OF LAEISZ IN THE 20TH CENTURY

PART II

THE HOUSE OF LAEISZ IN THE 20TH CENTURY

Chapter One: THE YEARS 1901 - 1914

DEATH OF CARL F. LAEISZ

Death of Carl Ferdinand

No one would have guessed that the man who in February had spoken these words so permeated with the Hanseatic spirit and received with such stormy applause, would suddenly be attacked by a virulent disease and marked for death! On August 22, 1900, people read in the obituary notices which the Hamburg Stock Exchange dedicated to those just departed a tribute to his personality which, with all its North German dryness, yet mirrored the deep impression left at his death by Carl Ferdinand Laeisz.

Chairman of Hansa Line

"The fruition and the esteem in which the firm of F. Laeisz rejoices, it owes not least to his ever-active creative thought and labor. Besides the purely mercantile business, the young Laeisz devoted himself also to the shipping interests of his house, and in addition found the time to place his notable ability for work at the service of the building up of a regular steam communication with the harbors of Canada for the steamship firm Hansa, which was established in 1881 and for which in the early years, he was a member of the executive board of administration and later chairman of the board of directors. The importance to the position of Hamburg which this line achieved during its lifetime was due altogether to the tireless activity of the deceased. He conducted its business uninterruptedly until altered circumstances made it appear necessary to unite the line with the Hamburg-American Packet Joint-Stock Company.

Head of the Seamen's Association

"After the first-named ship-owning company had liquidated in a way altogether satisfactory to the stockholders, the deceased had a large part of his time free, and from then on, therefore, he could devote himself with all the intensity he desired to the Seamen's Association, of which he had been the head ever since its founding on December 5, 1887. In this field, Carl Ferdinand Laeisz accomplished something truly great; as the regulations drawn up for the prevention of accidents to laborers and seamen, which were initiated in the year 1891 and significantly enlarged in 1899, were exclusively his work. The working out of provisions for the protection of widows and orphans of seamen grew out of his efforts; and after they become effective, the seamen will have reason to remember that this law for the benefit of their relatives and survivors is to be credited solely to the thoughtfulness of the deceased, so that his name will be forever inseparable from it.

Member of Citizens' Council & of Chamber of Commerce

"His untiring creative labor and the universal regard which Carl Ferdinand had won for himself caused his fellow-citizens, as a sign of their high esteem, to elect him in 1892 to the Citizen's Council, to which he belonged until his death, and in the work of which he always took a prominent part. But his most characteristic field of labor was the Chamber of Commerce, of which he was a member from the year 1884 and in which he held the vice-presidency from 1893 to 1894, after which, during the years 1895-98, the confidence of his fellow members entrusted to his hands the conduct of the presidency. In this realm, the deceased performed a distinguished service; especially is his conduct of the presidency to be pointed out as one of the most tireless and the most splendid. On this account, the merchants many times took occasion to express their deepest thanks to Carl Ferdinand Laeisz for his activity as presiding officer of the Chamber of Commerce.

"No one will forget the moment on the 31st of December, 1898, when in the meeting which 'An Honorable Merchant' customarily holds on the last day of the year, Mr. Lutteroth expressed the especial thanks of the assembled merchants to the man who was retiring from the presidency upon the expiration of the legal term of office, by walking across to Mr. Laeisz, who, as president, was conducting the meeting for the last time, and shaking his hand in token of the thanks of all the Hamburg merchants in the assembly.

"But the departed did not confine his activity and his joy in work to matters which concerned only the well-being of his native city, his nearest neighbors: his wider outlook embraced also every interest which might serve the great fatherland, and Carl Laeisz held himself always ready, whenever he was needed, to intercede for the universal good. Thus he at once responded to the call which summoned him to a place on the Industrial Board of the German Empire, and in this place too he acted with his best skill for the welfare of the state to which he belonged as well as that of his fellow-citizens."

Chairman of German-Australian Steamship Co., & of "Cosmos".

The obituary goes on to remind us that Carl Ferdinand Laeisz was chairman of the board of directors of the "German-Australian Steamship Company," that he sat on the board of the German steamship company, "Cosmos," was a member of the Association of "Naval Architects," and of "Lloyds" of London, as well as of the association for codification of law of nations, finally, that he belonged to the board of trustees of the Reichsbank (Imperial Bank), the board of directors of the North German Bank in Hamburg, and that of the Emigrants' Chest in Hamburg. In summing up, this tribute concluded:

Member Assoc. of Naval Architects, Lloyds of London, Reichsbank, etc.

"What Carl Ferdinand Laeisz meant to and did for his native city and for his fatherland will not be forgotten, and throughout the history of Hamburg, whenever the talk turns to the mercantile development of our community, the name of the deceased will receive a loud applause."

On March 24, 1899, the firm could look back upon 75 years of existence. Many congratulations from friends all over the world made clear what honor and affection the House of Laeisz enjoyed. Naturally, there was no lack of respect paid by official circles. The Chamber of Commerce handed the firm the "Chamber Of Commerce Golden Commemorative Medal" with a long congratulatory letter. From the state secretary of the Imperial Department Of The Interior, Count Posadowsky, came a letter written in the friendliest possible tone; and the German Kaiser likewise sent his congratulations through the Prussian ambassador, Herr Von Metternich.

Seventy-fifth Anniversary of House of Laeisz

THE SUCCESSORS OF CARL HEINRICH AND CARL FERDINAND LAEISZ

Appointment of Guardians

Since Carl and Carl Ferdinand Laeisz closed their eyes forever within a short time of each other, and 2 young boys remained as bearers of the great name, the 2 Hamburg senators, Drs. Predöhl and Westphal were appointed as their guardians. Proprietor of the firm until her death in 1912 was the widow, Mrs. Sophie Laeisz, née Knöhr, who for almost half a century had been the loyal and industrious life-partner of Carl Laeisz.

Appointment of Confidential Clerks

The work of 3 generations was taken over immediately by the confidential agents, P. Ganssauge, J. Reisse, and H. Strück. These men carried to completion the great tasks already begun. After the death of Carl Ferdinand, the plans for the greatest sailing vessel ever to be built by the firm were discovered in his desk, fully worked out. Carl Laeisz gave the commission for this to the Tecklenborg yards in Geestemünde before his death. He did not live to see her completion in 1902.

The services which the successive generations, Laeisz father, son, and grandson, had rendered to the shipping and commerce of their native city and to the larger fatherland led, immediately after the death of Carl Laeisz, to the idea of letting this family speak to the future as well through a memorial of metal and stone. On April 26, 1903, on the eve of the 75th birthday of Carl Laeisz, it was ready to be unveiled in the well of the court of the Laeisz-house beside the Trostbrücke. During the ceremony a friend of the Laeisz family, General-Consul Kothe, addressed to Mrs. Sophie Laeisz, with her 2 grandsons, to Burgomasters and Senators of Hamburg, to the President and Vice-President of the Council, to the President of the Chamber of Commerce, to the authors of the memorial, and to the relatives and friends of the House of Laeisz, from the entire industrial world of Hamburg, a speech of which the following sentences should be remembered.

"When we consider the entire life of the senior member, 'the old Laeisz', as Hamburg called him for many decades, it evolves somewhat according to a plan. Growing up under hard conditions in a hard era, he was able to overcome the difficulties occasioned by the building up of his own business and of many other enterprises far more easily than would have been possible to a man less steeled in the severity of life. 'Heads up!' 'Through struggle to victory!' This had been the youthful insignia of the old gentleman; this remained his inner guide through life. He did not stop with his own, always high-aimed enterprises; he overcame also the difficulties and problems of others. And in the same spirit, the father brought up the son, and both again brought up the excellent grandson. It is inspiring to read in the memoirs of this grandson concerning his grandfather how in bad times, in the crisis of the year 1857, the fruit of this upbringing unfolded into rarest blossom, how the father found in the courage of his son the finest support for triumph over those difficult days – and that not only for his own peace of mind, no, but for the blessing of the entire body of Hamburg merchants. That harsh time must have made a deep and enduring impression on the then 29-year-old Carl Laeisz. Through courage, skill, and labor, to alleviate the hardships of others, this was the result at that time of the efficient working together of father and son, and that remained their program, the Laeisz program, from then on.

"Skill, labor, and helpfulness! Was it any wonder that under such a program, the grandson, our unforgettable Carl Ferdinand Laeisz, should ripen into the splendid man that he was to us? Was it a wonder in him whom nature had also equipped with the most complete gifts of the spirit? Skill was evident in all his doings; labor from morning till evening was his happiest way of life; and what he accomplished in helpfulness, that is inscribed in golden letters in the history of the seamen's Association, which he initiated and developed into a model institution."

THE LAEISZ MEMORIAL

The plan of the memorial is simple, compact, effective. Before the background of a portal of flesh-colored streaked marble from the island of Skyros in the Aegean Sea, there arises a life-sized bronze group, whose 3 figures embody Shipping, Ship-building, and Insurance. A powerful outstanding male figure, the head covered with a pilot's southwester, symbolizes Navigation; to the right, at his feet, an earnest laborer, with a propeller fastened to a shaft, symbolizes Shipbuilding; and a female figure, who is searching in an open account book, Insurance. On the upper crossbeam of the doorway, in low relief, is a portrait of "old Laeisz"; on the right perpendicular support, that of Carl Laeisz; and on the left, that of Carl Ferdinand Laeisz. When the house burned down in a night of bombing in the year 1943, all 3 reliefs, which were in marble, fell into ruin, while the metal figures remained intact. The record of dedication of the memorial designed by the Hamburg sculptor, Caesar Scharf – the artist did not live to see the completed work – is dated April 26, 1903, in Hamburg, and signed by the following firms:

North German Insurance Company
Northwest German Insurance Company
Hanseatic Nautical And General Insurance Company
German-Australian Steamship Company
Assurance Association Of 1865
North German Bank In Hamburg
Neptune Assurance Company
Hamburg-South-American Steamship Navigation Company
Union Bank In Hamburg
Bd. Blumenfeld
Joint Stock Company "New Exchange"
Hamburg-American Line
General Nautical Insurance Company
German Levant Line
New 8 Insurance Company
Woermann Line m.b.H.
German East Africa Line
German Steamship Navigation Company "Cosmos"
Blohm And Voss
North German Coal And Coke Works, Joint Stock Co.
Shipowners' Stock Company Of 1896
The Directors Of The "Janus"
Association Of Hamburg Assurance Writers
In the Name of the Seamen's Association: Richard C. Krogmann, Chairman

This series of names is itself a memorial not less impressive than the symbolization of the accomplishments of the firm through the memorial in bronze and marble in the Laeisz-House by the Trostbrücke.

It was a testimony to the careful planning and solidity in the building up of the firm that the death of such important persons as were Carl and Carl Ferdinand Laeisz did not interrupt the flowering and continuous growth of the business. Not until the year 1912, therefore shortly before the World War, did the 2 sons of Carl Ferdinand Laeisz, Herbert and Eric, enter the firm. In 1917, Herbert, the elder brother, remained on the field of honor at the West Front. In 1913, with 18 sailing vessels which combined a net tonnage of 14,000 in round numbers, the firm was at the highest point that it had reached during its existence. It was the largest private ship-owning company in Hamburg. The régime of the confidential agents had done all that was possible. Not only the shipping business, but the other branches also took part in the expansion. The most convincing testimony to inner strength and unaltered enterprising spirit was given in 1908, 7 years after the death of Carl Laeisz, by a plan, emerging at first in outline, for the undertaking of a great overseas plantation for banana culture in the Cameroons. Its accomplishment, merely interrupted, not set aside, by the war, will occupy us in another chapter.

Chapter Two: FROM THE FIRST WORLD WAR UNTIL 1939

DISPOSITION OF THE LAEISZ FLEET AT THE CLOSE OF WORLD WAR I

The English Lubbock writes only a few sentences concerning the fate of the Laeisz firm in the World War and their conduct immediately thereafter; but these sentences, with their self-criticism are characteristic, especially in the mouth of an enemy:

"The war cost Herr Laeisz his whole fleet. . . .

"The great German shipowner, however, was not to be crushed out of existence by the simple method of confiscating his fleet. He at once set about buying back the pick of his ships from their new owners, who had no idea what to do with them and were only too glad to receive marks instead of ships. . . .

"Not only was Herr Laeisz not satisfied with getting his old ships back, but he began building again. . . .

"In 1918 Messrs. Blohm and Voss built the 4-mast barque PRIWALL* of 2,849 tons net.

"In June 24, 1926, Tecklenborg launched the splendid PADUA at Wesermünde.

"Wise in their generation, the Germans insist that their officers shall be sail trained, and accommodation was provided on the PADUA for 40 cadets.

"Only recently I had a sad letter from Chile lamenting the decay of the British sailor and remarking that amongst foreigners the British officer was not considered inferior on all points to the sail-trained Germans, Finns, Danes, and Souwegians generally. And this inferiority was put down to their ignorance of the primordial ways of the sea; in other words, they were navigators and engineers but not seamen or men of the sea."

At the outbreak of the World War of 1914-18, there were 16 sailing vessels with a combined tonnage of 42,000 gross, in round numbers, in the possession of the firm. They had the following fates:

PAMIR

1. PAMIR,[1] while on a return trip, received from another sailer the news that war had broken out. By departing somewhat from her usual route, she was able to reach the neutral waters of the Canary Islands unobserved and to anchor in a bay of the island Palma. There she remained during the entire course of the war. Then after the war, she was able to bring her whole cargo of saltpeter to Hamburg and unload it, and was then consigned to the Italians. They took the vessel with a cargo of coal to Genoa. There she remained idle, and in 1924 could be bought back again for the price of 7,000 pounds. The vessel remained in the service of the firm until 1931, and was then bought by the shipping firm of Erikson in Finland.

PARMA

2. PARMA was in Iquiqui in Chile, was delivered to the English on April 22, 1921, in Delfzijl (Holland), and on November 8, 1921, bought back for 10,000 pounds. This vessel sailed for the firm until 1931, and was then sold in Finland.

PASSAT

3. PASSAT[2] was in Iquiqui, was delivered over to the French on May 27, 1921, and bought back on December 22, 1921, for 13,000 pounds In 1932, this vessel also was sold to the shipping firm Erikson.

---

*Correction. PRIWALL was built as POLA, 1916-19, but not made ready for the sea until after the end of the war. — The author.

[1] [Capt. Jurgen Jürss - EDITOR]

[2] [Capt. Otto Piper - EDITOR]

4. PEIHO[3] was in Caleta Buena (Chile), was delivered with the PARMA to the English, and bought back on July 13, 1921, for 6,100 pounds. On March 16, 1923, this vessel stranded in the strait of LeMaire, not far from Cape Horn. *PEIHO*

5. PEKING[4] was in Valparaiso, was delivered to the Italians on May 10, 1921, and bought back on January 11, 1923, for 8,500 pounds. She sailed for the firm until the year 1932, and was then sold in London. *PEKING*

6. PELIKAN[5] was in Valparaiso, was unloaded on April 5, 1921, in Dunkirk, and then handed over to the enemy alliance. *PELIKAN*

7. PENANG[6] was in Hamburg, and was sold on October 12, 1917, to Bremen. *PENANG*

8. PERIM[7] was in Antwerp, and was sold on November 3, 1917, to a Hamburg firm. *PERIM*

9. PERKEO[8] was captured by English warships on August 6, 1914, and as the sailer, BELL, was sunk by German U-boats at the beginning of 1916. *PERKEO*

10. PETSCHILI[9] was in Valparaiso and wrecked there during a violent Norther on July 12, 1919. *PETSCHILI*

11. PINGUIN[10] was in Hamburg, and was sold on September 15, 1917, in Bremen. *PINGUIN*

12. PINNAS[11] was in Valparaiso, was unloaded in Dunkirk on February 21, 1921, and then delivered over to the enemy alliance. On December 22, she was bought back for the sum of 6,000 pounds. On April 27, 1929, this vessel had to be abandoned southward from Cape Horn. *PINNAS*

13. PIRNA[12] was at Hamburg, and was sold there on April 20, 1916. *PIRNA*

14. POMMERN[13] was in Valparaiso, was unloaded in Delfzijl on March 29, 1921, and then delivered over to the enemy alliance. *POMMERN*

15. PONAPE,[14] on September 20, 1914, was captured by the English and remained in English possession. *PONAPE*

16. POTOSI[15] was caught in the passage to Valparaiso, was sold right there to a Bremer firm,[16] but after that delivered to France, finally came into possession of the Chileans[17] under the name FLORA. On the 18th of September, 1925, not far from the Argentine coast, the coal cargo of the vessel caught fire, and the burned-out wreck was sunk by cannon fire from an Argentinian warship. *POTOSI*

THE COUNTING HOUSE FOR SAILING SHIPS, LTD.

At the close of the war, there lay along the shore of South America about 50 German vessels; of these, 9 sailers belonged to the Laeisz firm. By order of the Imperial embassy in Buenos Ayres, these vessels, in order to avoid enemy seizure, were rendered unfit for use by partial destruction of the rigging and sail-fittings.

---

[3] [Capt. H. Hamm - EDITOR]
[4] [Capt. A. Oetzmann - EDITOR]
[5] [Capt. H. Kaiser - EDITOR]
[6] [Capt. Gerke - EDITOR]
[7] [Capt. A. Holtzmann - EDITOR]
[8] [Capt. Hinrich Nissen - EDITOR]
[9] [Capt. A. Teschner - EDITOR]
[10] [Capt. B. Petersen - EDITOR]
[11] [Capt. A. Oetzmann - EDITOR]
[12] [Capt W. Ehlert - EDITOR]
[13] [Capt. H. Ravn - EDITOR]
[14] [Capt. C. Eckhardt - EDITOR]
[15] [Capt. Robert K. Miethe - EDITOR]
[16] [F. A. Vinnen & Co. - EDITOR]
[17] [Gonzalez, Sophia & Co. - EDITOR]

Since, at the close of the war, because of the scarcity of world tonnage, the freight prices had risen enormously – for example, saltpeter freight charge from Chile to Europe was something like ten times the pre-war average –, it would have been extremely rewarding to get all the vessels lying in the harbors of Chile as quickly as possible back into the return journey with their cargo. Two things worked against this, however: first, the damages taken into consideration by the higher powers, in the settlement of which the costs could not be determined without much ado, and second, the requirement of the Versaille dictation according to which all German commercial vessels of over 1,000 tons should be delivered over to the enemy powers. For the Laeisz firm, this meant that all its sailing vessels, including the recently built and not yet floated POLA and PRIWALL, as well as the steamships PUNGO and PIONIER, must be surrendered. Out of the firm's entire fleet, therefore, not one single vessel remained.

Capt. Petersen in Chile

At this blow, Paul Ganssauge took the precaution to send to Chile, as early as 1919, Captain B. Petersen, the ship-inspector for the firm, to make preparations for the possibility that the sailers could again be put into action. The circumstance that the individual enemy powers to whom the vessels would be assigned were hardly in position to produce the crews necessary to get the sailers under weigh, gave rise to the development of the idea of seeking ways and means to bring the vessels back to Europe on their own account and deliver them when here. After many discussions with the owners of other sailing vessels lying before Chile and with the government agencies – ministry of transportation, commission for delivery, etc. – an agreement was reached with the Imperial Government by which the owners, uniting in a pool of the sailing vessels, *might load the sailers lying on the West coast of South America for the home-coming passage to their own account.*

The Counting House For Sailing Ships G.M.B.H.

This agreement must, however, first obtain the consent of the "Maritime Board Of The Reparation Commission." For this, further negotiations in London were necessary, in which Paul Ganssauge and Emil Offen (G. J. H. Siemers and Co.) with representatives of the Empire and of a few other shipping firms, took part. They succeeded in reaching an agreement favorable to the German shipowners: those vessels which appeared to belong to the German owners might be loaded for Europe to their account. In the European harbors where the cargo was to be unloaded, the sailers, after the unloading and the repairing of the damages resulting from the return passage, must be surrendered to the respective power of the enemy alliance. For the central clearing house of all problems connected with the home passage, the shipping firms concerned established the Counting House For Sailing Ships, G.m.b.H., at Hamburg. (Limited Liability Company) As managers, Messrs. Paul Ganssauge and E. Offen were named; as confidential agent of the Counting House for all vessels on the west coast of South America, Captain Petersen. The conditioning of the vessels and the clearing up of special conditions arising from the war caused many difficulties; but in spite of that, all sailing vessels that could be reconditioned without unreasonable cost to the owners were brought to Europe and surrendered there. The firms paid for the reconditioning; what had to be paid in accumulated demurrages and other costs was in part taken over by the Government.

Through the discussions in Berlin and in London, much time was lost. Meanwhile, saltpeter freight rates dropped from 200 shillings a ton to 90-115 shillings according to location and the size and age of the vessel. Nevertheless, the arrangement was a complete success. In spite of the sometimes high costs of

(1) (NAUTICAL PHOTO AGENCY)

Steel 4-Masted Barque PONAPE ex REGINA ELENA, 2,318 Gross Tons
1911-1914

(2) (NAUTICAL PHOTO AGENCY)

Steel 4-Masted Barque PERKEO ex BRILLIANT, 3,765 Gross Tons
(1914)
As BRILLIANT

(1) (NAUTICAL PHOTO AGENCY)

Steel 4-Masted Barque POLA, 3,104 Gross Tons
As RICHLIEU

(2) (NAUTICAL PHOTO AGENCY)

Steel 4-Masted Barque PRIWALL, 3,105 Gross Tons

repair and conditioning, a considerable overplus remained for the shipowners. Out of the earnings from the cargoes of the 7 home-coming vessels, it was possible for the F. Laeisz firm, as noticed above, to buy back the PAMIR, PARMA, PASSAT, PEIHO, PEKING, and PINNAS from the nations of the alliance. With this fleet, a regular freight service from Hamburg to Chile and back could be started again.

It contributed much to the success of the entire operation that Captain Petersen had been sent to Chile at the right time, before it was even settled that the idea would prevail of setting the vessels free to carry freight to Europe in favor of the owners, and that he was able to set everything in working order on those vessels which were again to be made seaworthy. Paul Ganssauge could also point to a special success in London in that he succeeded in keeping the PRIWALL, which had not been entirely completed by the end of the war, out of the surrender-requirement, whereas POLA unfortunately had to be given over to France. Thus, with the 1 vessel, PRIWALL, the resumption of the West Coast service could begin, even before the return and re-purchase of the other 6 sailers. In 1920, PRIWALL took a part of the crew substitutes for the return passage out with her. Further recruits went out to Chile under very hard conditions in the steamer LUCIE WOERMANN, chartered for the purpose.

POSEIDON AND PLANET

Since, because of events of the war, the 2 large fruit steamers ordered by F. Laeisz in 1914 had to be given up to the Allies and, on the other hand, the plantations also were lost, the firm ceased after the war to build fruit vessels. Two turbine steamers were ordered from the dockyards of Joh. C. Tecklenborg Mutual in Geestemünde, which were finished in October and December respectively. These vessels had a freight capacity of about 9,500 tons and a speed of about 12 1/2 knots. They were especially well fitted for piece goods cargoes, and after a rather long dickering with the Hamburg-American Line, a deal was successfully made with it in accord with which the 2 vessels should be included on equal terms in the service to be re-opened by the Hamburg-American Line during the course of 1923 to the West Coast of South America by way of the Panama Canal or the Straits of Magellan. This agreement, which was of vital significance for F. Laeisz, was signed on November 8, 1922, on behalf of the firm of F. Laeisz by Messrs. Laeisz and Ganssauge, on the side of the Hamburg-American Line by the privy councilors Cuno and Peltzer.

After both vessels had made several passages to La Plata, POSEIDON, on the basis of this compact, was the first vessel to undertake the voyage to the West Coast of South America and back via the Panama Canal, leaving on August 12, 1923. The PLANET followed on November 1, 1923, with her first voyage to the West Coast of South America via Magellan Straits.

The agreement was drawn up for 20 years, running therefore to the year 1942, but was interrupted in 1939 by the outbreak of the Second World War. Note: F. Laeisz became F. Laeisz, G.M.B.H. (A limited liability company) between November, 1920, and February, 1951.

THE LAEISZ FLEET IN THE FIRM'S 100TH YEAR

When on March 24, 1924, the firm F. Laeisz was able to celebrate with festivities the 100th return of the day of its founding, it again possessed a notable fleet, namely:

Two steamers (PLANET and POSEIDON) each of 9,500 tons capacity, and 6 sailers (PAMIR, PARMA, PASSAT, PEKING, PINNAS, PRIWALL) of a combined capacity of around 26,000 tons (the PEITHO was unfortunately lost in March, 1923), therefore, altogether, a capacity of about 45,000 tons.

Introduction of Synthetic Nitrate

A fatality was already threatening the saltpeter trade in the years 1925-29, as the manufacture of artificial saltpeter-air-nitrogen, already prospering before the World War, became ever greater in extent and lower in cost. To the factories in Norway where this manufacture first took on great dimensions with the help of the plentiful water power, were added the highly efficient German factories. In fact, only their help had made it possible to carry on the war beyond the year 1915, when we would otherwise have had to surrender because of a lack of ammunition.

As the new shipbuilding showed, the management of the firm did not let itself be turned aside from the plan to rebuild its sailing fleet, and again in the year 1926 gave the Tecklenborg yards in Geëstemunde the commission for the building of the 4-mast barque PADUA.

At the end of 1923, Willi Ganssauge, now a partner in the firm, took his first voyage on the POSEIDON. It was a thrilling experience for him, since on this passage the new Laeisz steamer, POSEIDON, and the home-coming 4-masted barque PARMA[18] met in the English Channel on a radiant morning.

BUILDING OF THE LAST COMMERCIAL 4-MASTED BARQUE

Sailers Equipped As Training Vessels

In clear-sighted recognition of what was required for the highest possible security in the business of shipping, the management, after the surrender of their merchant fleet, still held fast to the proved belief in giving officers and captains their training on sailing vessels. The quick tempo of the rebuilding of our merchant fleet made it clear, moreover, that the few deep-sea sailers still afloat could not supply the new demand for seamen. Therefore they decided on the solution which for decades the North German Lloyds had proved useful; to build freight carrying school ships. One of the first to appear in this category after the War was a Laeisz sailer, the PADUA. Besides the usual crew of trained sailors, officers, and under-officers, there was space for 40 boys, who were to receive their first seaman's instruction in return for a modest compensation. After the second year, they were apprentice seamen and already drawing a small wage. The third year saw them proud sailors on full wage. From the PADUA, they went out to the other deep-sea vessels which still sailed under the German flag. Even the building specifications for the PADUA showed a division of living space new on the Laeisz sailers, since lodging had to be provided for the 40 ship's boys. Eventually the sailing vessels, PRIWALL, PEKING, and PASSAT were also adapted for the training of ship's boys.

Passages like that of the PEKING in the winter of 1931-32 demonstrated that even after the War, a tested, resolute leadership, could, with our newly recruited increase of seamen, turn out distinguished, yes, record-making performance. The F L sailing vessels have sent many qualified young seamen into German shipping. Also the Second World War again showed us that among the men of our U-boats and other warcraft who wore the knight's cross on their blue collars, many talked with pride of the time when on the slender decks of the handsome PADUA in the roaring gales off Cape Horn, they were first taught what it means to be a seaman.

[18][Capt. Toepper - EDITOR]

SOME POST WAR PASSAGES

In *Schiffe Und Schicksale (Ships and Destinies)* there is a record of several good passages made by the PEKING, PASSAT, and PADUA between Hamburg and the saltpeter coast in the years 1925-31. The timing to South America was as follows:

4-mast barque PEKING	1925:[19]	Channel-Talcahuano	74 days
	1926:[20]	Channel-Talcahuano	79 days
	1928:[21]	Channel-Talcahuano	77 days

The PEKING made the following really dazzling passages:
from Ushant (Channel) Dec. 27, 1931 to
Valparaiso, Feb. 24, 1932[22] = 59 days
from Taltal, Mar. 12, 1932 to
Santander, May 22, 1932[23] = 71 days

4-mast barque PASSAT	1927:[24]	Scilly-Corral	67 days
	1927:	Caleta-Buena - Channel	75 days
	1927-28:	Channel - Corral	73 days
	1930:[25]	Lizard - Talcahuano	72 days

4-mast barque PADUA	April 5, 1928[26] from Hamburg, April 10, 1928 from Scilly June 20, 1928 to Talcahuano	71 days
	August 1, 1928 from Mejillones Oct. 10, 1928 passed the Lizard	70 days
	1928-29: Lizard to Talcahuano	74 days
	1929: Channel to Corral	68 days
	1929-30: Tocopilla to Brugge	73 days
	1930: Lizard to Talcahuano	72 days
	1931:[27] Lizard to Talcahuano	62 days

The Australian Grain Trade

After the war of 1914-18, aside from harvest season in LaPlata ports, there were hardly any paying freights for the great sailing vessels anywhere in the world, except the passage to Australia. For the most part, the outward passage had to be made in ballast, unless one happened to secure a cargo of lumber for South Africa. So in those years there assembled in the ports of Australia as soon as the wheat harvest was gathered, the last champions among those once so proud representatives of the real romance of the sea. Most of them under the white, blue-crossed flag of Finland some under the German and Swedish flags, they set out, laden with wheat, on the passage "to the Channel for orders". With beating heart, every old seaman awaited news of the arriving vessel. With satisfaction, the German seamen of the year 1933 could greet as victor among 221 vessels the MAGDALENE VINNEN,[28] who had required only 76 days for the return passage. Second, with 83 days, was the Finnish 4-masted bark, PARMA. She too had sailed until 1931 under the black-white-red and the white F L flags.

[19][Capt. Oellrich - EDITOR]
[20][Capt. J. H. Piening - EDITOR]
[21][Capt. Jurgen Jürss - EDITOR]
[22][Capt. Hans J. Rowher - EDITOR]
[23][Capt. Hans J. Rowher - EDITOR]
[24][1927-1928: Capt. E. Müller - EDITOR]
[25][Capt. Hans. J. Rowher - EDITOR]
[26][1928-1930: Capt. J. Hermann Piening - EDITOR]
[27][Capt. Robert Clauss - EDITOR]
[28][Auxiliary - EDITOR]

TO SOUTH AUSTRALIA IN 67 DAYS

Record Passages of PADUA and PRIWALL

Then these accomplishments were cast far into the shadow by the latest 2 vessels of the glorious Laeisz fleet. After a long period of enforced rest in the port of Hamburg, the two 4-masters, PADUA and PRIWALL left their home anchorage on the same day with their goal Australia. On November 2, 1933, the 2 great seabirds swung out of their nest, at the mouth of the Elbe, to sweep, a few hours apart, out of the narrows of the Ärmelchannel into the endless space that is their true home. The race began. Both were lightly loaded, and thus at last had for once the same favorable conditions which formerly the tea and wool clippers always had on their fast wonder-voyages. And now the German youngsters demonstrated that on their much heavier vessels with far smaller crews, they could give at least the same performance as the wide-famed and far-sung "hard-case sailormen" of clipper times. At *least* the same!

The PRIWALL ran out of the Channel with a small lead; but naturally that signified nothing on a race-course of more than half the earth's circumference. In the North Atlantic, the 2 P-liners were already showing their class. From noon of the 13th to noon of the 14th of November, the PRIWALL ran 293 nautical miles. At more than 12 miles an hour, she flew along before the brisk northeast trade wind with the speed of a good steamer, and 2 days later, the PADUA reached about the same speed. In exactly 3 weeks from the Channel, they had crossed the Line on the same day. Using the wind-system of the North Atlantic shrewdly, they arrived in 2 weeks more in the latitude at which the clipper ships had formerly made their astonishing passages. The 2 great workhorses, which our modern deep-sea sailers really are, now demonstrated that they were of the same blood as the slim racers of the past century. Almost side by side, they flew along toward the east, their towering pyramids of sails spread stiff as boards before the brave west wind of the "roaring forties". From December 14, 1932, until New Year's Day, 1933 - that is, 17 continuous days - both held an average of 11.9 miles an hour; 529 kilometers per day for one of these blockish sailers is really an accomplishment that must inspire enthusiasm in every expert. That demands a control of the vessel which has mastered even the most secret skills of handling huge tackle; it demands a crew that carries out every command with intelligence and lightning speed. That means hours of clear-eyed watching for pitfalls; it means hauling on braces and sheets that crack the joints; it means wet tackle and wet berths; it means "Free-watch on deck!" when at last possible moment the topgallant sails must be secured against the invading squall. That demands iron arms and steel sinews, an indestructible sense of humor, and enthusiasm for the profession. For to run a course like that for 17 days on end implies that the sails must not be hauled down one minute before it is absolutely necessary.

So they lashed their racers eastward, the captains Clauss and Jürss, like those damned Yankee skippers of the tea passages, and their "hard-wood" sailors stood on the rolling decks and toiled at least as valiantly as the "iron" men of the clipper days. For where 4 stood then, now there were at most 2, and every extra 2 arms mean a lot in the fastening of a lashing top-gallant sail! On the 5th of January, both vessels stood before the entrance to the Gulf of Spencer, PADUA some 60-70 miles behind PRIWALL. Then the air became impenetrable. PADUA hove to, but PRIWALL kept on, and thereby ran into the destined harbor a day ahead of her rival. 62 days from the Channel - a new record for the Australian passage was set up. And German the ship, and German to the last ship's boy the crew it bore!

We will complete this presentation of the wheat-voyage of the 2 Laeisz vessels with the report of the commander of the PRIWALL, Captain Robert Clauss, on the decisive last lap of the sailing race before the entrance into the Gulf of Spencer.

"On January 4, the PADUA is 129 nautical miles south of us. Then a stiff west wind sets in, and we both brace four-square for the last spurt. Our positions at noon on January 5 are:

PADUA 36 degrees 33 minutes south, 134 degrees 15 minutes east,
PRIWALL 35 degrees 53 minutes south, 135 degrees 33 minutes east.

Whereas the PADUA stands 116 nautical miles southwest-by-west off South Neptune Island, the sentinel of Spencer Gulf, we have still 43 nautical miles northeast-by-east to sail to the same point. And from there are still 17 nautical miles to the entrance to Spencer Gulf, to our goal. Ridiculous 60 sea-miles, the remainder of 15,000! And yet this last remnant was to become a severe test for vessel and for man. It happened this way. In the morning, it had blown stormily, but a laughing sun looked down through the rifts in the hurrying clouds. This allowed good astronomical observations. PRIWALL went rushing over the white-striped blue sea till our hearts laughed in our bodies. It was as if she realized that the final struggle was beginning.

"Shortly after eleven o'clock, a dark cloud comes flying up from the west. 'Who knows how it will look in an hour!' I think, and begin to take the sun's altitude regularly. When, at noon, everything is overcast, then I revise the last good altitude to a near-meridian latitude. Combined with the recorded morning observations, I shall arrive at a reasonable estimate of the vessel's location. Neptune means well by us. To be sure, it grows ever darker over our masts; yet some 10 minutes before the culmination, I succeed in getting one more really good and accurate observation of the sun. Now I have the necessities for reckoning an exact ship's location, a great comfort when standing for land. PRIWALL, during the morning watch, has ploughed 55 nautical miles through the water. At the change of watch, I have to take both lookouts off the royal. The vessel lays herself over and clips toward her goal at a steady rate of 14 1/2 knots. Then comes a series of sharp gusts which bring with them much rain and invisibility. This keeps me back on the deck a good deal. Therefore the vessel has again laid 11 nautical miles behind her on her old course, north 63 degrees east, before I have finished reckoning the noon position: 35 degrees, 53 minutes south; 135 degrees, 35 minutes east. I set down the corrected point.on the local chart, which gives a picture of the entrance into the Gulf of Spencer. A grasp at the parallel rules: north 40 degrees east from us South Neptune's Island. Where is the circle? Aha! Exactly 43 more nautical miles before the light-tower of the island is abeam. From then on, there are only 17 miles more. I set down the new course, north 15 degrees east, and go on deck.

"The weather does not clear up again; one rain squall follows another. Harder and harder they drive through the rigging. Then the drama really breaks loose. A sharp clap on the after-deck. A couple of times the mizzen-topsail flaps thundering up and down, then flies away in shreds before the howling squall. Would it not be better we should begin to clew up? But to make secure the upper and lower topgallant sails, the giant lower sails, and the dozen staysails now? Caramba! That would take hours! And PRIWALL is rushing through the water as if she were sporting happily like a dolphin, speeding over the high seas. Heave the vessel to now?

"Another look at the chart. Thunder and lightning! The situation is certainly far from comfortable! On our lee-side, Kangaroo Island. Northeast of us the York- and northwest the Eyrie- peninsulas. Ahead, the cliffs of the Neptune group, of the Gambier Islands, and a half dozen or a full dozen more of sharp little rocks. And PRIWALL is flying at 14 or 15 knots toward them, the speed of a torpedo boat for the captain of a deep-sea sailer steering toward land! Thereto rain and thick air all around, and a clear outlook only for minutes between. But to heave to and waste unknown stretches of time – that now would be just as miserable. Finally, why has one gone to school and studied navigation? Why through long years has one accumulated ocean experiences? After all, this should bring certainty. All that one has observed and reckoned, and with it that sure feeling in the fingers' ends, that must count for something, if navigation as a whole is to make any sense!

"Quietly, I go over my reckonings in my mind once more, the sun-altitudes in the morning and shortly before mid-day. I assure myself once again of the correctness of my instrument readings at the latest observation. And what about our chronometer? – is not that to be trusted? But we have also had exact controls during these last days through the wireless signals from Adelaide. Por Dios! If there is anything in this whole business of observation and reckoning, then my vessel's position must be right, for everything has been carried out carefully. And since leaving Hamburg, no drop of alcohol has passed my lips, not the smallest drop of beer. Even the fragrant Christmas punch could not make me waver in my principles. This is to be a severe testing; a decision of the utmost responsibility hangs upon it. But everything assures me that the reckoning is right. So I will sail into the Gulf of Spencer though it rain cats and dogs.

"I go on deck. Jonni Jungblut stands at the helm. Ever since Hamburg, he has been apprentice pilot, the true blond son of his home on the lower Elbe. He is sixteen; but with his bearlike strength, he holds the rudder easily. And how the vessel obeys him! That one is born for a sailor. When he steers, he has his hand on the soul of the vessel. And she runs for no one else as she does for his rudder-turning. He will hold a good course, that boy!

"'Jonni, watch the steering well. Now comes the worst!'

"Jonni smiles. At 15 knots, the PRIWALL races between the bristling cliffs. Squall after squall whips howling over the blue-black sea. The visibility has become a trifle better. Silent we stand on the high deck and stare into the fleeing vapors. The first officer is with the watch on the forecastle, and the second is making the anchor clear for letting go. Again the storm howls in from the west. The air shuts us in like thick wet cloths, the rain strikes rattling on the deck. Slowly, far too slowly, the gray side-drops draw rustling to the east; ahead, it is gradually becoming clearer. If my reckoning is right, South Neptune should now come into sight to the larboard. If my reckoning is right! If the High Powers were favorable! If the chronometer was correct! If the log spoke truth! But no – everything was in agreement. Clear as glass was every consideration. The tower *must* come into sight now – right away!

"My eyes bore into the clearing air. There is something lying low, gently rounded, before us there, 3 points to larboard – South Neptune Island! Clearly the sharp stripe of the slender lighthouse tower rises now from the gray-blue background. 'See him there, Jonni, there he is!' There it was, exactly where we were expecting it to be. With the most complete aids of modern navigation, we could not have steered straighter for it, the first bit of land that we have seen for 15,000 miles, since the passing of Start Point. We, the old-fashioned sailing navigators!

"Without pausing, PRIWALL flies toward her goal. About 15:05 o'clock, South Neptune measures west, 3 nautical miles away. Carried on by the roaring

(F. LAEISZ)

Steel 4-Masted Barque PADUA, 3,064 Gross Tons
1926-1945
Leaving Elbe River, Germany, 26, July, 1929

west, the giant rigging all one singing and humming and quivering, wide-dashing spray before the gleaming prow, so swings the 'Flying P-Liner' at 16 o'clock over the line of Thistle Island and Gambier into the quiet inland water of the Gulf of Spencer. Not quite 62 days since we left the English Channel, we have reached our goal."

We would not close this chapter on the firm of F. Laeisz without recording a testimonial in the form of a report from the German *Seewart* (Marine Watchtower), vol. 12, 1939, on the last 3 passages of the PADUA, who acquired a certain fame among all friends of deep-sea navigation. These 3 passages, 1 from the Channel to Chile, 1 from Valparaiso to Australia, and 1 from Australia to England, were completed in a series, one right after the other. The report reads:

THE LAST VOYAGE OF THE PADUA

"The 4-masted bark, PADUA, under command of Captain H. Richard Wendt, left the port of Bremen on October 14, 1938, with an average draught of 17 feet, bound for Corral, which was reached on December 22. On December 26, the barque sailed off for Valparaiso. Arrived there December 30. On January 14, 1939, PADUA stood out to sea from Valparaiso to sail to Port Lincoln in South Australia. This time in ballast. On the eighth of March, she let fall anchor in the ballast roads of the aforesaid harbor. After emptying her ballast, she began to take on a cargo of wheat, which was aboard by March 31. Altogether, 4,484 tons in 52,804 sacks. On April 3, the sailer left the outer roadstead of Port Lincoln to begin the passage to Queenstown for further orders. On July 8, 1939, the vessel was made fast in the unloading port of Glasgow. With this, her passage ended. The complete voyage had required 8 months and 23 days."

When one remembers that in the days of sailing vessels, such passages frequently required from 14 to 16 months, it should be worth while even today to become familiar with the details of that passage. Yes, in one respect a passage of that sort still deserves a certain attention. For it was the opinion in official circles that, with the dying business of shipping by sail and with the dying state of seamanship, the time of fast passages was also over. In the following, the most important dates of the 3 laps of the voyage – from Europe to the West Coast, from the West Coast to Australia, and from Australia to England – will be repeated. As bases, the notes of the meteorologic, hydrographic daily record of the German *Seewart,* no. 8173, kept aboard the PADUA, and the ship's log of the PADUA, which was obligingly placed at our disposal by the shipping firm of F. Laeisz.

From the English Channel to Corral

After Ushant was brought astern on the afternoon of October 22, favorable northeast winds soon set in which allowed the sailer to enter the northeast trade winds, just 6 days later, at about 29 degrees north latitude and 22 degrees west longitude. On November 11, at 1-3/4 degrees north latitude 27-1/2 degrees west longitude, the beginning of the southeast trade winds was noted. On the following day, the Line was passed. Time of this first lap, 21 days. A good, encouraging start.

At 34 degrees south latitude, canvas was temporarily reduced due to a Pampero squall. For the rest, the passage kept its normal course, with no stormy winds. On December 5, PADUA passed latitude 50 at 63.6 degrees west longitude. On the evening of December 8, she passed through the straits of Le Maire; on the morning of the 10th, she reached the longitude of Cape Horn. The sailing around the Cape, with prevailing light to moderate winds from varied points including the East, presented no especial difficulties. On December 15, she reached latitude 50 in the Pacific Ocean. Time of circumnavigation of the Cape, 13 days. Since the captain had gained sufficient west latitude, he could stand merrily to the north, under dominant west-northwest winds. At noon of December 22, the vessel lay at the buoy in the harbor of Corral.

Overall time from the English Channel	61 days
Overall actual distance	9,390 nautical miles
Average day's run	154 naut. miles
Average hourly speed	6.4 knots

The greatest average speed was made between 53 degrees 55 minutes south latitude, 83 degrees 18 minutes west longitude, and 49 degrees 39 minutes south latitude, 80 degrees 21 minutes west longitude, with wind 262 nautical miles at a wind average of Beaufort 5, with wind athwart. This passage is probably the fastest made in the present century by German sailing vessels to Corral, according to those meteorological logs of *Seewart.* Outside the years between 1904 and 1934, appear the accounts of 12 fast passages, of which the shortest took 64 days, the longest 124. It seems noteworthy that both passages, that of 64 days and another fast passage to Corral of 62 days – thus the second in speed – should have been made by the PADUA.

A tabulation follows of the 3 passages of the PADUA referred to, 1929 under Captain Piening, 1936-37 under Captain Clauss, and 1938 under Captain Wendt, in which the length of time from the Channel to the Equator, from the Equator to 50 degrees south latitude in the Atlantic, from there around Cape Horn to 50 degrees south latitude in the Pacific, and finally to Corral, are compared with each other. The agreement of these 3 passages by the same vessel under 3 different captains is striking. It is justly deduced from this that: "When one and the same vessel is able to make 3 such outstanding passages over the same course under 3 different commanders, it speaks equally well for the sailing powers of that vessel and for the value of that school of navigation which is the practice of this firm."

From Valparaiso to Port Lincoln

PADUA left Valparaiso January 14, 1939, in ballast, and worked her way up immediately toward the northwest, in order to get into the realm of the southeast trade wind. She started at 25 degrees south latitude 86 degrees west longitude. Duration of passage to that point 9 days. The trade wind is weak, in accord with the summer season: it will not exceed a force of 4. At 20 degrees south latitude 124 degrees west longitude, the first trade breezes announce themselves. The weather, as was to be expected, declares itself for variable at the approach to the Low (Paumotu) Islands and throughout their passage and remains essentially so: changeable winds, rain showers, thunderstorms. At 29 degrees south latitude 172 degrees east longitude, a fine trade wind is again indicated, but seems not to have lasted long, PADUA is now nearing the Australian mainland. On March 8, anchor is let down in the Port of Lincoln, after a passage of 52 days, 12 hours.

Overall actual distance	9,014 nautical miles
Daily average distance	172 nautical miles
Average speed throughout	7.2 knots

The distance sailed is about 377 nautical miles less; herein is expressed the almost daily calculated westward instrumental displacement, a welcome gift of the southern equatorial drift.

This passage, too, can be pointed out as a very good one. Among 75 Australian passages made in the period from 1905 till 1914, the fastest was 46 days (full-rigged ship ALSTERTHAL, Captain M. Looks, January into March, 1912, from Mejillones to Sydney). If we allow only 1,500 miles for the greater length of the PADUA course and use the average as a basis of reckoning, the PADUA theoretically would have undercut the ALSTERTHAL by almost 3 days. A medium length of passage from the west coast of South America to the east and south coasts of Australia has been reckoned on the basis of as yet unpublished material as 71 days.

FROM PORT LINCOLN TO QUEENSTOWN

Although Queenstown is customarily named as the end of the first passage, it should be added that the course merely crossed the Daunt lightship (51 degrees 33 minutes north latitude, 8 degrees 0 minutes west longitude): in reality, the passages ended on July 8 at Glasgow. 93 days presents a good result if one remembers that the average length for a medium – that is, a medium-good – passage was considered 112 days. For the longest passages, such figures as 144 days are given; the fastest is still that of the PARMA, which in 1933, sailed from Port Victoria to Falmouth in 83 days.

Concerning the portion of the passage from Australia to Cape Horn, the following records will probably be of interest. The distance covered was 6,668 nautical miles, the daily average distance 202 nautical miles, the average speed 8.4 knots. The greatest distance in one day was 290 nautical miles; that is, a good 12 nautical miles an hour. The wind during that day seems to have been mostly level aft; the medium strength of the wind was 6.5 Beaufort.

For the entire passage – from Australia to Queenstown – the distance was 14,962 miles, the daily average 160 miles, the average speed 6.7 knots. If we compare this result with that of the passage from Europe to the West Coast, on which the speed-average was 6.4 knots, we realize that actually the homeward passage with a full vessel was better than the outward passage with a light vessel. The explanation must lie in the unique situation presented by the Southern Pacific with its good west winds. All in all, the entire passage signifies a complete success, which is to be valued much more highly as being the first passage by a young captain, who won his spurs by it.

When the PADUA reached the port of Glasgow in 1939, the clouds of the Second World War were already gathering. In a particular realm, that of the long voyage with sailers, the shipping firm of Laeisz had in the course of a century risen from small beginnings to its later height. It was, however, not alone commerce with sailing vessels that they included in their circle of interest. We saw how already the great grandfather of the man who now represents the great name of Laeisz was concerned with setting up solid overseas establishments as supports to his business. So, too, the firm later founded business houses and plantations in widely separated places across the ocean, in Central

(F. LAEISZ)

Paul GANSSAUGE
1866-1937

(F. LAEISZ)

Erich F. LAEISZ
1888-

(F. LAEISZ)

Willi GANSSAUGE
1901-

(F. LAEISZ)

Frau Christine Von Mitzloff-LAEISZ
Daughter Of Erich F. Laeisz
1916-

STEAM VESSELS OWNED AND OPERATED
BY REEDEREI F. LAEISZ BETWEEN 1825 AND 1946

WEST COAST OF SOUTH AMERICA ROUTE

	No.	Name	Dimensions	Gross/ Net Tons Reefer Space	Engines	Crew/ Pass.	Built	Builder	Ac-quired	Ac-quired From	Fate
	83	PUNGO	380.0x49.4x29.9	4,722 2,966	Tecklenborg T. 3Cy. 400NHP 14 Knots	--- ---	1914	J.C.Tecklen-borg A.G., Geestemünde, Germany	1914	Builder	1914: Requisitioned by Imperial Navy. Famous as raider MÖVE. Became GREENBRIER, then OLDENBURG.
	84	PIONIER	387.5x49.1x22.6	4,689 2,929 ---	Tecklenborg ---- 14 Knots	--- ---	1915	J.C.Tecklen-borg A. G., Geestemünde, Germany	1915	Builder	1915: Requisitioned by Imperial Navy. Became MIAMI and returned to PIONIER
Sisters	85	POSEIDON	450.8x57.2x27.0	5,864 3,655	Tecklenborg 2 Steam Turbines 1 Sc. 762NHP 12½ Knots	42 12	1922	J.C.Tecklen-borg A. G., Wesermünde, Germany	1922	Builder	1939,[1] Oct. 22: Sunk by crew when chased by 2 British auxiliary cruisers N. of Iceland.
Sisters	86	PLANET	450.8x57.2x27.0	5,821 3,554	Tecklenborg 2 Steam Turbines 1 Sc. 762NHP 12½ Knots	42 12	1922	J.C.Tecklen-borg A. G., Wesermünde, Germany	1922	Builder	1945:[2] Sunk by magnetic mines in Bay Of Swinmünde

[1] [Master: W. Nielsen - Editor]
[2] [Master: Joh. Behrens - Editor]

America and the Cameroons. To one of these 2, the African Fruit Company, because of the impressive growth which it achieved, we shall have to devote a special chapter. The other, far older, in Guatemala, began its work in the seventieth year of the preceding century and was able to continue it until the beginning of the outbreak of the Second World War. This too will be discussed in its place.

LAEISZ IN GUATEMALA

In 1885, a foster son of Carl Laeisz, commonly called Hermann Laeisz, founded the firm Laeisz and Company in Guatemala as a branch of the firm of F. Laeisz. Its original location was in Retalhuleu on the south coast of Guatemala. Later, the principal location was moved farther into the interior to Quezaltenango. Besides this, there were establishments in Coatepeque and Mazatenango. The latter was given up in 1936. The export and import business handled by the firm was managed by F. Laeisz in Hamburg. The exports to Guatemala were chiefly iron ware and textiles; the imports from there to Germany were hides and pelts, coffee, honey, and gum.

Hermann Laeisz died in Guatemala in 1906. He had been in partnership with a native, José Prochazka. After the death of this man in San Francisco in 1917, Mr. Bruno Schumacher took over the guidance of the firm Laeisz and Co. until his death in the year 1930. Until 1906, he had worked for the Guatemala branch with the F. Laeisz firm in Hamburg and after that became confidential agent for Laeisz and Co. in Guatemala. After 1930, the firm was taken over by the previous confidential agent, Mr. Conrad Franke, and, according to the prevailing law in Guatemala, renamed, "Laeisz & Co., Successors, Conrado Franke & Co." The business had not attained a very wide compass in Central America, but, especially after the World War, it made a good foundation for the rebuilding of the overseas connections of the Hamburg firm. During the Second World War, the establishment in Guatemala was sequestered by the local government. It is still in existence today, however; only, the possession and property rights have been taken out of German influence. Franke died in 1952. But even during his lifetime, the firm Laeisz succeeded in building up an agency with its former enterprise in Central America.

THE PARTNERS AFTER 1912

In 1912, the two sons of Carl Ferdinand Laeisz, Herbert and Erich Laeisz, became partners of the firm. Herbert Laeisz went into the World War in Oels, as a reserve officer with the 8th Dragoons, was at first in the East, then in 1917 joined one of the newly created infantry regiments in the West. There he fell on April 18, 1918, in a charge attack on Meteren, a little place between Hazebrouck and Bailleul in the French Department of the North.

Mr. Paul Ganssauge Taken Into Partnership

Until 1923, the great grandson of the firm, Erich Laeisz, now remained its only owner. On October 13, he took into partnership, effective January 1, 1924, the previous confidential agent, Paul Ganssauge, he who, as it states in the introduction to the contract signed with him, had guided the firm "independently and with great success for many years." Paul Ganssauge was born, in 1866 on January 1, the same day of the month as the founder of the firm, Ferdinand Laeisz, in Frankfurt-an-Oder, and

Mr. Willi Ganssauge Taken Into Partnership

on October 1, 1890, entered the firm of F. Laeisz as an employee. Only 11 years later, he was, as has been related, called to a high position as one of the 3 confidential agents entrusted with the temporary guidance of the firm. Exactly a year before his death in January 1937, the partnership was extended to his oldest son, Willi Ganssauge, born 1901, who had entered the service of the firm back in 1920. In the founding and in the upbuilding of the African Fruit Company, interrupted for a long decade by the war, and to which we now turn, the deciding personality was Paul Ganssauge.

Chapter Three: THE AFRICAN FRUIT COMPANY, LTD.

BANANAS IN THE WEST AFRICAN CAMEROONS

The Region

The African Fruit Company was founded by the firm of F. Laeisz at the incitement of friendly parties for the purpose of making Germany independent of the need for importation of foreign bananas. In the year 1911, the Hamburg shipowner and broker, Ernst Russ, drew attention to the possibility of banana culture in the Cameroons.[1] The land in question was at the southward pointing foot of the great Cameroon Mountain, which for some years already had been increasingly occupied by German plantation associations. Here lies a funnel-shaped inlet which is protected by out-jutting tongues of land and into which several streams flow, the Cameroon Basin, from which the Cameroons get their name, as well as from the narrow projecting crags of the Portuguese Camarões. In general, it is not unlike the Gulf of Stettin. Its water is shallow; only a narrow channel is navigable by large vessels. Numerous branches of water, called krieks (from the English "creek") penetrate the muddy, boggy, mangrove-wooded region along the shores of the basin. In the basin, opposite the mouth of the river Wuri, lies the chief harbor-town, Duala.

The landscape on the Cameroon basin is dominated by the mighty Cameroon Mountain. It is completely volcanic, about half covered with woods, and with its 13,123 feet, it reaches the height of our Alpine peaks. Its shape, however, is flattened, and the whole mass is built up of lava and ashes hardened into stone. Volcanic rock is changed by weathering into especially fruitful soil, for which the tropical planter seeks eagerly. The fertility is further increased by the tropical abundance of rain. The annual rainfall in Middle Europe averages around 23.6 inches. On the Cameroon Mountain, it reaches 393.7 inches, and 9 to 13 feet are normal at the foot of the mountain. The tropical primeval forest, which must be felled in order to start plantations, looks entirely different from the German forest. On the bottom spreads an impenetrable thicket into which no step is possible except where elephants have trod a path or a bushwhacker has cut a passage. Over this mass of undergrowth rise leafy trees of medium height, and above this second floor of vegetation the real primeval giants reach 164 to 196 feet into the air. Most of these types of trees have soft wood and, in spite of their height, are easily cut down; only the so-called ironwood is so hard and so heavy that it sinks in water. For laying out a plantation, it is advantageous that the ironwood be not too numerous.

In the first years of German colonial policy,[2] there was much uncertainty concerning the best use of the colonies. The first thought was of trade with the natives in the hope of mineral wealth, but obviously there was none of this in the Cameroon woods. Not until the middle nineties did the idea arise of laying out plantations such as were earning great profits in tropical America, in the Dutch Indies, and similar overseas provinces. Experiments in coffee brought disappointment, and vanilla culture was not taken up seriously. On the other hand, cacao, oil palms, caoutchouc, and especially bananas, produced outstanding results. It was not easy to find investors for plantations in the Cameroons, since,

[1] [In West Africa, South of Nigeria, in the Gulf of Guinea - EDITOR]
[2] [Acquired in 1884 - EDITOR]

for example, the cacao tree, first considered, does not bear fruit until the fifth or sixth year. Bananas, on the other hand, bring in a harvest in less than one year; but the use of bananas was at that time very slight in Germany. Nevertheless, up to the outbreak of the war of 1914, the number of German plantations on the Cameroon Mountain increased to 40, 17 of them large companies. The experience was the same as that with the German colonial policy and colonial policy as a whole, namely that the period of backwardness and unsuccess was much shorter with us than with older colonial peoples in the beginning of their activity.

Growth of Plantations

The south and southwest slopes of the mountain were covered with plantations, which together possessed over 284,165 acres of land. Of these, more than 69,188 were under cultivation; over 27,181 were of bearing age. About 32,123 acres were planted to cacao, about 17,247 to caoutchouc trees, about 12,355 to oil palms, perhaps 2,471 to bananas. The relative size compared with German agricultural holdings may be more clearly realized when one considers that 284,165 acres here are almost a half million Prussian acres, and that 1,000 to 2,000 acres in Germany amount to a manor.

These were the conditions under which Ernst Russ made the proposal to start banana cultivation in the Cameroons. An important condition for this project was that in the mean time the taste of the German public for bananas had developed and that there was already a certain amount of importing business in bananas. At first it was mostly the bananas from the Canary Islands that were eaten; with time, however, the bananas of the United Fruit Company gained the lead even in Germany. The first thing that had to be done for the plan proposed by Ernst Russ and taken up by the Laeisz firm was the testing of the soil and of the varieties to be planted. In 1908, at the southeast foot of the mountain, in the Tiko plain, banana shoots from the Canary Islands and from Central America were planted. Only 350 shoots arrived in fit condition for planting, but these throve and multipled fast. The next step was the founding of a German banana syndicate, which, through an expert, conducted closer research into whatever concerned the soil for the proposed undertaking, and also into shipping possibilities.

Founding of the African Fruit Co., Ltd.

The result was the choice of a piece of land, of about 12,355 acres to begin with, in the Tiko plain. One factor in this decision was the fact that ocean-going vessels could come up as far as Tiko through Bimbia Creek, one of the many brackish branches through which the delta waters of the Mungo River mingle with the water of the Cameroon inlet. The syndicate brought together its experience and the contracts and adjustments concluded with the German government concerning the acquiring of land or such requisites into a new enterprise, "The African Fruit Company GmbH," whose seat was at first to be in Berlin, but was soon moved to Hamburg.

The region around Tiko had so far been very little settled. There was only a negro village, whose inhabitants had been brought in in 1910 because of the proposed planting. After one year, the picture changed to that of a growing European settlement on an ordered plan. In part decisive in the choice of Tiko as the location for the African Fruit Company was its location on the creek. At first the idea was to transfer the harvested bananas to the transports by means of lighters; but it soon became evident that fortunately there was a deep-water landing place at hand on the outlying island of Keka, and so a strong dike was made across the 722 feet of the creek between the shore and the Keka Island. On this dike a narrow gauge railroad spur was laid.

Bananas produce no seeds, but increase by shoots from the roots. The first brought to Tiko were from Central America, but an attempt to get further planting material from the Canary Islands was unsuccessful. So Tiko remained dependent on itself. The work advanced rapidly, however. In the regular Association meeting of August 19, 1913, the first annual report of the AFC was presented. According to this, the European personnel active in the district of Tiko consisted of: a planting foreman, 3 planters, a barber-surgeon, and a master carpenter. In August 1912, a captain sent out by the firm of F. Laeisz and 3 European manual workers were employed on the preparatory work for the landing pier to be built as an extremely important feature of the undertaking. The working conditions were at first not favorable. Among the native workers, who averaged about 500, bad health conditions prevailed. This led at the beginning of 1913 to the installing of a physician and to the improvement of the sanitary arrangements. At the end of 1912, there were some 1,483 acres under cultivation and 11.6 acres in planting. At the beginning of 1913, the Imperial Colonial Jurisdiction gave the concession for the building and use of the landing pier, and the firm of F. H. Schmidt in Altona received the commission for building it. At the close of 1912, a steamer chartered by A. F. C. went direct to the Keka Island with all the material for the pier, iron rails for the track, and other goods, altogether 1,300 tons of cargo.

In the annual report for 1913, it was already possible to give comprehensive information. The landing pier on the Keka Island was completed, also a number of houses for the European and native workers, a sawmill, and a place for the drying of the peeled bananas, so-called fig-bananas. The tracts planted with banana trees *in bearing* at the end of 1913 amounted to about 1,087 acres, which produced a harvest of more than 12,000 bunches. The harvested fruits were pared and dried to fig-bananas and shipped to Hamburg. .Since July, 1913, regular consignments had been shipped of some 400 boxes, each one of 661 lbs. These wares found good sale at rising prices.

By the end of 1913, the number of workers had grown to the neighborhood of 800, and by June, 1914, to nearly 1,200. At the end of 1913, the European personnel consisted of 1 planting foreman, 1 merchandising foreman, 5 planting assistants, a barber-surgeon, a master carpenter, and a building engineer. Unfortunately, the planter's assistant, Genrich, died on August 17 in the hospital at Duala, and the planter-foreman, Mr. Weiss, on November 23 in the hospital Victoria, as a result of an unregulated use of quinine. "We lost in the deceased," the report said, "two conscientious workers, whose memory we shall always honor. The state of health of the other Europeans was on the whole, satisfactory. We have followed all recommendations of the physician, and no cost has been spared in the realization of the importance of this question of improving the sanitary conditions on our plantation. Europeans and workmen have been moved into well ventilated houses with sheet-iron roofs. Filters have been installed for the improvement of the drinking water, and a Hamburg well-digging company experienced in tropical well-digging is here at present for deep drilling after good drinking water on our plantation. As a result of this costly care, we may happily record an essential falling off of sickness and death among the workers."

These observations bear testimony to the difficulties with which all beginning agricultural enterprises in tropical lands newly cleared from a primeval forest have to cope. They also bear witness, however, to the readiness for precautions and the feeling of responsibility of German business pioneers. In the year 1913, the management of A. F. C. in Hamburg undertook a research journey to Central America and there engaged a new head planter, Mr. Witthuhn, a German who had had many years of experience in banana culture in Costa Rica. In the years

1913-1914, verbal agreements were made with neighboring plantations concerning the cultivation of bananas and their delivery for shipment by the AFC. Also the organization of an enterprise devoted to their sale in Germany, which went by the name of "Cameroon Banana Company GmbH" was almost completed by the summer of 1914. This company was to be endowed with a capital stock of 250,000 marks, of which AFC was to supply 51% and 5 Hamburg fruit-merchants were to make up the rest. It was agreed with the harbor authorities that a special place at the wharves should be arranged for the AFC and leased to them for the more rapid turnover of banana shipments. Two special steamers PUNGO and PIONIER, were so far along in building that by the end of 1914 they could be put into use.

In the business year of 1913, the capital of AFC was raised first to 1,250,000 marks and later to 2,000,000 marks, and supplied mostly by the Laeisz firm. At the outbreak of the war, the business managers of AFC found themselves in the Cameroons with no way to get back to Germany. Since its Hamburg representative was called into the army, Paul Ganssauge, acting chairman of the directors' board of AFC, was appointed manager.

LOSS OF THE PLANTATIONS IN WORLD WAR I

Effect of World War I and Loss of Plantations

Such were the pre-war beginnings of AFC. Shipments could have begun, but the outbreak of the war made the continuation of the work impossible. The steamers, PUNGO and PIONIER, each of 3,000 tons, were chartered by the Imperial marine. And since, as special vessels for the banana trade, they were notably faster than the usual freighters, they were in every way suited to be used in the war against commerce as auxiliary cruisers. PUNGO was put into service November 1, 1915, as "auxiliary steamer 10." and later, as auxiliary cruiser, received the name of MÖWE. The command was given to corvette Captain Graf of Dolma-Schlodien. There stood beside him on his staff also a series of officers and captains of the merchant marine in their capacity as officers on furlough, with their thorough knowledge of the locations and the peculiarities of the paths of international shipping over the oceans of the world.

The event proved how cleverly both vessel and staff had been chosen. The great vessel of 4,788 gross tonnage with her crew of 235 men sank on her 2 trans-ocean passages, of 66 and 120 days respectively, 182,200 tons in all of the enemy's available shipping space, and besides this, destroyed with the action of her mines the British liner, KING EDWARD VII, a giant of 16,350 tonnage.

Re-purchase of Plantations

At the close of the war, both vessels, in accordance with the provisions of the Versaille peace treaty, had to be surrendered to England. During the World War and in the following years, the firm of F. Laeisz had provided the necessary means for the support of the AFC in Hamburg and had fulfilled the current responsibilities, especially toward the personnel, although it was at first not clear when or if the work could be begun again.

The unfortunate outcome of the war led to the loss of all German colonies. The plantations on the great Cameroon Mountain were seized by England. After some years, however, there appeared to be a possibility of buying them back and picking up the business again under the control of the British mandate. As soon as this possibility became apparent, the firm sent Mr. Walter Richter to Cameroon to learn the situation in regard to the plantings and other conditions. Thereupon it was decided to begin work again. When the re-purchase was

(1) (F. LAEISZ)

S. S. PIONIER, 4,689 Gross Tons
1915

(2) (F. LAEISZ)

S. S. PUNGO, 4,722 Gross Tons
Launch At J. C. Tecklenborg's Yard At Geestemünde, Germany, In 1914

(1) (F. LAEISZ)

The Second S. S. PIONIER, 3,264 Gross Tons, Of 1933

) (F. LAEISZ)

Growth In Size Of Laeisz Sailers Between 1856-1892
PUDEL (1856) - PARSIFAL (1882) - PLACILLA (1892)

completed, Mr. Walter Richter and Willi Ganssauge were appointed managers. As was natural from the development of circumstances, a close official connection was set up with the firm F. Laeisz, whose partner, Paul Ganssauge, senior, had furthered and sustained the undertaking from the outset.

REBUILDING

Now the rebuilding was begun with the same aims as before the war. In 1926, the capital fund of 1,750,000 marks was collected up to 700,000 marks, and then in 1927 raised to 1,750,000 again through cash instalments covered mostly by the F. Laeisz firm. Since the plantation had been almost completely ruined during the wartime and the after-wartime under English régime, the AFC, in recommencement of its work, could not count on any possibility of harvests of its own. Just as little could it reckon on any speedy supply of bananas from other plantations, since after years of neglect all were in the same situation. Apart from the partly preserved buildings and - what was essential - the landing wharves and railway spurs, it was therefore practically a new beginning.

In a memorandum made for AFC, during the war, on the consumption of bananas in the United States, England, and France, it was shown how fast banana-consumption had increased. For the year 1915, a consumption in the United States of 55 million bunches was estimated, at a value of 22 million marks, and in England immediately before the World War, 8 million bunches at a value of 40 million marks. The figures for consumption in France and Germany were much more modest. At Hamburg, the only German port that counted in the importation of bananas, the figure had not reached 11,000 bunches in 1899-1900. By 1911-12, it was already almost 1,000,000 bunches, and in the first half of 1914 it was something over 1,000,000 bunches, in value over 9,000,000 marks. A correct picture of the possibilities of increasing the use of bananas in Germany required a comparison with the population figures of the countries just named. According to this, each American consumed on the average 90 fruits a year, each Englishman 25, a German only 4, and a Frenchman 3 1/3. If the immediate goal were set at the same figure as in England, this would mean the importation of 12,000,000 bunches at a value of fully 100,000,000 marks. Even after the attainment of this goal, each inhabitant of the German Reich would have only 1 banana to eat every two weeks! Concerning the healthfulness of the use of bananas, we need waste no words.

In the afore-mentioned memorandum from which these facts are taken, reference was made to the great economic advance in the culture of bananas in the Canary Islands, in Jamaica, and in Costa Rica, also to the subsidy which an English shipping firm, Elder, Dempster, and Company, had received from the government for a steamship service established by them for the transport of bananas. "We, on the other hand," the report goes on to say, "have undertaken the culture of 19,768 acres out of private means without any financial assistance; yes, even further, we have ourselves carried all expenses connected with the transportation of suitable varieties as well as the preliminary work and research trips. Also we have ourselves built great steamship wharves for the shipping facilities. The possibility of transportation by means of fast modern steamers built and arranged for the purpose was supplied to us by the shipping firm of F. Laeisz, again without government aid".

The principal emphasis of the memorandum was placed on the evidence as to how capable of development, according to the examples cited, banana consumption in Germany might be considered, and on the values to be gained in the realm of production by banana culture on a great scale. These considerations were conducive to the AFC having the courage, even after the loss from the war, to again risk a large capital in the Cameroon plantations. As was to be expected, the first years after the World War demanded great expenditures, which were at first only slightly offset by profits. In 1926-27, the gross intake ran to only about 90,000 marks, in 1928-29 to about 252,000; but by 1929-30 already to 250,000 marks. The fiscal year of 1930 still showed at its close a loss of 150,000 marks, which might, however, already be covered by the expected gain of 1931. The years of 1932, 1933, each showed gains of 4,000 marks. 1934 brought a gain of 100,000 marks. In 1935, for the first time since the founding of the company in 1910, a dividend was paid of 6%, and in the following year one of 8%. Payment of loans could be undertaken on a modest scale for the first time in 1930. Not until 1934 did this reach a point corresponding to the need. This favorable development made it possible for the AFC as early as 1929 to order built to its own account the vessels needed for the growing banana trade, since the earlier attempt to transport bananas in the current shipping space of other lines had not been successful. The building of its own vessels led the AFC in 1930 to transform itself into a stock company and to raise its capital to 2,250,000 marks, about 3/5 of which was contributed by the firm of F. Laeisz, about 2/5 by the firm of Ernst Russ, and the remainder by separate small stockholders. The Bremer Vulkanworks delivered the steamship PANTHER (2,171 gross tonnage) in October 1930, and the second steamship, PUMA (also 2,171 tonnage) in December of the same year. With the predominant interest of the firm F. Laeisz, it seemed natural that this firm should not only take over the entire required shipbuilding business under its flag, but that also in the naming of the vessels the old tradition of the "Flying-P-Line" should be adhered to. For these vessels, Otto Höver in his book, *Das Schöne Schiff* (Beautiful Ships) has the following words to say:

"It seems as if the German shipyards, after the lapse of the depression years, had taken to the medium freighter type with special affection. Such were the motor vessels produced for the African Fruit Company of Hamburg for banana transportation from the Cameroons. In view of these distinctive and outstandingly successful vessels, one could almost say: the old banana swingboat has become a yacht. The shipping firm once known for the proudest and fastest sailing vessels is now equipped with new P-lines, which, as motor-vessels, are of a similar nobility of appearance with the earlier full-rigged ships and 4-masted barques. The firm has remained true to the names with the initial "P" even with the fruit-racers of the Cameroon passage.

PANTHER, PUMA, PIONIER, PELIKAN, PONTOS, PALIME; some of these newly-builts have slightly curved beak-heads, an approach to the prows of the clipper ships. One can easily believe that Laeisz's crews could transfer not unwillingly from the deep-sea sailers of the firm to the new fruit-runners. The lines, the general shape, and the upper structure of these vessels are blameless and have found the highest approbation in all of their ports of call".

This bright enthusiasm over the complete esthetic picture that the banana-steamers present is the more convincing in that – coming from the lips of an art-historian – it repeats the impression which these vessels make on an eye trained in the sight and appraisal of harmonious lines and forms. Here it is once more evident that the highest fitness to purpose also implies beauty. For the bent bow of the banana transport has no reason to preserve the memory of the soaring clipper prow. Shipbuilding is not guided by emotion. It is rather the consideration of the construction best fitted for an end, the nature of which is first noticed in the vessel in dock, but of which the true effect is only to be observed in the vessel in motion on the sea. Aside from the favorable effect on the marine properties of the vessel, a prow of this sort offers still another advantage. If it should come to a collision of the bow with another vessel or a docking place, the resulting damage is usually above the waterline of the vessel. It is hardly necessary to explain what that signifies. And the white color of the deck wall, which lends the vessel something of the appearance of a yacht, expressive of a festive spirit, that also is suited to a purpose: white reflects the sun's heat, and bananas must be kept cool! And now back to our theme after this philosophic flight!

At the beginning of the year 1933, the price of bananas had reached such an unforeseen low, far below the prices which had encouraged the building of the 2 special vessels with the accompanying increase of capital shares of the AFC to 4,000,000 marks, that there was serious deliberation whether to risk the building of more vessels for the transportation of the ever-increasing harvests. The decision for the positive was due to the assumption that the new régime which was setting in with the opening of the year 1933 would succeed in virtually putting an end to the tide of unemployment. It was obvious that in such case a rise in banana consumption in Germany was to be expected.

In March 1933, the building of the third vessel was decided. It received the name PIONIER (about 3,300 gross tonnage) in memory of the building of the first banana steamer before the war. It was the first major shipbuilding to be started since the full outbreak of the world economic crisis in Germany, and it was likewise the first motor vessel of the shipping firm.

No state aid was given to this shipbuilding. With the induction of the PIONIER into service, the gross profits of the enterprise rose from 1934 on, and the opportunity-favoring conditions of the following years led to its full financial recovery.

The leadership of AFC felt no hesitation about investing the earned increase in capital in new vessels. In January and October 1935, the motorships PELIKAN (about 3,300 gross tonnage) and PONTOS (about 3,400 tons) and in the beginning of 1936 the fourth motorship PYTHON (about 3,700 tons) were sent into service. Thereby the preparations for a significant banana export from the Cameroons and the ability of the AFC to conduct this were definitely assured. Between Hamburg and Tiko a regular 8-day line service was established. In 1937 came the building of the motorship PALIME (about 2,900 gross tonnage), and of PORJUS, the little transfer steamer for transporting bananas from Hamburg to the Scandinavian lands (about 750 tonnage). In July 1938, the motorship POMONA (about 3,500 tons) was put into service. But this belonged not to AFC, but in common to the firms of F. Laeisz and Ernst Russ, who chartered it to AFC. When, in 1925, the work of rebuilding began under the control of the English mandate of the Cameroons, there were only 2 English firms active there. Since their agency posts were insufficiently supplied, a trading post was erected in the planting territory of the AFC in order to take care of the essential needs of the personnel. The business soon increased of itself, however, and thus came about the establishment of further settlements on other Cameroon locations. The rapid development of the trading post enterprises led, as early as the year 1926, to the result that the trading business became independent. These exchanges were brought into the AFC commercial department G.m.b.H. with a provisional capital of 20,000 marks. The close connection of the AFC with the firm F. Laeisz was evident again in the commercial department since the firm took over 55% of the capital. The firm of Ernst Russ assumed 25% and the AFC itself the remaining 40% of the company shares. The new enterprise took charge of all the purchasing for the AFC, supplied it with the required wares, and was commissioned by it with the sale of the products of the Cameroon plantation. This process proved successful. Since the turnover increased from year to year, the capital had to be raised in 1927 to 100,000 marks. The branch established in Duala, in the district of the French mandate of Cameroon, developed well.

As long as the plantation did not produce any noteworthy quantity of bananas, the purchase and sale of such Cameroon plantation products as cocoa, palm kernels, palm oil, and fig-bananas played the chief role in the commercial department of the AFC. Proper sales organizations were lacking at first. Therefore a new task fell to the company when in 1930 the sale of fresh bananas had to begin. Much money was spent in learning how. At first, selling by auction was tried, with entirely unsatisfactory results. Unsold, left-over quantities of bananas were handed over to individual fruit merchants to ripen in a temporary erected structure. This business, too, closed at a loss. So other ways must be sought, and even, repeatedly, that of co-operation with the English Jamaica Producers Marketing Company, Ltd. At the close of 1935, an agreement was reached with the English firm concerning the sale in England, Holland, and Belgium, as well as on supplying the market in Southeastern Europe, Scandinavia, and Finland. The World Depression, which had already begun sharply in 1931, worked unfavorably on the sales; also the name Cameroon-bananas, had not yet gained favor. The incoming consignments frequently had to be left on commission, so that the gain in the first 5 years was but slight. However, during this time, the confidence of the trade was earned, and in the principal buying centers, the necessary distribution places were created that should in the future prevent serious trouble from the interruption of sales or from too heavy imports. In the agreement with the "Jamaica Producers", it was fortunate for both sides that the principal harvest seasons for bananas in the Cameroons and in Jamaica were widely separated. There was therefore a good understanding over the occasional exchange of Jamaica and Cameroon bananas according to insufficiency or superfluity on the one or the other side. Altogether, it had cost much trouble and repeated changes of organization by the time the "German Cameroon bananas" were actually introduced into the German and foreign markets.

Paul L. Ganssauge and Co.

The favorable development after 1935 then led at the end of 1937 to the decision to remove the banana sale in the German market from the commercial department of AFC and to hand it over to a new enterprise: the branch company of the firm of Paul L. Ganssauge and Co. Corresponding to the ratio of investment by the partners interested in the new company, 70% of the capital stock was taken up by the firm of F. Laeisz, 30% by the firm of Ernst Russ. The taking over of the banana sales in Germany required a plan of management. From now on, the firm of Paul L. Ganssauge worked in the German market, while the sale of bananas in the foreign market remained with the commercial division of AFC. The partner personally answerable was the third son of Mr. P. Ganssauge senior.

At the close of 1930, the business concerns of AFC and its daughter company gained further expansion through the salvaging of Bibundi Stock Company, an important Cameroon enterprise which was not fortunate in rebuilding after being bought back from English possession. In 1935, the AFC was offered the opportunity to acquire a large parcel of shares of the German-West African Trading Company. Both companies united at the close of 1935 in the founding of an association with the wide-reaching aim of bringing under cultivation the lands belonging to the German-West African Trading Company. A large banana planting, rapidly developed, gave expectation of fortunate harvest results for the year 1940 – but it was not destined to get that far. In 1937, the AFC also acquired a part of the shares of the German Togo Company, which again was itself closely connected with the Molive Plantation Company. Its possessions lay, like those of the Bibundi, within the region of the German plantation enterprises at the foot of the Cameroon Mountain.

The history of the AFC, together with the firms which arose in connection with it after the resumption of German work in the Cameroons, shows clearly that both the founding and the continuance of the enterprise rested throughout on the initiative of the firm F. Laeisz in friendly co-operation with the firm Ernst Russ, and it still rests there. It is also demonstrated that AFC succeeded in realizing, under the completely changed conditions of the post-war period, an aim set very early, namely in 1908. The position at which the enterprise had arrived by the year 1939 is above all due to the persistence of the firm F. Laeisz. The funds spent by them and a few friends during 30 years for the Cameroon banana business, inclusive of the shipbuilding, reach a sum of far over a million marks. Very few persons hold so firmly, tenacious and unconfused, to the originally chosen goal. The success of this privately undertaken activity consists in the creation of productive plantations as well as in the building up of fleets of special vessels unknown before in Germany, which kept up a weekly shipping service between Hamburg and Cameroon, and thereby assured to the German plantations in Cameroon their sales in Germany.

The AFC had not used its swift growth to become a monopoly, nor cramped the production of other German plantations in the Cameroons. It worked much more as an example, in that other German planting companies had taken up the cultivation of bananas and by that means were on the way to becoming secure against depression. Banana farming here had also proved that, once the sale is assured by the help of a transport fleet and by a suitable sales organization, it brings in good profits and thereby makes it possible to build up comfortably in spite of a series of unprofitable years those long-term planting operations which require more years to come into bearing, such as cacao, palm-oil, and caoutchouc. This development, which, had it been spared the misfortune of the second World War, would presumably have gone forward splendidly, was essentially due to the activity of the chairman of the board of directors of the AFC, Paul Gans-sauge senior, who died in 1937, and of his sons. It was he who fought with all his might after World War I to build up AFC again. His courage and his foresight justified themselves, and Mr. Walter Richter, appointed as a member of the board, who in his early years even before 1914 had been active in the Cameroons, took charge of the practical carrying out of the economic program.

Summary of Cameroon Enterprises

Let us repeat in summarizing: The AFC carried on a plantation business in the Cameroons, principally banana culture, but tied in with the planting of cacao, caoutchouc, and oil palms. It took part also as a partner in other plantations and bought the products of other banana farms at established prices. It forwarded with its special vessels the products of all these plantations to Europe; therefore practiced also a comprehensive shipping business, carried the Cameroon products to Europe and brought back wares to the Cameroons. In so far, it was also a considerable commercial undertaking. For the management of its vessels, it employed the services of the firm F. Laeisz; for the sale of bananas in Germany, the branch firm Paul L. Ganssauge and Co.; and for all other business matters, the African Fruit

Company, Commercial Department G.m.b.H. The division of the separate functions of the company – production, shipping, selling, other commercial business – grew necessarily out of their actual variety. In the workings of the AFC, the German economy received equivalent value from its import activities. 80% of the Cameroon banana exports could be distributed on the German market duty-free. Besides, the duty-free import of a tropical fruit not unimportant to the nourishment of the German people, there was an activity which, as practiced by the AFC, was of significance to the development of worth-while colonial improvements without direct assessment of taxes. This was demonstrated in the Cameroons by the plantations of oil palms, caoutchouc, and cacao already established or still in upbuilding. For this income-producing business, banana culture was the necessary forerunner. Thus it came about that the business of AFC, as well as that of the other German planting companies in the Cameroons at whose head AFC stood, was preparing a large number of young Germans with practical experience in the tropics for a future colonial husbandry under the German flag, as was still the hope in those days.

REMINISCENCES

Reminiscences

We have followed the history of the firm of F. Laeisz from the Hamburg hat factory that Ferdinand Laeisz started in the year 1824 up through 130 years. The age of the proud sailing voyages during the half century before the first World War saw the evidence of the firm's spirit of adventurous undertaking, its high technical skill, and the economic results of these together with the rise of Germany in world commerce and world economy. Even the first World War could not keep down the will and the ability of the losers to renew themselves through their own power.

Then, when changed circumstances of the time put a halt to the growth of the sailing business at its former rate, that creative force which had never failed in the course of 4 generations brought into growth, thanks to newly won additional strength, an enterprise like a strong fruit-bearing tree, though at first thought of only as an overseas side-branch of the firm. This was the African Fruit Company. The hope for regaining and expanding our business undertakings on German colonial soil was destroyed by the second World War. It has, however, sprung up as a new hope in another part of tropical West Africa under a neutral régime, and it may be that in the course of unforeseeable years the events and experiences, the pictures of labor and the results of labor, may be repeated, both in the large and the small, even if under altered conditions. Therefore it may be permitted, in this book of memories, as a postscript to that portion which deals with the AFC, to restore a selection of these pictures taken from the time when the American Fruit Company stood at the height of its performance and success. From such a record, the young manhood which has now entered into the new undertaking can form an idea of what was experienced on similar ground 15 to 20 years ago by their forerunners in the field. May it prove acceptable that herein the comfortable and the cheerful, the serious and the adventuresome shall alike come to expression.

TO TIKO ON THE PANTHER

Brinkmann of PANTHER

All the banana vessels of the African Fruit Company sailed under the Laeisz flag. Captain Otto Brinkmann of the PANTHER, in his book, *Captains Report*, pictures the outward passage between Hamburg and

Reports On An Outward Passage

the principal lading port of Tiko, in the Cameroons, the loading of the banana cargo, and the return. We omit the lively presentation of the passage through European waters. From Las Palmas on, we shall give the report in Captain Brinkmann's words.

". . . We have mastered half the stretch. Tomorrow we shall be by Cape Blanco, and there our sailcloth open-air bath will be built up. And the next morning will see us by Cape Verde. (It does its name small honor. The 2 grounded steamers whose wrecks still lie on the outjutting rocks show that it does not look 'green' to the mariners.) In our cargo-spaces, sulfur ovens have been set up. The hatchways are shut fast, and all 24 hours thick clouds of sulfur bite to death the mould fungus and all the little creatures that a fruit cargo brings with it.

"Along the African coast now goes our course. To be sure, we see the land only in a few places, but the water has an entirely different coloring. The clear crystal blue has faded into a sad, opaque brown. Yesterday, the PANTHER was still swimming over 3,281 feet of water, and today we sound a scant 1,469. The air is damp. In the evening the western heavens glow a threatening copper red. The desert sand of the Sahara, eddied up by storms and whirled on upward many thousand feet, spreads itself here from a great height over the ocean. It is harmattan weather. Everything on board is covered with a light brown layer.

"A strong harmattan can make orienting extremely difficult: the coasts and their lighthouses can then hardly be made out a mile away, and the height of stars can no longer be measured. For the driving machinery of our South African Line, the harmattan likewise brings hardship, for the fine emery-hard dust works itself into the motors.

"From Cape Palmas with its high green hills and waving groups of palms, our course now goes almost east to Cape Nightingale. We have still 1,000 miles before us. But here the Guinea stream runs our way; PANTHER makes 360 miles in 24 hours. The cooling machine is set up to cool the holds and to store up a supply of cold in the insulation chambers. We are ordered by radio to Fernando Po, to load bananas there. For 2 days we steam through the ovenhot Gulf of Guinea. No vessel meets us; only rarely does a school of hogfish enliven the pool-quiet water. The sun burns. At the least movement, sweat breaks out. Our bathing reservoir hardly offers refreshment now. When it is filled afresh in the morning, the water registers 29 (i.e., C.). At noon it has risen to 33. In that, let him bathe who wishes! Now comes into sight the green coast of the Spanish island, Fernando Po, and about 2 o'clock in the afternoon, our anchor falls in the harbor of Santa Isabel.

"We lie here as in a kettle; the rock walls rise almost perpendicular on every side. Our passengers are shown the sights of the town and the environs by an agent. Meanwhile, a large lighter has come alongside with 5,000 bunches of bananas. The side hatches swallow bunch after bunch, as the black laborers reach them up. The officers stand by the hatchways and check the loading. The rejected bunches are simply thrown into the water. In 3 hours everything is settled, the passengers come aboard again, the bass note of our steam whistle echoes threateningly from the shore, and we steam out again toward Victoria.

"We must hurry in order to arrive before dark. Against the cloudless heaven, the cones of the Great and Little Cameroon Mountains rise clear; even the lava stream from the latest volcanic outbreak is plainly recognizable as a distinct stripe. Victoria and the little islands in front with the silhouette of the mighty mountain in the background offer a delightful picture. With the last of the twilight, we come to the place of anchorage, where already the black harbor- and customs- officials are waiting for us.

"The plantation foreman of the African Fruit Company, who has come from Tiko in his auto, greets us heartily. He has brought 2 German planters with him, who will assist us in the transferring of the bananas. We lift anchor and steam out in the soft tropic night toward Meme. At first the lighthouse of Debundscha serves as a finger post, but after that, all is dark and a pair of cat's eyes were not to be despised. The water is shallow here, and as we steam across the bar, the PANTHER wallows sullenly from side to side and can not be steered correctly. We go into the satin darkness of the river's mouth, into which our headlight throws its milkwhite wedge. Carefully we feel our way in the stream past the many built-up fishing contraptions of the negroes. Then a faint light gleams before us, and another. Our anchors go rattling to the bottom. Immediately lighters filled with bananas are again lying alongside, and for 3 hours, to the singsong of the niggers, the green bunches wander into the belly of the PANTHER.

"As morning dawns, the loading is finished. Again we go up river, past Victoria and on into the mouth of the Bimbia. For 2 hours, our vessel winds her way between mangroves and primeval forest; then suddenly the landing wharf of Tiko comes in sight. Carefully the PANTHER slips up to the shore, there sticks her snout deep into the marshy bush; white is the foam below her afterdeck, and slowly and carefully she feels her way backward to the mooring place. The heaving lines clatter against the wooden pier; thick yellow manila hawswers creak out of their boxes. The narrow foot-plank is shoved out to land, and, held by gravity, the black revenue officer strides aboard. The outward passage is ended.

"The clearing usually fulfils itself painlessly. The revenue officer thumbs through the pile of lists that our Third shoves under his black nose, impresses the stamp of the British Empire upon them, and the thing is done. But woe if one thing is lacking! Even under the palms, St. Bürokratius demands his sacrifice.

"Then let not the cigars and the glass of beer be forgotten! That is the most important part of the whole transaction. But no 'dash'! Our black customs officer is an 'educated black gentleman', no common bush nigger. Oh, yes, even here are class distinctions. He must be entertained as a guest. He is a man proficient in writing and extremely scrupulous within the framework of his activity. Many of these customs officials have a mastery over the English speech in word and writing and command a good knowledge of French, but unfortunately seldom of our tongue. The negroes from the days when the Cameroons were still German are old people - in the tropics, man ages rapidly. If they are well-to-do, that is if they have succeeded in earning 2 or 3 wives who have born them children, preferably numerous daughters, then the sale of these daughters offers them through the payment a sure income for the evening of life. Every negress is proud if she brings a good price, and she looks with scorn on her neighbor who was 3 pounds cheaper.

"English law makes the negro and the white man equal, and the missionary associations work zealously to give the negro the conviction that he is just as much of a man as his white Massa. The law which the negro actually respects and fears, however, is that which is practiced by his medicine men with all possible magic tricks and which holds him in a fearful belief in ghosts. The Djudju, the magic of the medicine man, is irresistible. Woe to him who dares defy the Djudju! For then, with the aid of poison and other diplomatic means, sickness and death are invoked to demonstrate the power of the Djudju. Usually the mere use of a magic charm is sufficient to make the negro docile. And cases have been known when the mere magic curse of the medicine man made people die without the use of poison. Their unshakeable belief and their fear of the Djudju killed them.

"Our customs official has drunk his beer, and, with the lighted cigar in his mouth, he goes to land with his loose-jointed legs, again held to the plank by gravity – the fellows never really bend completely at the knees. Thereupon the vessel is free for business, the unloading may begin.

"Again the side-hatches are opened. On their necks, the 'boys' drag out the cargo: chests and boxes, codfish bales and sacks of rice, bricks, cement, lime fertilizer, and whatever other splendors there are. Six of the chocolate fellows have pulled the crate of 12 living turkeys to the shore. The distressed creatures are protesting excitedly. Then one fellow squats down and imitates the gobble of the turkey-cock, the 12 turkeys join in, and the niggers almost die laughing. They have completely forgotten their task, stretch their necks up to their ears, beat about with their arms, roll their eyes – but none thinks any more of working. First must their Massa intervene with his 'tuning fork', a not too slender switch.

"Our passengers have greeted relatives and acquaintances, the passports are checked, the customs investigations completed. Now their luggage is swaying ashore on the woolly heads of the boys, and then the 'trollies' start for the various lodgings. These trollies, railway carts with seating capacity and brakes, are indispensable here. The boys shove. Down hill, they jump up behind. The wagon rattles on and is controlled only by the brake. These vehicles have the advantage over the auto of being independent of the condition of the street. The Cameroon roads in the rainy season are true rivers of mud. And unfortunately the English government does practically nothing about maintaining the ways. Now most of the plantations are in German possession, likewise the great pier at which we are lying, and the outspread net of narrow-gauge railways. The Germans must help themselves here.

"The cargo is unloaded; already 600 sacks of cacao and 5,000 boxes of fig-bananas have been loaded on. Now the hatches are closed in order to cool off the hold again. Meanwhile it has gotten to be 8 o'clock in the evening. The men have liberty until midnight; then the loading of the fresh bananas is to begin.

"A few try to sleep a little. They have bound handkerchiefs around their foreheads; otherwise the sweat would run into their eyes. The majority renounce this sleep, which does not refresh one anyway and which leaves one at the mercy of mosquitoes and the tiny but no less stinging sand fleas.

"A man spends his time better by going over to the village. Tiko-town, it calls itself proudly. Today much is going on, since this is Thursday, and the folk are coming from near and far to the market, bringing their miserable products with great clamor to the man. Especially interesting are the 'mammies' of marriageable daughters, who are standing here on the market for sale, like hens with us at home. In the evening, business must give way to the fine arts. They stand around in a great circle while in the center a couple performs a highly imaginative love dance with much dislocation of their bodies, which in the matter of elucidation leaves nothing to be wished. All clap and sing with them. During this, much palm wine is drunk. So it goes the whole night through, especially in the full of the moon. Then bag and baggage are again loaded onto the old women, and they take the homeward way. Balancing a heavy tone-jug on her head, a corded bundle clasped under each arm, while 2 live hens dangle from her back, the old woman drags herself painfully along the path. Three steps behind, goes her lord and master with the 'walkerstick'. To carry more, his dignity forbids. Again 3 steps behind him goes his young wife. She has been given a gay scarf, which she drapes alternately and picturesquely over her head and around her hips. She too carries nothing, for she has the so dearly prized 'kakka-bobbies,' youthfully firm breasts, and must be spared, else her worth as ware will lessen. Punctually at 12 midnight, the palaver breaks loose. A banana train has brought about 500 boys, all young lubbers of 15 to 18 years. There is a chattering like a cage of parrots. Each has a tattered cloth of indefinable color on his body. Elsewhere, one hole after another makes a net, but with the negro, it makes a costume.

"Now the guard arrives, '4 line,' that is, by fours. The common speech is pidgin English. Negroes of different tribes often cannot understand each other. So this jargon is the tongue with which one may get along everywhere, deep into the land. Outside of a few of the older negroes, one finds none that speak German; only now and then one hears scraps that have been picked up. Their word-treasury is for the most part exhausted with 'komm-komm-komm!' 'los-los!' and 'pass auf!'

"Assigned by the Massa, they assume their places; a whistle shrills over the dark stream, and the banana train rolls up. Passed from hand to hand from the wagons, the bananas are manned into the vessel through the side hatches until the packer, as the last man, stows them away skilfully. One of the sailors takes charge of each gang. The whole operation is controlled by the officers, who also, together with the planters, check each bunch for its fitness for shipping. Every second or so, there is a splash. One gang is singing a sad nigger-song. We do not understand the sense or the words – only the peculiar sounds impress us; one hears the repeated humming as *ndjanga - ndjamba*. At the other gate, they are singing a song in pidgin-English, in which the massas are given nicknames which mostly remain unknown to them. Away up front, 2 are quarreling and throwing a hail of abusive words at each other's heads; the air is shrill with 'You monkey!' 'You bushman!' 'You damn bushnigger!'

"Toward morning, the tempo of work slackens. To be sure, the 8-hour day has been introduced, but most of these people worked long hours yesterday on the plantation gathering bananas. More and more often one hears the planter's encouragement, 'Pass banana – pass banana!' But it will not run so smoothly any longer. In the brief pauses between passes, the boys lie down. Now we simply cannot tolerate any loss of time with our precious and easily damaged cargo. Before dark, we must be at sea.

"When anything goes wrong on board, the first officer must always jump to the rescue. It is so on the China coast; it is so in Chile and Australia; whether we are dealing with coolies, Javanese, or the crew boys. So here too, the First appears: 'Come on, boys, come on– no be tired– pass banana– give us a song.' And he himself with his booming sailing-ship voice starts it, the beautiful song, *Ambas bay,* and the entire company roars out enthusiastically with the refrain:

'Ambas bay,
money no the'e– pass banana

Time very long,
give us a song– pass banana

So so work,
Black man to talk– pass banana

Black man like shop,
Work never stop– pass banana

PANTHER go home
money will come– pass banana–'

Now the ban is broken, all weariness flown; at all the hatchways, there is a singing and shouting: 'Pass banana- pass banana!' The work goes on swimmingly, and at 8 in the morning comes the relief.

"At 5 p.m. the PANTHER is laden. The clearing outward follows exactly the same lines as the clearing in, with stamp, beer, and cigars. The customs official is the last to leave the vessel.

"'Loose the lines!' 'Heave anchor!' Yard by yard, the PANTHER frees herself from the pier. Messages are called out; up ahead the capstan rattles. 'Engines slow forwards, rudder hard to starboard!' Three long notes from the steam whistle in farewell. 'Full steam ahead!' A last signal, and Tiko bridge disappears behind the mangroves. Again through the twistings of the Bimbia, with many a 'Starboard 5 - port 10 - rrrecht sooo!' Past Farm Point, where Mr. and Mrs. K. send us the last greetings from Africa with flag swinging and scarf waving; past Cape Nightingale - and again we have reached open sea.

"We are carrying 4 passengers: 2 planters, and 2 merchants. Besides these are 2 chimpanzees, Max and Jonny, aboard for the zoo in Münster. The Africans have also all kinds of cattle with them- long-tailed monkeys and rickitickis, a bushcat, and African squirrels named kakaorats. On the afterdeck are plants for the colonial exhibit. "To the south, shimmers the lighthouse of St. Isabel, and above the peak of St. Isabel, glows the level-lying sickle of the moon. God be thanked! At last, fresh sea breezes blow out of the cabins the smell of Africa, which nested throughout the vessel like the smell of a horse stable. Out here, one can breathe free again.

"Again we are in the 4th latitude, but now driving west against the Guinea current. The engines must work hard to keep up a good mileage here. Sinewy forms are those who down below there in breeches and wooden shoes are swinging the slice bars with hard fists and shoveling coal almost without pausing into the never sated fires. Two men at a time, they must shove 30 tons into the boiler mouths in 24 hours. Only completely healthy, strong men can endure that.

"At 12 midnight, the Third Officer goes into the 'fruit alley' to check the temperature in the banana holds. Regularly every 6 hours now the 50 thermometers are read. Captain and officers take turns. Aside from this, the engine-room personnel continually regulates the cooling system, for bananas are sensitive, and the temperature in the hold must be kept exact to 1/2 degree.

"Next morning, we have reached the longitude of Lagos. The sun burns singeing hot, yet under the awnings in the fair breeze it is bearable. In the afternoon, the sky becomes cloudy, the air is oppressively sultry; all signs point to a tornado. After sunset, the lightning begins. Unbroken it flames and flickers over the entire heavens, single flashes flame sharply, yet the thunder is only moderate. Toward 10 o'clock, the typical deep-black, sharp-edged clouds come up in the northeast. Soon after, the wind sets in and in a few minutes swells to storm strength. It is sensibly cooler. Now the downpour of rain breaks loose. The flashes quiver blindingly; the thunder rolls hard and crashing over the foaming sea. The palaver keeps up for an hour; then all is again peaceful.

"We are making good daily time now. The fruit is cool below us, the coolers are running slowly. On deck, the painting has begun. Masts and smokestacks gleam with fresh color. One day, we pass our youngest, PYTHON, who is making her maiden voyage. With the aid of the wireless and the beam compass, we can mark our place in this unending space to a yard's exactness. It is clear weather. The German flag and the company flag flap in the breeze. We pass at 2,000 feet distance and hoist in sport the signal, N D P. In words, this is: Nanny- Dora- Paul. It is the body and belly drinking toast of their captain:

'Na, then, God bless you!' PANTHER rushes on northward. Straight ahead is the north star, and it climbs a mile higher every minute. Cape Verde lies directly behind us. Still sleeps the trade wind, and we mention him only in whispers not to awaken him. We have come pretty well through the rainy zone. Only one day of rain, after which the deck was at once thoroughly scrubbed with soda and sand.

"Near Cape Blanco, a stiff trade wind sets in, which had previously announced itself only by the swell. Now it whistles through all the keyholes. Doors and windows are closed. It is so cold one must put on woolen underwear. The Africans drink grog. For 2 days, we box against the trade wind; then Teneriffe comes in sight. Silvery the cone of Pico de Teyde rises against a cloudless sky. Once more, from a distance, we see banana fields.

"As we had hoped, north of the island the wind lets down, but the swell increases. The wind now blows stormily from the west. Helped by the rollers, a high sea has developed rapidly. Heavy swells roll sidewise at us. PANTHER turns bravely and evades them neatly so that only spray whipped up by the storm scours over us. The Africans have given up the struggle and do not come to meals any more. Two days the trouble lasts. Then we run into the Channel with the wind astern. The rolling of the vessel has stopped at once. The wind has turned northwest, and here in the protection of the English coast, the sea is subsiding quickly. In 22 hours, we flit through the Channel. One can see everything. The EUROPA passes us. Mirror-smooth, the North Sea welcomes us— it is a little misty, but not too much for us to continue to run under full power. On board, there is a swarming of all possible birds of passage. Chiefly they are starlings and finches, but there are also titmice, larks, and water wagtails.

"In the afternoon, about 5 o'clock, at Elbe I, the pilot comes aboard; the ocean voyage is ended. Around midnight, we make fast to the quay in Hamburg. 'Welcome to Hamburg, Captain! Did you have a good passage? How are the bananas?'

"'Thanks! Satisfactory!. Bananas sooo. . .!'" (Meaning in best condition.)

THE CONDUCT OF THE FRUIT BUSINESS IN AFRICA

Bananas

"Among the plantations bought back from the English at that time were small ones found in private ownership of some 247 acres, middle-sized with an area up to 2,471 acres, and large ones that comprised 24,710 acres. Among these was the AFC. On each 2 1/2 acres stand between 500 and 1,000 banana trees in bearing. The cultivated banana no longer brings forth seeds. During a thousand years of cultivation, it has, like the rose, lost the capacity for that. The increase is through offshoots. When the plant is 5-6 months old, the mighty inflorescence appears, and after 2-3 months more, the fruit can be harvested. This, however, must be done before the ripening, and furthermore, the fruit must not ripen during the transportation overseas. As soon as the ripening begins, it proceeds so rapidly that the fruit should be used as soon as possible. The banana trunk is a trunk only in appearance; it consists of layers of leaves rolled together, and it dies off as soon as the fruit is formed. In a banana plantation, the plants in bearing and the offshoots of every age stand always side by side. The cut-back shoots, to which even rough handling at the root end does no harm, are about as high and thick as a strong fore-arm. The lower, club-shaped end is put into the ground. Above, in the midst of the oblique cutting-surface, in only 12 hours, appears a new growth, shooting out like a white candle-end. Not long, and the leafy growth begins also. So powerful is the growing urge of the plant in fertile ground.

Personnel

"Africa requires much new learning and experience, and the beginner is given no long time for contemplation. It is better to learn from the spade up. Often, soon after arrival, one must take over the independent leadership of a group of a hundred and more workers. The novice soon learns the nature and peculiarities of his people. He assigns to the younger and weaker the light field work, to the proficient the transport service, to the experienced the planting and sowing, to the strong the cutting and grubbing out of the virgin forest.

"Piece by piece, the axe lays low this primeval forest. The planter's path from his dwelling to the work-place grows longer with every 2 1/2 acres of planting land gained. Often he goes 3 times a day back and forth over the fallen giant timber and through bare-laid gullies, for road-building begins later with the planting of the new land. In the midst of the newly begun preparatory work, a dwelling is built for the young assistant. Gradually, it acquires the character of its owner. The garden is tended and yields its quota of provisions for the kitchen. If at first the boy, the cook, the washerman were merely occasions for embarrassment, a relationship with them grows with time. Boy and cook discover the habits of their master and what he requires to make him feel comfortable.

Language

"He who is able can learn to talk with the blacks by round-about methods. Among these is the so-called negro or pidgin English. The European finds it difficult to learn the various native languages, and there is not much point in it either. Pidgin English contains some hundreds of words mostly much corrupted. Also something of Portuguese and the Bantu tongue are mixed with these.

"This curious material is put together, not according to a European grammar but according to the negro's feeling for speech, into sentences and turns of phrase which often strike the white man as very funny. Even the natives who come from inland learn the pidgin rapidly. To understand it in the mouth of the blacks is at first much harder than to speak it oneself. But whoever masters it thoroughly can get along splendidly with his workmen and with his native overseers. One must feel out what sort of turn catches the fancy of the people. They are very receptive to little jokes, and more still are they delighted when the white man has an ear for their private affairs. Thus it is possible to build up such a good relationship between the white man and his black column that the workers will follow a transferred assistant from farm to farm in order to keep him as their boss.

"One firm principle in running a plantation is that the control must never slip. Therefore, the work-column must be continually superintended. When the established task is done, the worker is free and at liberty; but for the planter, much still remains to do. When he comes home, a whole line of people stands waiting: the workers. Cooks wait for the maintenance certification in order to receive from the warehouse the rice and codfish they are entitled to; others ask for an advance to buy something in the agency store or for a slip of paper entitling them to treatment at the plantation hospital. Then there are personal desires, for leave of absence, etc. Finally the overseers approach, to report on the completion of work and to get their directions for the following day. Not until all have been made content, can the planter go to his own work: the keeping of the account book, report on the harvest, the work accomplished, the count of people, notes for the monthly report, checking of the instruments for weather observation. Then, at last, usually when it is growing dark and 12 hours have rolled around, the day's work of the planter is done.

"Whoever keeps some self-respect and is not willing to let the African bush become his master changes before the evening meal from his workclothes – khaki, leather shoes, spatterdashes – into the white suit and white canvas shoes. About 5 o'clock, the day's heat lessens, and if the work is done up to then, there is time for a small, comfortable, cool drink before eating. It does not need to be alcohol; the consumption of strong drink today in the Cameroons and everywhere in the tropics is much less than formerly – partly for sensible reasons of health, partly because alcohol in Africa is a costly pleasure. Whoever wishes to have something above the cost of maintenance must be sparing with the 'drinks.' In the main counting house of a large plantation, the employees often eat together in one mess; on the smaller farms, they eat alone or 2 together. Who feels the need looks up a neighbor for an hour of conversation or for exchange of useful information. The medium of intercourse between plantations is the trolley, the light-rolling little cart which is pushed by 2 blacks over the narrow-gauge railway spurs that run everywhere.

The Company Trading Post

"It has already been observed that plantation labor is not the only branch of business that the African Fruit Company built up in the Cameroons. There is, besides, the trading post. This deals not only with the buying of the products of the native farms, principally cacao, but also with the sale of European wares to a trade that is made up for the most part of natives. From the main store, trading posts were pushed out as far as possible along the paths that led to the interior. These outposts were supplied with black clerks. They had to be able to read and write, and were from time to time inspected by the head manager. A main store of the AFC was situated on the river Mungo, which empties into the Cameroon inlet.

A Flood On The Mungo

"One day in the rainy season on the Mungo, it poured not only for a few hours in the afternoon, as was customary, but for an entire night, an entire day, and the following night. The Mungo rose, as always after a hard rain. Differences in the water level of 16 1/2 feet and more were still within normal experience, but this time things became dangerous. The water was already licking close to the warehouse, a large circular metal building in which the goods for the exchange were stored. The most valuable among these is the cacao brought by the native producers. The beans have to be dried out again at the exchange, and after that are stacked in 133-lb. sacks one above another in the warehouse. One thousand sacks is no unusual stock. Among the wares in the exchange are books, and yard goods to suit the taste of the black women; shirts and hose, hats and shoes for the men; coverlets, sugar, salt, tobacco, codfish, and petroleum in large metal containers. One very important ware is the hand lanterns protected by woven wire rings. In the primeval forest, there are no lighted pathways, and a half hour after sunset at the latest, it is pitch dark in the tropics, so that for every step outside of the house, one needs a lantern. Of the work tools bought by the natives, the most important is the machete, the heavy broad hewing knife.

"The dwelling of the white employees in the Mungo exchange stands many steps up on the plateau through which the river has cut its way. After the noon meal, the men came down to look at the height of the water. A rod was rammed into the tossing, onrushing flood to make sure if it were still rising. There was no doubt about it: the water level was coming up. The warehouse already stood on a water-surrounded island.

"Now there was nothing to do but empty it. The working force was mobilized. Most important was to carry out the cacao sacks and to store them in a high spot. But there was not only cacao in storage; there were also boxes and sacks of soap, sugar, and rice. They piled the casks of petroleum, which the water cannot harm, one above another, and on top of them the boxes of soap, the sacks of sugar and rice. The water was rising rapaciously. Soon the blacks were wading breast-high in the inrushing, gurgling brown flood. A troop of workers attacked the cacao sacks to carry them out. All at once the entire mass of cacao sacks, piled 6 deep and 14 high, lost balance and fell splashing into the water, as the ground on which they rested was undermined. Had any of the men been standing at the foot of the wall, not one of them would have escaped with his life. The whole mass of cacao was lost at once. What might perhaps be rescued by drying out again was doubtful.

"In the storehouse, the boxes were tumbling about. The water rose and rose. One could reach the storehouse only by swimming; the work had to stop. Night came on. The Mungo and the rain roared in competition, and soon no one could see, not for an instant, whether the warehouse were still standing or whether its ruins and its contents were being rolled outward by the Mungo. Therefore: swim over and find out. One of the 2 white men takes a lighted lantern, holds it with his left hand on his head above the water, and propels himself with his right hand over toward the warehouse. The light of the lamp dances on the water; the young wife and the comrade watch it, troubled. Now the light disappears. Is the swimmer in the warehouse or is he struggling out there in the Mungo? Calling across brings no answer that can be heard.

"Therefore: out after the first swimmer! The method is the same: the lantern on the head, swimming with the right arm. At last comes a comforting sound from the warehouse. It is still standing! But everything movable is floating. The sugar is hopeless; even the thoroughly soaked rice will hardly be salable now. The money-chest is entirely in the water. It has airholes on the under side, but fortunately it contains only metal money, shillings and pence; pound notes are too large for the wage payments and for the small trading with the blacks.

"At last toward morning, the rain lets up, the Mungo begins to go down. Now it is a matter of saving out of the ruined content of the warehouse whatever can yet be saved. Ropes are strung back and forth, and the cotton and imitation silk cloth hung up to dry. A grove of bright-colored stuff waves in the sun. The colors have run together, but that will not disturb the customers too much. The soap is a pretty poor risk now, but the damp cacao a much worse one! It can still be saved from moulding, but hundreds of sacks are of use only to make cocoa butter. The fat content of the beans is not affected by the wetting and redrying, but the aroma is gone.

"On such occasions, when everything goes wrong, the white man must first of all show himself a man. If the black men see that the Massa goes with them into the water and lays hold of every task, he can expect much help from them. If the master has succeeded in keeping his people in the mood and temper for the daily work, they will not forsake him in time of need. Then it becomes clear what sort of position the business leader and his assistants have among them. In Africa, the European may find daily opportunity to prove whether he has grown capable of dealing with suddenly appearing situations for which there was no preparation in the homeland. Whoever can stand such tests, he will make good in Africa, he may call himself an 'African,' not merely a European living by chance in Africa. The AFC can say that they have nearly always made good with their employees, and have had the finest of experience with their responsible leaders."

STEAM VESSELS OWNED AND OPERATED
BY AFRIKANISCHE FRUCHT CIE A. G. AND REEDEREI F. LAEISZ BETWEEN 1825 AND 1946

WEST COAST OF AFRICA ROUTE

	No.	Name	Dimensions	Gross/ Net Tons Reefer Space	Engines	Crew/ Pass.	Built	Builder	Acquired	Acquired From	Fate
Sisters	1	POMONA	394.0x52.7x24.7	3,457 1,764 220,000	Machinfbrk, Augsburg-Nürnburg 6 Cy. oil $16\frac{1}{2}$ knots	35 12	1938	Deutsche Werft A.G., Bet Finkenwarder, Hamburg, Germany	1938	Builder	1939, Sept. 3: Taken by British as prize of war. Later sunk as EMPIRE MERCHANT
Sisters	2	PANTHER	394.0x52.7x24.7	4,876 2,811 220,000	Machinfbrk, Augsburg-Nürnburg 6 Cy. oil -------	35 12	1939	Deutsche Werft A.G., Bet Finkenwarder, Hamberg, Germany	1939	Builder	1941: Reqi-sitioned by Navy. 1945- SALZBURG 1947- EMPIRE MOLE Now REVENTAZON

Note: 1, September, 1939, the following were on order: 1 freighter (about 9,500 tons), 3 refrigerated vessels, and 1 15,000 ton tanker.

STEAM VESSELS OWNED BY AFRIKANISCHE FRUCHT CIE A. G. AND OPERATED BY REEDEREI F. LAEISZ BETWEEN 1910 AND 1946

No.	Name	Dimensions	Gross/ Net Tons Reefer Space	Engines	Crew/ Pass.	Built	Builder	Ac- quired	Ac- quired From	Fate
1 (Sisters)	PUMA	319.1x45.5x15.4	2,171 988 100,000	Bremer Vulkan T. 3Cy. 394 NHP	-- --	1930	Bremer Vulkan, Vegesack, Germany	1930	Builder	1939: Sold to Navy.
2 (Sisters)	PANTHER	319.1x45.5x15.4	2,171 987 100,000	Bremer Vulkan T 3Cy. 394 NHP	-- --	1930	Bremer Vulkan, Vegesack, Germany	1930	Builder	1939: Sold to Navy.
3	PIONIER	352.8x44.8x24.0	3,264 1,933 148,000	Bremer Vulkan 5 Cy. 975 NHP 14 Knots	35 12	1933	Bremer Vulkan, Vegesack, Germany	1933	Builder	1940, Sept. 2:[1] Torpedoed and sunk with loss of 400 lives
4	PELIKAN	352.8x44.8x24.0	3,264 1,933 128,000	Bremer Vulkan Oil 5 Cy. 975 NHP 14 Knots	35 12	1934	Bremer Vulkan, Vegesack, Germany	1934	Builder	1940, March 3: Requisitioned by Navy. Later Elders & Fyffes vessel.
5	PONTOS	366.0x44.8x24.0	3,410 2,032 146,000	Bremer Vulkan Oil 5 Cy. 975 NHP $14\frac{1}{4}$ Knots	35 12	1935	Bremer Vulkan, Vegesack, Germany	1935	Builder	1940, Feb. 8: Requisitioned by Navy. Later EMPIRE MOWDDACH

6	PYTHON	362.6x47.1x24.9	3,664 2,163 160,000	Maschinenfbrk. Augsburg- Nürnburg Oil 5 Cy. 975 NHP 15 Knots	35 12	1935	Deutsche Werft A.G., Bet Finkenwarder, Hamburg, Germany 1935	Builder	1939, Dec.:[2] Requisitioned by Navy. Later held up by British cruiser in the S. Atlantic while supplying U-boats and sunk by crew.
7	PALIME	293.0x30.0x29.0	2,863 1,487 166,000	Oil ------- ------- 16 Knots	35 12	1937	Deutsche Werft A.G., Bet Finkenwarder, Hamburg, Germany 1937	Builder	1940, April: Requisitioned by Navy.
				NORTH AND EAST SEA ROUTE					
8	PORJUS	199.3x31.2x11.7	764 355 ---	Deustche Werke Kiel 8 Cy. 179 NHP 12 Knots Engines Aft	15 --	1937	Lübecker Flender Werke A.G., Lübeck, Germany 1937	Builder	1939, Sept.: Requisitioned by Navy. Later John Schuchmann of Kiel, Germany
9	PALOMA	196.5x31.6x17.7	932 617 ---	Klöckner- Humbolt Oil 6 Cy. ------- ------- Engines aft	15 --	1941	Smit & Zoon, Westerbrock, Germany 1941	German Government In exchange for PRIWALL	1946, April 5: Allocated to U.S.S.R. Became RONSKÄR, later LANGERON

[1] [Master: Th. Thayer - Editor]
[2] [Master: Gustav Lüders - Editor]

Chapter Four: BEGINNING AGAIN

WORLD WAR II

World War II

For the firm of F. Laeisz, a very hard time began on August 25, 1939, when general shipping orders came from Berlin to find safe harbors at once. The catastrophe started quickly after the outbreak of war and caught the POMONA first, which at the end of August 1939 lay at London for the delivery of a banana cargo. Immediately, on August 26, the vessel was prevented from leaving, and at the outbreak of the war was seized as a prize. The 9,500 ton turbine steamer, POSEIDON, was captured near Iceland at the beginning of September by an English warship, and sank herself.

The motorship, PIONIER, on the other hand, was able to get from Tiko to Fernando Po in safety, to break out from there in the course of November 1939, and to reach Germany by a roundabout course. PELIKAN and PALIME, which were on the return passage from the Cameroons, also succeeded after the outbreak of war in getting to German havens by a long detour via Nurmansk and Scandinavia. It would take us too far afield to follow the sometimes romantic wanderings of these vessels. PIONIER was later rebuilt and taken into the marine war service, and still later torpedoed. The banana motorships, PYTHON, PLANET, and PALIME, were lost during the war through enemy operations. The 4-masted barque, PRIWALL, which was caught at Valparaiso, was taken over by the Reich and given to the government of Chile. As a substitute, the firm received from the government authorities the motorship, PALOMA, of 1,000 tdw., built in Holland. As an end-result, the war brought to the firm the complete loss of all its vessels as well as of its foreign possessions in the Cameroons, Guatemala, and Brazil. The counting house burned to the ground in the year 1943 as a result of a bombing attack, and also the private home of Mr. E. F. Laeisz on Harvestehuder Way with its valuable art treasures was completely destroyed by bombs. At the end of the war, the 3 remaining banana vessels, PELIKAN, PONTOS, and the newly built PANTHER, as well as the sailer, PADUA, and the motorship PALOMA, had to be surrendered to the Allies. The motorship, PORJUS, was made a wreck by enemy operations, and sold as such after the war.

It was out of these ruins that in 1945, at the end of the war, the rebuilding had to begin. In the lack of any overseas connections, which had been the soul of the enterprise, this was a hard thing to undertake.

F L Starts Rebuilding

The building of new vessels was at first forbidden to the Germans, yet repairs could be made. At the bottom of the Elbe lay a wreck belonging to the AFC. This was raised and could be sold. Thus the firm was ready to start rebuilding when permission was given by the Allies to build at least German fishing cutters. That was the first connection with shipping made after the war, and it was the only possibility of giving employment again to a part of the shipping personnel. Two newly built fishing cutters were for a long time the remaining link with shipping, since the possibility of rebuilding a proper shipping company did not come during the first after-war years. Trade with foreign lands could be carried on only through an arrangement with the Allies, "Joint Export-Import Agency" (JEIA). On the basis of the possibilities offered through this, however, Swedish and Norwegian vessels could be chartered by F L for German importers, to which AFC also belonged, and with these an import and export trade could be begun. Aboard these vessels, old captains of the firm were to be found as super-cargoes. The first major contracts were in relation to the importing of bananas from Columbia.

Then, in 1950, when, on the grounds of the arrangement with St. Petersburg, possibilities for greater shipping activity were indicated, permission was gained for the building of 2 fast refrigerator vessels. Meanwhile, the limitations on tonnage and speed still in force at the beginning of this building were removed. In consideration of the great war-losses of AFC and the Laeisz firm, aid in the form of credit from the national government and from Hamburg made the financing of the new building easier. The 2 new vessels were put into service under the names, PROTEUS and PERSEUS. Herewith the tradition of the earlier P-liners of the firm was resumed. As a substitute for the POMONA, lost as a result of the war, permission and financing could also be obtained for the MS PEGASUS, which was put into service on December 30, 1951, in partnership with the firm of E. Russ. PROTEUS, PERSEUS, and PEGASUS were improved types of the fruit-refrigeration vessels built before the war. At present, they are among the swiftest vessels of the German merchant fleet, and they enjoy popularity among both shippers and passengers.

With the employment of these 3 vessels, began a general reviving of business. In the course of the year 1953, F. Laeisz, as correspondent-ship-owner for 2 part-owners, put 2 more small vessels into service, namely, MS PARNASS and MS PELION, which were planned for use purely as ventilated freight motorships for the European commerce, especially for the importing of fruit from Spain and Italy.

AFC Resumes Activity

The African Fruit Company A. G. resumed its activity in the banana trade purely as an importer; gradually it could take on a certain share of the combined banana imports first from Columbia, later from Ecuador and Guatemala. A group of fruit importers got together, to which the African Fruit Company also belongs, and which transfers the incoming fruit to the wholesalers.

Since the year 1948, the African Fruit Company has been in the hands of Mr. Bundies, an old African planter who, during the Second World War, lost his possessions in the most productive region of what was formerly German Africa. He too has kept the tradition of the firm not to neglect any task once undertaken as soon as conditions permit its resumption and promotion. In accord with this tendency was the agreement to a proposal by the government of the Free State of Liberia in West Africa on the testing of the possibility of growing bananas there. These enterprises have been in progress since the end of 1952, and an important bridgehead has already been erected in Liberia.

One can count on it, on the basis of what has already been done and what is planned, that in a foreseeable time a new field of activity will develop there as a direct continuation of the African Fruit Company from the year 1910. Moreover, the company has been functioning since April 1, 1951, as a joint stock company. Mr. Bundies is the personally responsible partner, and the firms F. Laeisz and Ernst Russ are silent partners.

Mrs. C. Von Mitzlaff-Laeisz becomes a Partner

The mother-firm, F. Laeisz, under the leadership of its partners, Erich F. Laeisz and Willi Ganssauge, has thus since the war resumed its activity as a shipping firm. On January 1, 1954, the daughter of the senior member, Mrs. Christine Von Mitzlaff-Laeisz, was taken into the firm of F. Laeisz as a partner.

Old and new foreign connections have been knit and are leading to growing activity in general export and import business. The insurance department might be renewed and promises rising returns.

(1) (F. LAEISZ)

M. V. PLISCH
With Her, In 1947, A New Start Was Made

(2) (F. LAEISZ)

M. V. PERIKLES
The "Flying P" In The 1950's

(1) (NAUTICAL PHOTO AGENCY)

Steel 4-Masted Barque PISAGUA, 2,852 Gross Tons At Dover, England, March, 1912
1892-1912

(2) (F. LAEISZ)

Steel Ship POSEN Ex PREUSSEN, 1,761 Gross Tons
1891-1909

The badly damaged Laeiszhof has been restored with painstaking labor and without help of insurance, and now, years after the fire-catastrophe, shows handsomer than before.

Thus the experience, the perseverance, and the vision of a goal to be attained have not been lost in the firm F. Laeisz, which in 1954 can look back on 130 years of an existence full of vicissitudes, and it is to be hoped that they will in the coming years continue to bear good fruit.

Also the rebuilding of a plantation – this time in Liberia – was begun in 1952 and is striding forward.

SAILING VESSELS OWNED AND OPERATED
BY REEDEREI F. LAEISZ BETWEEN 1921 AND 1946

Serial No.	Official No.	Const. & Rig	Name	Dimensions	Com. Load Gross/ Net Tons	Built	Builder	Ac- quired	Ac- quired From	Fate
79	RWGL	S.4m.bq.	POLA	322.5x47.2x26.5	3,104 2,878	1920	Blohm & Voss, Hamburg, Ger.	1920	Builder	1921: Allocated French Gov. 1927: Scrapped after explosion in Baltimore.
80	RWIN/ DIRQ	S.4m.bq.	PRIWALL	323.0x47.1x26.3	3,105 2,849	1919	Blohm & Voss, Hamburg, Ger.	1920	Builder	1941: Given to Chilean Navy by Third Reich. 1945: As LAUTARO Burned in Pacific.
73	RBWN	S.4m.bq.	PARMA ex ARROW	327.7x46.5x26.2	3,090 2,971	1902	A. Rodger & Co., Port Glasgow, Scotland	1921	Gen. Steam Nav. Co., London, Eng.	1931, Oct.: Sold syndicate headed by Capt. R. deCloux, Mariehamn, Åland, Finland. 1936: Hulked in Palestine.
69	RCDF	S.s.	PINNAS ex FITZJAMES	267.1x40.1x23.6	1,946 1,790	1902	W.Hamilton & Co., Port Glasgow, Scotland	1922	French Gov.	1929, Apr. 27: Dismasted off Cape Horn and abandoned.
72	RCDM	S.4m.bq.	PASSAT	322.0x47.2x26.5	3,091 2,882	1911	Blohm & Voss, Hamburg, Ger.	1922	French Gov.	1932: Sold G. Erikson, Mariehamn, Åland, Finland. Now German training vessel.

Serial No.	Official No.	Const. & Rig	Name	Dimensions	Com. Load Gross/Net Tons	Built	Builder	Ac-quired	Ac-quired From	Fate
66	RNHB	S.s.	PEIHO ex ARGO ex BRYNYMORE	275.0x41.5x24.2	2,131 1,980	1902	A.McMillan & Son, Dumbarton, Scotland	1922	British Gov.	1923, Mar. 16: Stranded near Cape San Diego, Straits of Le Maire. Total loss.
71	RDFT	S.4m.bq.	PEKING	322.1x47.1x26.5	3,100 2,883	1911	Blohm & Voss, Hamburg, Ger.	1923	Italian Gov.	1932, Sept.: Sold to Shaftesbury Homes & Arethusa Training Ship, Medway, Eng.
65	RDWC	S.4m.bq.	PAMIR	316.0x46.0x26.2	3,020 2,777	1905	Blohm & Voss, Hamburg, Ger.	1924	Italian Gov.	1931, Nov.: Sold G. Erikson, Mariehamn, Åland, Finland. Now German training vessel.
79	RFDT/ DILZ	S.s.	PELLWORM ex FAITH ex MARÉCHAL SUCHET	281.1x40.7x22.7	2,270 1,991	1902	Chant. & Atel. De St. Mazaire Penhoet, St. Nazaire, France	1924	Soc. Des Voiliers Français, Havre, Fr.	1926: Sold Syndikatsreederei, Hamburg, Ger. 1943: Sunk as Luffwaffe target.
80	RFVQ/ DTRR	S.4m.bq.	PADUA	320.5x46.1x25.4	3,064 2,678	1926	J.C. Tecklen-borg, Geeste-münde, Ger.	1926	Builder	1946: Allocated U.S.S.R.

STEAM VESSELS OWNED AND OPERATED BY REEDEREI F. LAEISZ BETWEEN 1946 AND ----

No.	Name	Dimensions	Gross/Net Tons Reefer Space	Engines	Crew/ Pass.	Built	Builder	Ac-quired	Ac-quired From	Fate
87	PLISCH	-------	--- --- ---	--- --- --- ---	--- ---	1947	----- ----- -----	---	---	Sold to Eastern Zone of Germany.
88	PLUM	-------	--- --- ---	--- --- --- --- --- ---	--- ---	1949	----- ----- -----	---	---	Sold to Eastern Zone of Germany.

STEAM VESSELS OWNED AND OPERATED BY
AFRIKANISCHE FRUCHT CIE A. G. AND REEDEREI F. LAEISZ BETWEEN 1946 AND ----

EUROPE TO AFRICA AND THE AMERICAS ROUTE

	No.	Name	Dimensions	Gross/Net Tons Reefer Space	Engines	Crew/ Pass.	Built	Builder	Ac- quired	Ac- quired From	Fate
Sisters (3, 4)	3	PROTEUS	-------	3,500 --- 218,000	Oil --- --- --- 16½ Knots	40 12	1951	No. 626: Deutsche Werft A.G., Bet Finkenwarder, Hamburg, Germany	1951	Builder	
	4	PERSEUS	-------	3,500 --- 218,000	Oil --- --- --- 16½ Knots	40 12	1951	No. 627: Deutsche Werft A.G., Bet Finkenwarder, Hamburg, Germany	1951	Builder	
	5	PEGASUS	-------	--- --- 216,000	Oil --- --- --- 16½ Knots	40 12	1951	No. 951: Howaldtswerke, Kiel, Germany	1951	Builder	
Sisters (6, 7)	6	PELION	-------	--- --- ---	Oil --- --- --- 12½ Knots	23 1	1953	No. 554: Werft Nobiskrug, G.M.B.H., Rendsburg, Germany	1953	Builder	
	7	PARNASS	-------	--- --- ---	Oil --- --- --- 12 Knots	23 1	1953	No. 555: Werft Nobiskrug, G.M.B.H.	1953	Builder	

	No.	Name	Dimensions	Gross/Net Tons Reefer Space	Engines	Crew/ Pass.	Built	Builder	Ac- quired	Ac- quired From	Fate
Sisters (8, 9)	8	PERIKLES	-------	--- --- 191,000	Oil --- --- --- $16\frac{1}{2}$ Knots	38 12	1954	No. 678: Deutsche Werft A.G., Bet Finken- warder, Hamburg, Germany	1954	Builder	
	9	PIRAUS	-------	--- --- 191,000	Oil --- --- --- $16\frac{1}{2}$ Knots	38 9	1955	No. 682: Deutsche Werft A.G., Bet Finken- warder, Hamburg, Germany	1955	Builder	
	10	PORTUNUS	-------	--- --- 220,000	Oil --- --- --- 17 Knots	40 12	1955	No. 1013: Howaldts- werke, Kiel, Germany	1955	Builder	
	11	PARTHENON	-------	--- --- 190,000	Oil --- --- --- $16\frac{1}{2}$ Knots	--- ---	1956	No. 689: Deutsche Werft A.G., Bet Finken- warder, Hamburg, Germany	1956		

PART III

THE CHILEAN NITRATE TRADE

PART III

THE CHILEAN NITRATE TRADE

Chapter One: THE "FLYING P" LINE

Under the goal-conscious leadership of Laeisz father and son, the shipping firm turned decisively in the last quarter of the previous century to the building of steel vessels and the formation of a regular liner-service from Hamburg and Antwerp to the ports of the South American West Coast. This route led around Cape Horn, and that meant that the old vessels could no longer carry sail in bad weather, but lay heaved to and waited with sails furled until the wind abated. But this method did not suit either Laeisz. To sail in heavy weather, to hold the course under canvas stiff as boards in spite of howling squalls and whistling westerlies down under there at the last outpost of the South-American continent — that required strong tackle on strong vessels, and such vessels could be built only of metal.

The firm of Laeisz was not itself the first to undertake passages to the West Coast of South America. A cousin of Carl Woermann's father, David Fr. Weber, carried on in the forties and fifties an export business of Westphalian linens to Chile for tropical clothing. In the year 1864, the firm of Weber and Co. expired as a shipping firm; but as agents in Valparaiso of the shipping firm of F. Laeisz, they remained closely connected with the West Coast linen trade until the outbreak of the Second World War. Also the Sloman shipping company and the firm of Zeiss Brothers sent occasional vessels to the West Coast, but could not keep up the undertaking. On the other hand, the sailers under the white flag with the red F L took the Cape Horn way ever more numerously, and one can say that from the nineties on, the firm concentrated its shipping business on the trade with the West Coast of South America, even in successful competition with the steam transports.

Early in 1892, the entire world of shipping listened to the news that the great 1440-ton barque, PAMELIA,[1] had taken only 67 days from Dover to Iquique. Many men of the profession thought it a newspaper hoax. Still more astonishing was the report that the PLACILLA,[2] built by Tecklenborg in Bremerhaven, a powerful 4-master of 2,900 gross tonnage, had run out from the Channel on March 2 and arrived at Valparaiso on April 29: 9,500 nautical miles in 58 days, an average of 164 miles a day. Only 4 times could this performance be topped later. The publicity for the nitrate carriers began to interest people. With growing amazement, they followed the passage of the Hamburg deep-sea sailers. Thus the PAMPA made the following noteworthy passages:

[3]1892:	Dungeness - Iquique	67 days
[3]1893:	Dungeness - Valparaiso	64 days
[3]1893:	Dover - Valparaiso	65 days
[3]1894:	Dungeness - Valparaiso	64 days
[4]1898:	Iquique - Cuxhaven	69 days

[1] [Capt. H. Dehnhardt - EDITOR]
[2] [Capt. Robert Hilgendorf - EDITOR]
[3] [1892-1897: Capt. J. Steineck - EDITOR]
[4] [Capt. J. Jensen - EDITOR]

Under Captain Schröder in 1905, the vessel achieved her best passage going out through the Elbe through the difficult fairways of the North Sea and the English Channel to Valparaiso in only 61 days, and returning as far as the Isle of Wight in 75 days. The full rigged ship POSEN—until 1902 called PREUSSEN—can point to similar performances under Captain Petersen:

[5]1893:	Channel - Iquique	68 days
1895:	Iquique - Dover	71 days
[6]1898:	Hamburg - Valparaiso	69 days
1898:	Dover - Valparaiso	63 days
1900:	Iquique - Isle of Wight	68 days
[7]1904:	Elbe - Valparaiso	68 days

On October 14, 1909, this [8]vessel burned in mid-Atlantic. It had on board a gunpowder cargo, took fire and exploded. Its crew was picked up on the same day by the English steamer, EARL OF CARRICK, and taken to Pernambuco. In 1895, the powerful POTOSI was completed. Her monstrous pyramids of sail towered over 197 feet. On July 26, she ran out from the Elbe, to sail past Ushant on August 1, into the open Atlantic for the first time. In just 3 weeks, she reached the equator, and on October 6 let fall her anchor at Iquique. The great vessel, under Captain Hilgendorf's control, had required just 66 days. Within 20 days, the vessel was unloaded and loaded again with 6,000 tons of saltpeter. That also was an unusual performance, which testified to the vigor of the vessel's management. On the evening of October 26, she was at sea again, and on November 14 she had passed Cape Horn. Two days before, the English wool clipper, CIMBA,[9] had passed by on her homeward journey from Australia. The CIMBA enjoyed a reputation because of her fast passages. At first the courses of the 2 vessels lay a little apart. But on November 27, the 2 came in sight. Immediately the English sporting spirit awoke. Those on the POTOSI could see how over there the last bit of sail was spread, although the wind blew stormily. The race had begun. For 3 days, the wind-dogs remained in sight of each other; for hours their officers stood at the rail, observing jealously every maneuver of the other vessel. Yet it was clear that the German was the nimbler. Steadily, she gained ground, and by the evening of the 30th was entirely out of sight. On January 17, the CIMBA passed the Channel entrance. She had a very good passage from Cape Horn behind her, and there were strong hopes aboard that the POTOSI was not yet in. Nevertheless, on entering London harbor, the Britons had a mighty disillusionment. For there they learned that the POTOSI had already lain almost a week at Hamburg when the CIMBA first entered the Channel. 15 days before, on January 2, her rival, the POTOSI, had shown the Lizard her identification signal. From Cape Horn to the Channel, the famous wool clipper had been beaten by more than two weeks! To be sure, the German vessel had flown through the latter part of her passage with unbelievable swiftness. For 11 days on end, she had rushed toward her goal with an average speed of fully 11 knots, that is $12\frac{1}{2}$ m.p.h., the speed of the best freight steamers of that day. Once again, in October 1902, the POTOSI,[10] in sport, overtook the CIMBA,[11] on the outward passage. Following is a brief summary of the wonderful passages of this racer:

[5] [1893-1897: Capt. H. Schmidt - EDITOR]
[6] [1897-1901: Capt. Boye Petersen - EDITOR]
[7] [Capt. A. Schütt - EDITOR]
[8] [Capt. E. Paulsen - EDITOR]
[9] [Capt. J. Fimister - EDITOR]
[10] [Captain Schlüter - EDITOR]
[11] [Capt. Holmes - EDITOR]

(1) (F. LAEISZ)

Steel 5-Masted Barque POTOSI, 4,026 Gross Tons
1894-1920
Launch At J. C. Tecklenborg's Yard At Geestemünde, Germany, September, 1894

2) (Capt. Robert K. MIETHE)

Steel 5-Masted Barque POTOSI

(F. LAEISZ)

Steel 5-Masted Barque POTOSI: Fore Deck

(1) (Capt. Robert K. MIETHE)

Capt. Robert Karl MIETHE
1877-
Master Of PROMPT, PAMPA, PITLOCHRY, PAMIR,
And POTOSI: 1905-1920. Photo Taken On Board POTOSI In 1916

(2) (F. LAEISZ)

Steel 5-Masted Barque POTOSI: Main Deck

(1) (Capt. Robert K. MIETHE)

POTOSI: Valparaiso, 4, Aug., 1919

(2) (NAUTICAL PHOTO AGENCY)

FLORA Ex POTOSI
Burned Out And Beached At Comodoro Rivadavia, Argentina,
On 2, October, 1925

	OUTWARD PASSAGES		HOMEWARD PASSAGES	
[12]1896	Lizard - Caleta Buena	65 days	Caleta Buena - Lizard	78 days
1896/7	Lizard - Valparaiso	59 days	Iquique - Lizard	79 days
1897	Isle of Wight - Iquique	70 days	Iquique - Dover	77 days
1897	Isle of Wight - Iquique	62 days	Caleta Buena - Cuxhaven	74 days
1898	Channel - Iquique	62 days	Iquique - Channel	74 days
1898	Dover - Iquique	68 days	Caleta Buena - Isle of Wight	70 days

Then, in 1900, came the record passage to Valparaiso, which was never to be beaten. On March 15, the vessel left the port of Hamburg and was towed down the Elbe. Before passing Cuxhaven, she cast the tug loose and rushed out into the green North Sea under full sail. The Isle of Wight faded away into the evening twilight of March 21, the first day of spring. After the unbelievable period of 55 days, the vessel let fall her anchor on May 15 in the roads of Valparaiso. The daily records which the sailer sped through on her way north after rounding the Cape are unique in the history of shipping by sail. The POTOSI laid behind her:

from midday to midday on	9-10 May	278 nautical miles
	10-11 May	378 nautical miles
	11-12 May	322 nautical miles
	12-13 May	345 nautical miles
	13-14 May	283 nautical miles
	Total	1,606 nautical miles

The day's run from the 10th to the 11th of May is the greatest distance ever covered in 1 day by a sailer up to that time: 378 nautical miles are 434.9 land miles. This stretch corresponds to the distance from Wiesbaden to Copenhagen or from Danzig to Vienna. Driven only by the wind, this powerful vessel roared on with the speed of a freight train. In order to get an idea of this accomplishment, one must compare the distances covered daily with distances on land. Let us think of the vessel at midday of May 9 as at Tripoli on the coast of Africa. At noon of the 10th, she had reached Palermo in Sicily; on the 11th, Florence; on the 12th, she stood off Stuttgart; on the 13th, at Flensburg; and on noon of the following day, at Oslo, the Norwegian capital. 120 hours from Tripoli to Oslo!

In the English newspaper, *The Field,* among the memoirs of an English captain, appeared an account of a meeting with this famous vessel, which demonstrates the ungrudging admiration of the professional for the "Flying-P liners". The writer was at the time still Second Officer on an English steamer bound for Hamburg. As his vessel entered the Channel, the POTOSI, on her way home, passed the Lizard simultaneously and let wave the gay standards of her identification signal. The wind blew fresh from the southwest. A white squall came up between the two vessels. Then it grew foggy, and the Englishman saw nothing more of the great sailer. At 10 knots an hour, the steamer plowed up the Channel and the North Sea. On the second day after the meeting, at 2 in the afternoon, she came to the mouth of the Elbe and picked up the pilot. The English captain turned to him and remarked, "We saw the POTOSI abeam the Lizard. There has been a good wind since then; she will probably be here toward evening!" A slightly ironic smile passed over the weather-tanned features of the

[12] [1895-1901: Capt. Robert Hilgendorf - EDITOR]

German seaman, as he replied: "The POTOSI? She came in this morning, Captain." (This story was also told by Lubbock in *The Nitrate Clippers*.)

In the year 1902, the largest of all square-rigged vessels without auxiliary engines was completed in the shipyards of Tecklenborg A.G. in Geestemünde, the 5-masted full-rigged ship, PREUSSEN. The masts, 9 feet in circumference at the base, rose to a height of 213.9 feet above the keel; the combined length of steel wire used in stationary and running gear amounted to more than 15 miles, that of hempen rope, 10½ miles. Besides this, there was 10,000 feet of reserve cable and hawser, so that the length of cordage required for the rigging amounted to 28 miles. Besides this, the rigging used 2,296½ feet of chain and 1,260 wood and steel blocks. Among all the 43 sails, the vessel spread the largest span of sail-surface ever yet carried: 59,848 feet. She had a capacity of 8,000 tons, that is 160,000 hundredweight. Under the strenuous conduct of Captain B. R. Petersen, she had achieved for the company flag a world reputation as the swiftest sailing vessel. Her first passage employed only 65 days from the Channel to Iquique; the home passage, 79. It was the general test by which her commander became certain of what he could demand of his steel racer. The following is the fastest passage which was ever achieved by a sailer. Leaving the Channel[13] on March 5, she reached the harbor of Iquique on May 1, in the space of 57 days, a record never before conceived of as possible. Although the POTOSI took only 55 days to Valparaiso, the distance to Iquique is fully 800 nautical miles longer; so that with the two extra days, the PREUSSEN'S passage is still the faster.

From the Channel to the equator, the PREUSSEN had used only 13 days and 8 hours, several days less than the previous record for this stretch. If the luck of the great 5-master had held good, she would have reached her goal in slightly over 50 days. But she had to win her laurels with honor. Heavy west and southwest storms threw themselves upon her on her way around the Cape. From 50 degrees south latitude in the Atlantic to 50 degrees south in the Pacific, she required 11 days, whereas in 1910 she was to cover this same stretch in 7 days. But Captain Petersen cudgeled his ship forward into the teeth of the howling counter-wind, mercilessly getting the last bit possible from ship and from crew. And they made it in spite of hailstorms and heavy roaring seas. On one morning watch between 8 and 10, they logged 17 knots. The ship had raced 126 km. in 4 hours through the over-rushing rollers! And the glorious outward passage was worthily completed by the homeward one of 68 days to the Channel, exactly 74 to Cuxhaven.

Twice more the PREUSSEN raced in 62 days from the Channel to Iquique, and twice she returned in the same brief time from Taltal and from Tocopilla to the Channel. Then, in the spring of 1908, the giant sailer was chartered for a passage by the Standard Oil Company. With a full cargo of petroleum, she left New York on May 27; 73 days later, she passed through the Lombok strait between the islands of Lombok and Bali, and in 112 days, her anchors rattled down in the harbor of Yokohama. It was a remarkable passage considering the circumstance that the ship's crew was not acquainted with eastern Asiatic waters. In the South Atlantic and the Indian Ocean, in the "roaring forties" (that stretch of sea between South Africa and Australia, cut through by latitude 40 and stormy winds), the ship had shown what was in her. Here, where the tea- and wool-clippers had once run off their great daily records, the heavily loaded giant vessel produced results that placed her as a rival of equal rank in the line of the best clipper ships. In the 11 days between July 21 and 31, she had flown 3,019 nautical miles before the icy squalls of that latitude — 3,483.7 miles, 64½

[13] [Hamburg on 16, February, 1903

(1) (F. LAEISZ)

Steel 5-Masted Ship PREUSSEN, 5,081 Gross Tons
Building At J. C. Tecklenborg's Yard, Geestemünde, Germany, 27, January, 1902

(2) (F. LAEISZ)

PREUSSEN: Launch
7, May, 1902

(F. LAEISZ)

PREUSSEN
Outfitting At Tecklenborg's: June, 1902

(F. LAEISZ)

PREUSSEN
1902-1910
Berthed At Blohm & Voss, Hamburg, Germany

(F. LAEISZ)

PREUSSEN

(1) (AMOS & AMOS)

PREUSSEN
Ashore: 7, November, 1910, Crab Bay, England

(2) (F. LAEISZ)

Steel Barque POTRIMPOS, 1,273 Gross Tons
Stranded Long Beach, Ilwaco, Washington, U.S.A., In December, 1896,
And As She Appeared 2 Years Later

miles more than the POTOSI achieved in her famous 11 days in the North Atlantic. From Yokohama, the PREUSSEN then sailed away in 75 days to Taltal, and came from Tocopilla to the Channel with a full load of saltpeter in 69 days. On April 3, 1910, she arrived again in Hamburg. It was to be the last time, for on her next outward passage, the most powerful and swiftest of all great-sailers was stranded close off Dover and lost. Other vessels of the Flying-P Line too have made noteworthy passages, even though they were outshone by the 2 "cracks" of the firm.

SALTPETER

At times during the Chile voyages, other passages were made also, if the circumstance could be used with special profit in the freight market, or if a Laeisz vessel were chartered by another party. That, however happened rarely. The dominant word was *Saltpeter,* for the demand of agriculture for nitrogen fertilizer was constantly growing. To explain what saltpeter is and where it comes from, we must branch out a bit. The West Coast of South America is for the most part without rain, because a cold ocean current from the South Pole prevents dampness that comes in from the sea from condensing. Wherever, close to the shore, high peaks project, the dampness in the air does thicken to rain. This happens in the southern part of Chile; but farther north, the Cordilleras stretch into the interior, and between the coast and the high mountains there lies a gradually rising region several hundred miles broad which remains rainless, since the damp sea air cannot thicken above it. Thus has come about the Atacama desert, and in it lie the saltpeter fields, which can develop and maintain themselves here because there is no rain; for saltpeter draws dampness strongly, and a little dampness is sufficient to dissipate it.

Nitrate

Where the saltpeter in the Atacama Desert comes from is a question as yet unsolved. Since it also contains iodine, which appears in sea water, perhaps the saltpeter beds may somehow be connected with an earlier ocean-covering of this region. They begin in the south near Taltal, a harbor three days north by steamer from Valparaiso, and they reach northward to the neighborhood of Arica and 19 to 50 miles inland to a height of 3,281 to 8,202 feet above sea level. Taltal, Antofagasta, Tocopilla, and Iquique are the most important shipping ports. From each a railway leads inland up to the fields; these are bound together by the northern branch of the great Chilean mainline railroad. It leads, for the most part, through an absolute desert: bare mountains, with flats overstrewn with broken rocks, sand, dust, and caliche fields. "Caliche" is the name of the raw material out of which saltpeter is taken. Where there is enough caliche, there rises an "oficina" with its great boiler plant, its dwelling houses, administration buildings, layout of railroads, gleaming white masses of prepared saltpeter, and the mountainous heaps of the remaining stuff poured out by the cauldrons.

The mining of saltpeter proceeds in this manner: the bed of caliche is broken up along a strip by blasting, then the blasted fragments are made smaller with a hammer, and the broken masses are carried on a railway spur to the oficina. The tracks disappear in the underpart of the workshop building, the carts empty their content, it is broken up still finer by machinery and then raised to the upper floor where the cauldrons stand. Each cauldron is lined with steam pipes, and now is charged with caliche and water and filled with hot steam. After 24 hours, the saltpeter content is to some extent freed from a quantum of caliche. The residue containing no saltpeter is thrown on the heaps: the solution runs into large basins, in which the saltpeter separates itself in cooling. Then it is shoveled out and goes to the storage place, where it is stacked in long gleaming white mounds. Now it is ready to be stuffed into sacks and transported to the harbor. The waste land in which all these plants are erected is a complete desert. The procuring of water is difficult. Many works have a plant on the coast for the distilling of sea water and pump up the distilled water through pipes many miles long. At the beginning of the 20th century, there were still large German saltpeter works, which, however, were later sold to American capital. The largest German concern was the Sloman works, which could take the water for their business from the salty Loa-River, the only one which, coming down from the Cordilleras, flows through the desert to the sea. For human use, also, and for the watering of the little gardens which adjoin the home of every employee, the water must be distilled.

The discovery of saltpeter was decisive for the progress of the Chilean state. Dr. A. Plagmann records that the discoverer of saltpeter was a Portuguese named Negreiros. A sudden flaring up of his campfire is said to have startled him. He was searching among the ashes on the ground for his forgotten or charred powderhorn or something of the sort, when he discovered to his astonishment that it was the ground itself that was melting and breaking up in hissing flames. He had stumbled on caliche! From 1810 to 1812, Negreiros established 7 small refineries in Tarapaca in the province of Iquique, and his combined outtake per year amounted to about 3,000 tons. About 1835, the first sacks of saltpeter were shipped out of the port of Iquique — no one dreamed then that in a few years this insignificant stuff would far surpass all the other minerals of Chile. By the turn of the century, almost 90 saltpeter works were operating in the desert of Atacama. In the year 1908, the total income of the Chilean state was 233.6 million gold pesos, of which 62.2 million were for the export tax on saltpeter alone. How could the economy of Chile have developed without saltpeter?

THE NITRATE WAR

Bolivia-Chile-Peru War

When the saltpeter export from Iquique began, the borders of Chile lay about where Antofagasta lies today. The provinces of Tarapaca and Arica farther to the north were Peruvian, and between Peru and Chile lay a broad Bolivian corridor as outlet to the sea. Chilean enterprise and Chilean labor gave that dead land life during the saltpeter and copper boom. A German scientist investigated the Atacama on commission from the government. Now the Bolivian government, too, saw the welcome possibility of procuring here for itself a new source of income, and heavy taxes were laid on the Chilean saltpeter works. In 1866, an agreement was reached, but a secret understanding between Bolivia and Peru directed against Chile led to conflict. Chile landed troops in Antofagasta, the Bolivian officials were driven out of the city, and Peru now mixed in the war. Peru's superior strength on the sea seemed to give matters a turn unfortunate for Chile. But then came that memorable sea-fight before Iquique in which 2 small wooden Chilean vessels conquered 2 far superior Peruvian ironclads. Therein Captain Arturo Prat and his gallant crew found a hero's death, and since then the Chileans gratefully celebrate these men as their national heroes. The continual threat from the sea against the Chilean troops operating on land was over. Iquique could be

(1) (Capt. Robert K. MIETHE)

Master's Saloon Of PITLOCHRY At Tocopilla, Chile, In 1909
Left To Right:

Mr. Puls, Agent Of Ago Slomann
Capt. (Unknown) Of (Unknown)
Mr. Von Der Ago Slomann
Capt. Reitzmeyer Of MELPOMENE
Capt. Robert K. Miethe Of PITLOCHRY

(2) (Capt. Robert K. MIETHE)

The Great Valparaiso Norther Of 12 And 13, July, 1919
Photo: 13, July

(1)

Valparaiso - 1916

(2) (Capt. Robert K. MIETHE)

Valparaiso Hinterland
Left to Right:
Capt. H. Mehrkens, 4 m. Bq. ISEBECK First Engineer, Rettig S. S. NEGADA
Capt. Kagelmacher, S. S. NEGADA Capt. H. Kaiser, Bq. PELIKAN

(1) (Capt. Robert K. MIETHE)

Valparaiso - 1916

(2) (Capt. Johannes F. SCHMIDT)

Capt. Max Jürgen Heinrich JURSS
1881-1935

(1) (Capt. Robert K. MIETHE)

POTOSI: Nitrate Loading Apparatus
Captain H. Kaiser Of PELIKAN

(2) (Capt. Robert K. MIETHE)

IQUIQUE

occupied forever, and almost a year after the ocean battle, on May 28, 1880, the picked troops of Bolivia and Peru were blotted out in the murderous slaughter at Tacna. In January of the following year, Lima fell, which had been besieged for 2 years until Peru agreed to surrender to Chile the 3 provinces being fought over. In another year came the peace treaty with Bolivia, who renounced forever her passage to the sea. From then on, Chile was master of all the Caliche fields on the Pacific coast.

A half generation after that nitrate war, this salt was to play a rôle in the history of another great war. Dr. W. Kuhnhenn, Docent in the higher technical academy in Berlin, wrote concerning it: "The most infamous lie in the Versailles dictation was undoubtedly the guilt-lie, by which Germany alone was made guilty of the outbreak of the World War. This lie is today patent to the whole world, yet let us recall one fact which of itself would be sufficient to contradict it. It is perfectly evident what can be proved by the export statistics of a distant land, namely Chile. Germany had no reserve in saltpeter, yet without saltpeter, not a single shot is fired today. The ammonia synthesis and that of Leuna saltpeter according to the Haber-Bosch process were, as is known, first developed during the war, since Germany, in her constant leaning toward peace, had not thought to import saltpeter supplies for a war need. Although, when the need arrived, our genius for invention made our homeland independent of the need for Chilean saltpeter, yet this solution was impossible to foresee."

THE WEST COAST

History of Chile

About 1,367 miles lie between Cape Horn and Arica. Between these 2 points lies the land of Chile, which is one's first thought on hearing the words, West Coast. First to anchor there were the Spanish silver ships, that with the burden of their treasure sailed diagonally across the ocean to Manila. They were followed by the sailers of the 18th century, whose more modest desires were concerned only with copper. Later, the bird dung, the guano of the Peruvian Chincha Islands, won world renown and produced splendid family palaces within which fabulous wealth celebrated princely festivities. Hamburg, through the house of Von Ohlendorff, also played a leading rôle in this business. Even since the middle of the previous century, active relationships had sprung up between Germany and the West Coast, especially Chile. Her central and southern ports, through their pleasant climate and not least through their irresponsibility of living conditions, drew worthwhile emigrants. A school friend of Bismarck, Wilhelm Frick, settled in Valdivia in 1842. In the fall of 1848, the apothecary Anwandter from Kalau said to his grown sons: "Our beautiful dream of a free and united Germany is now dreamed out! With us, the wind blows backwards; therefore we should seek Germany in foreign lands." And thousands thought the same. Karl Anwandter became the founder of the German school in Valdivia, still one of the most important in that country. Valdivia has been, from the beginning, the favorite city for German life in Chile. The first shipbuilder of the country was Emil Ribbeck, who, as early as 1870, built in Valdivia vessels for the coastal service. Later, the shipyards of Behrens, Oettinger, and Schneider achieved distinction. One of the most important men in the opening up of the south, of the island world on the Magellan straits and the Tierra del Fuego, was Bernard Philippi, the brother of that scholar who, on government commission, investigated the region of the caliche beds. Chile's Little Germany — be it spoken with regret — unlike the German groups in North America, has remained pure German and has brought up its children to be Germans. The sailor, who comes in touch with people in all parts of the world, is a good judge of that. Nowhere else abroad does one have so clearly the feeling of being "at home", even under the palms of Valparaiso, as during an evening in a hospitable circle of Chile-Germans.

Chilean saltpeter had for decades found only limited favor on the world market. It was again a German who helped it to gain greater significance. The teachings of the chemist, Justus Von Liebig, pointed out to agriculturists the usefulness of certain minerals to increase the productivity of the soil, and soon after that, the demand for Chilean saltpeter set in so strongly that the export rose by leaps and bounds. Dozens of large companies were established, unheard-of names of little nests in the mountains of northern Chile rang out in the talk on the great stock-exchanges of Europe and North America. Whole armies of workers of all shades and colors streamed to the caliche fields and oficinas; in the van were the native Indians and mestizos more or less descended from these. New ports developed, villages shot up over night where until then had been only legions of pelicans and of dirty seals rolling themselves in the sand. Along the nitrate coast, "cities" were built, on every bit of sand beach, even where there was hardly room for a child's playground. Through the ankle-deep sand of the streets, endless caravans of mules dragged saltpeter or copper ore to the loading place. The houses were level with the earth, thrown together with boards patched with the inevitable petroleum cans, lime-washed in harsh colors, with wooden paths before them, filled with a crowd of mostly cheerful and always hospitable people. This is how the typical nitrate West Coast presented itself to the sailor. Only the larger harbors possessed stone houses of more than one story.

Wherever they were, they would probably not withstand the next strong earthquake. It required many horrible experiences to teach man to build massive buildings which could endure the wrath of a "terremoto". On May 13, 1647, the falling houses of Santiago buried more than 4,000 of its 12,000 inhabitants. In 1730 and 1751 two quakes so far destroyed the city of Concepcion that its discouraged inhabitants emigrated to the river Bio-Bio and there created a new home for themselves. Eighty-four years of quiet were granted to them there; then a single hour of terror laid in ruins the flourishing town together with its port, Talcahuano. Shortly after an earthquake, a high wall of water usually pours along the coast and finishes the work of destruction. Thus in the year 1877, Arica, Pisagua, and Iquique were visited by gruesome flood catastrophes. Even before the first World War, sailors could see high on the beach of Arica the remains of the wreck of a gunboat of the U. S. A., which the earthquake of 1868 had torn from its anchor and thrown far up on dry land. With the fearful earthquake which in 1906 destroyed large sections of Valparaiso, the ever-dreaded flood was fortunately lacking.

There is one other peculiarity of the West Coast which, among other things, accounts for the absence of blessing on the lips of commanders of sailing vessels in this uncertain region. It has already been mentioned that here a powerful ocean current runs parallel with the coast from south to north, the Humboldt stream, that farther on is called the Peru stream. This makes it necessary in steering into a harbor to figure closely on every possible eventuality. A sailing vessel which has sailed even a few miles too far north may seek in vain to get back over the ridiculously short stretch to a mooring place. Here, near the shore, the wind is almost always very weak; often it slumbers completely, and meanwhile, unceasingly, the current carries the vessel farther northward.

Tugs? They unfortunately knew only too well in what a jam such a poor misguided "windjammer" had gotten herself and, unashamed, demanded huge sums for the towing in. And at most of the saltpeter havens, there were no tugs strong enough to hold a great sailer against the current. Then only one thing remained to do: to draw off in a wide curve, to stand away from the coast again until a fresh wind could be found, to sail south with it, and then to steer for the land again with the mostly west or southwest winds, and carried by the now friendly Humboldt current, to approach the harbor once more. This could cost whole weeks!

The Nitrate Ports

Thus Nature had seen to it that a mariner bound for the West Coast could not be too arrogant! Also, in the time of the saltpeter trade, no harbor was safe from the high rolling swell of the open Pacific. Not until the twenties, was the mole-protected haven of San Antonio completed, in which, even in stormy weather, work can proceed in security. Valparaiso also, and farther north, Callao, have been built up into all-weather havens at enormous cost. The saltpeter vessels in their time, however, lay at anchorages which offered little or no protection. Here and there, small islands held off the on-rolling swells somewhat. But what help could the island before Iquique offer? Or the Alacran island before Arica? They lie south of the roads where anchorage must be made, and the swell rolls in mostly from the west. In other cases, land promontories gave to certain places the proud name of havens, as at Mejillones and Tocopilla; yet even these held guard only toward the south and southwest; the places of anchorage lay open to all that came to them from the north and northwest—and it was thence that the northers came! In order that the vessels should lie at all quiet under these circumstances, they were fastened to the bottom with 4 anchors, 2 at the bow and 2 at the stern. We may picture this as when an infant lies on his stomach on the turf, stretches out all 4 limbs and grabs into the grass with his fingers and toes. Since often 40 and more sailers lay at one time in the bustling ports, it often happened that the anchors and chains of neighboring vessels would get entangled — a source of much anger and many hours of hard work.

Loading Nitrate

And then began the taking on of cargo. It was brought alongside in lighters, the so-called launches. From the deck two coco-ropes were thrown to the "lancheros", with which they made the lighter fast to the vessel. Then the "lancheros" sat themselves patiently on the saltpeter sacks, waited until their turn came, and — smoked! After one has once seen how easily saltpeter burns and how wildly it flares up, then one may get an idea of the complete peace of mind that filled one of these lancheros. But the man has yet to be born who has accomplished the task of making this sort of people respect a "no smoking" ordinance. On board, naturally, care was taken. No one smoked on deck so long as the hatchways stood open; also the flight of any stray sparks from the chimneys of the galley was prevented and barrels of water stood ready in which saltpeter had been dissolved. That was the only way to put out a saltpeter fire, once started, for clear water is as good as useless, since, in burning, saltpeter sets free large quantities of nitrogen.

In the "classic" procedure of loading, a cargo of saltpeter was heaved sack by sack over the railing by handwinches. There on a platform a man stood ready to stick in the hook on the end of a rope that ran through a block over the hatchway and was serviced by 2 sailors. Through a simple trick, the hoisted burden was transferred to this rope, on which it was now conducted to the storage space. Four men turned the wheel of the handwinch, and although they were nearly always good creatures with the careless lightheartedness of the sailorman, yet it should not be concealed that often enough remarks occurred in which the hard word, "bone-mill", played a leading part accompanied by many decorative adjectives, as colorful as only the West Coast can produce them. It is interesting that the actual stacking of the cargo in the hold was taken over by 1 man. Saltpeter is a heavy cargo; its specific weight is from 2 to 2.2. If one should load a vessel with this in the same manner as, for example, with sacks of grain, only the lowest part of the hold could be filled before the limits of the vessel's capacity would be reached. Also, the weight of the cargo would lie very deep, and in an uneasy sea that is dangerous to the conduct of the vessel. In order to get the point of gravity to lie higher, this kind of cargo is stacked in a pyramid. To be sure, the entire floor of the hold is covered; however, the side walls remain free. That lets the possibility of a new danger arise: the cargo can shift; that is, lose its equilibrium with the rolling of the vessel among swells and shoot to one side, which, under unlucky circumstances, may result in the loss of the whole vessel. Therefore, the stacking of the cargo must be done according to an exactly planned method developed through long years of experience; herein lies the art of the stevedore. He comes on board with 2 helpers, who, at the beginning of taking on the cargo, erect from the first sacks heaved aboard a pile about shoulder-high under the hatchway. On this, they remain standing, and work from this, doing nothing more than place the sacks as they come down on the shoulders of the stacker. Working out from the base under the hatchway, he now lays a flat layer over the entire bottom of the vessel. This has, to be sure, been made ready for business by a "garnishing", a covering of pieces of wood, laths, and mats of rushes or bast, which leaves a space beneath free for the running off of bilge and sweat water, thus keeping the cargo from dampness beneath. Layer by layer, the stacker now places the stacks, bringing each layer a bit farther in from the walls. With each layer, the helpers build up the tower on which they are standing one layer of sacks higher. So grows the pyramid of cargo gradually to the rectangle of the hatchway without the stacker having put even 1 sack into position by hand. As soon as the burden is laid on him, he runs off with it like a weasel. Yes — runs! With little tripping steps, he flits to the farthest corners. A swift jerk of the lean body, and the sack falls into the position that it is to keep for the entire journey — exactly to an inch. With such precision is the drawing in of the sacks at the edges made that at the end the sides of the pyramid are in a completely straight-lined flight from the border walls to the hatchway rim. And so interlocked are the individual sacks with the spaces, so sensitively laid lengthwise and crosswise that the entire giant mound grows into one immovable body. There has no case been known of a saltpeter lading stacked in the manner described and by a trained stevedore having toppled. Even the sky-high seas at Cape Horn could not bring these artful pyramids out of equilibrium.

The weaving of this stack is a kind of inherited monopoly; the father initiates the son, but him only! Outsiders have attempted to break into the circle of this guild — in vain. After a few days, they gave it up, more dead than alive. And the vessel too was cheated. Everything that the bold experimenter had "stacked" had to be taken out again and stacked by a genuine stevedore, in order not to put the vessel in danger. They look so simple, these saltpeter pyramids — but those of Gizeh do too,— right? And yet no one has ever tried to build any like them... Seriously, let us try to be clear for once what sort of a labor such a man performs. For to the loading of a vessel of the size of the barque, PENANG, go about 30,000 or more sacks. If you saw such a man at work, slender, usually under medium height, rather to be described as lean than as lank, then you would wonder what could have piled up all this energy in so unpromising a body. Perhaps the good Chilean red wine that he drank with his fish and beans?

Yet it is understandable that in this kind of cargo-loading, weeks went by before a middle-sized sailer was loaded. And one can imagine that this situation did not much please the ambitious pair in the Laeisz counting house in Hamburg. Finally, what sense was there in record passages around Cape Horn if the racing storm bird had to be transformed every time on the West Coast into a patiently brooding hen? The firm of Laeisz therefore began to build up their own loading and unloading organization on the West Coast. In a few years, the firm could thank a skillful choice of agents and of personnel among the "lancheros" and stackers and the unresting watchfulness and energy of the Laeisz captains for a swiftness in the clearance of their vessels which up to then no one would have thought possible — above all, in a land in which a great many people have sworn allegiance to the belief in putting off every kind of work to a happy tomorrow. The vessels themselves were equipped with "modern" loading machinery, the antediluvian handwinches replaced by "donkeys", little coal-heated, steam-kettle contraptions that also relieved the crew of the trouble of heaving anchor. Later, simple motors came into use for this. It throws a revealing light on the many-sidedness of Captain Hilgendorf that he invented an improved, simplified type of shiploading winch that answered the test splendidly and accelerated the business of loading. Also in other respects, the loading machine was developed. A complicated system of hoisting wires, turning windlasses, and counterweights dancing up and down on cranes excited the astonishment of all the older vessels. In the hands of skilled and trained crews, they made possible the loading in an undreamed-of time. So it came about that the land organization took care of the frictionless delivery of the cargo, whereas at need a beneficent thunderstorm from the lips of a captain accustomed to command hurried up the business in the counting house. And the ship's officers understood how to arouse a high degree of sporting competition — one can call it nothing else — among their own personnel who handled the loading machinery as well as among the unhurried Chilean people. The P-Liners worked like the devil! To outdo another sailer of equal size and likewise saltpeter-laden was a trifle. Naturally now there could no longer by any question of a single stevedore stacking the vessel; rather, it soon became necessary to set 2 men to work in every hold at building the vessel's saltpeter pyramids. And it was not unusual for one of the great 4-masters under the Laeisz flag which had reached her landing place at the beginning of the week to set her sails for the homeward passage on the morning of the following Sunday.

The taking on of the final sack of a saltpeter lading used to be the occasion for a little ceremony, which reached its peak when the captain let "the mizzen sheet be hauled",[14] meaning that every man was to receive a free schnapps from above. This was only the touch-off for the traditional celebration on the evening before the homeward passage. It was solemnized with song and drinking rounds, to which good friends and acquaintances from the crews of other vessels came as guests. A prominent rôle was played by the "cheeren", an antiphonal shouting of toasts from vessel to vessel amid strokes of the great ship's bell in the forecastle. A ceremonial handed down from old times was observed during this, and if the right kind of vessel with the right kind of crew aboard lay at the roads, the evening became a glorious feast of comradeship, filled with the brotherhood of the wide open sea. Lubbock closes his book on *The Nitrate Clippers* with a somewhat sentimental passage in which he says:

"Alas! that the good old West Coast days have passed! When the WILLIAM

[14] ["Spliced the main brace": English version - EDITOR]

MITCHELL, the last square-rigged windjammer belonging to the port of London, loaded a nitrate cargo at Tocopilla in August, 1927, on what proved to be her last voyage, there was not another sailing ship in the anchorage.

"And when her crew, keen as mustard to keep up all the old customs of the sea, went through the ceremony of cheering ship as the last bag was hoisted aboard, not one of the dingy steamers lying around her even took the trouble to ring her bell! ...

"In the days of sail, the sea was a great commonwealth. Sailors, whatever their colour, whatever their nationality, were all dipped in the same tar bucket, ground in the same mould, and tested and proved by those three mighty character makers, wind, sea and canvas.

"They were loyal to their ships because they loved them; and they were artists in their profession, that great profession of sailorising which is now almost defunct.

"Seafaring is now given over to deck sweepers and brass polishers — to men with sweat rags round their necks — to men in overall suits of dungaree, whose hands, ingrained with oil and coal-dust, would make a sad hash of stowing a topsail in a gale of wind.

"And what do they think of British seamen on the West Coast in these troublous days?

"Letters have reached me telling the distressing but unbiased truth. In those very ports where once the British sailorman was considered beyond compare, now he is considered in the C-3 standard of his profession and only the officers and men of the German "P" boats are rated A-1.

"No wonder that so many are agitating for sail training once more under the Red Ensign."

PERSONNEL

Now the times are most likely gone forever when a half dozen or a whole dozen of great sailers under the German flag rode rocking on the rollers of Iquique. Many were the foster-ships she saw, the old West Coast, and many and many of these sailers had crews fully tested to the last man, who dared to shorten sail and to control their vessels when the wildest of the storm devils roared forth around the farthest cape at the end of the world. But always among the best governed vessels with the most capable crews and captains were the sailers from whose mainmast top flew the white flag with the red F L. They were indeed masters in the high school of seamanship of the passage around Cape Horn to the West Coast. It was one of the peculiarities of the age of the sailers that the captain of a sailing vessel often was young with her and grew old with her. From the building, from the keel-laying-on, he knew his vessel to the last plate, the last bolt, and the long, lonely sailing voyages led to a growing together of man and vessel which rarely comes about on the vessels of the machine age. The crew, too, in the hands of the sailing captain meant something other than on the many-horse-powered steamer. The continual common struggle against wind and sea welded officers and crew more closely together, and with good, serviceable people, the length of the passage also worked toward the same end. Not seldom, in spite of the strictness of discipline, there was a truly patriarchal relationship in the best sense of the word. The experienced, weather-worn, bear-sinewed sailor, often a stranger in the world from his birth, saw in his captain not only his superior, but often also the fatherly friend

(Hans DULK)

Capt. Robert HILGENDORF
1852-1937
Master PARNASS, PARSIFAL, PROFESSOR, PIRAT, PERGAMMON, PALMYRA, PLACILLA, PITLOCHRY, And POTOSI: 1883-1901

(1) (J. T. WENDLER)

Capt. Johannes Thomas WENDLER
1878-1953
Master PIRNA And PASSAT: 1907-1914

(2) (Capt. Robert K. MIETHE)

Capt. Paul Edmund OPITZ
1852-1933
Marine Superintendent: 1891-1922. Photo
Taken At Hamburg In 1910

and trustworthy counselor in all the difficult questions which his restless seaman's life brought to him.

The captain of a great sailer must be cut from sound wood, and the great progress of the firm during the years in which Carl Laeisz was its leader rested not least upon the sureness with which he chose his captains. A classic type was Robert Hilgendorf, who, in January 1879, at the age of 27, entered the service of the firm and two years later, in 1881, was promoted to captain. His figure is as much a part of the shipping company of F. Laeisz as that of the senior-chief, Carl Laeisz, and therefore this man may be chosen as a type in the long line of Laeisz captains, among whom not a few may recognize themselves in the personality of Hilgendorf.

Capt. Robert Hilgendorf

Hilgendorf was the most famous not only of all the Laeisz captains, but also of all the commanders of sailing vessels of his time. He was born in 1852 in Stepinitz on the bay of Stettin. Even at 12 years, he managed independently his father's cutter when his father took the field as a soldier against Denmark in the year 1864. At 18, he came to Hamburg and took service on various vessels of the Sloman shipping company. He had a primary school education, and as the child of poor parents, he must earn the money himself before he could enter the school for mates. In his service with the Navy on the corvette, ARCONA, during her 2-year circumnavigation of the globe, he gathered together enough savings to enter the navigation school in Altona. Two years after he had earned his letters patent there as an officer, he took his examination for captain and presented himself to Laeisz. As a Laeisz captain, he commanded 9 vessels in all: PARNASS, PARSIFAL, which he lost off Cape Horn, PROFESSOR, PIRAT, PERGAMON, PALMYRA, PLACILLA, PITLOCHRY; and since 1895, the 5-masted barque, POTOSI, the building of which he had already kept watch over at the Tecklenborg works in Geestemunde.

Hilgendorf was every inch a sailor and a go-getter, who made great demands on his crew, but even greater on himself. Sixty-six times, he sailed around Cape Horn, and on no passage did the rounding of the Cape, from 50° south latitude in the Atlantic to 50° south in the Pacific, take longer than 10 days. Also, he fulfilled an almost impossible wish of Carl Laeisz, namely, to accomplish 2 round voyages between Hamburg and Chile in less than 12 months. As early as the 'eighties, the wildest rumors were circulating among English and Australian seamen who met with the Laeisz vessels in both the Atlantic and the Pacific oceans. They called him "the devil of Hamburg", "the flying German", and in the harbor-taverns of Hamburg, Antwerp, Sydney, Iquique, and Valparaiso, the most fantastic fables were told of him and his voyages.

Hilgendorf seemed born to the seaman's calling. With his disciplined crews and carefully cared-for vessels, he beat even the records of the English tea-clippers, which till then had counted as the swiftest sailing vessels and which, moreover, always carried crews 2 or 3 times more numerous than was possible at the turn of the century. His always firmly upheld principle was "the best of speed in the interests of the firm". Therefore, he held his crews to a strict discipline. Such loose discipline as not seldom appeared among the colorfully assembled sailing crews of that time, he would not tolerate; and drunkenness just as little. "One can never drink too little — but easily too much!" he was accustomed to say. "Hard work, but good food!" became a watchword on his vessels. Because of his unsurpassed performances, Hilgendorf, who was no less just than strict, became the most trusted man in his shipping company. He achieved his masterpiece as a seaman in the year 1888, when he rigged up the PIRAT, almost completely unmasted in a Pamperos squall, which he did for the most part with deck material eked out only by cordage supplied by a passing vessel, and brought her back safely to Hamburg.

In 1901, while the PREUSSEN was still in building, Carl Laeisz died, and Hilgendorf, who resigned from his service with the firm on the death of his chief, was appointed senior navigator by the Hamburg Senate, which means, nautical expert of the Chamber Of Commerce. This honorable call resulted in his complete severance aboard. For 25 years, from his 50th to his 75th year, he discharged the duties of the office, and active to the last, he was able to enjoy another 10 years of well-earned retirement. Shortly before he left the service of the firm, he received the Kaiser as guest aboard the POTOSI, and on his 80th birthday, he received from Wilhelm II, from the house at Doorn, a telegram of greeting and a picture of the Kaiser with friendly words recalling the visit to the POTOSI. Nor did the senior master of German shipping fail of other signal honors during his long life.

Captain Paul E. Opitz

With the building of the Laeisz fleet of deep-sea sailers for the West Coast passage, the name of Paul Edmund Opitz is also associated from the beginning of the 'nineties. He was for 31 years Inspector for this most famous of sailing-ship firms at the turn of the century; and, surprisingly, he was an inlander, born in April, 1852, in Berlin. This boy from the lower sixth form of the Friedrich-Wilhelm Gymnasium transformed himself in July 1869 into a ship's boy. When war broke out in 1870, he reported at once as a volunteer for armed service. After the declaration of peace, he sailed on several vessels, took the test for deep-sea navigator in 1880, and in 1881 entered the service of the firm of F. Laeisz as First Officer. After he had for 10 years commanded various of the firm's vessels and made several passages as supercargo on steamers which the company of F. Laeisz had chartered from the Bremer-Hansa Line, he was appointed inspector for the company. It was the year of the first 4-masters; PLACILLA and PISAGUA were built at Tecklenborg, PERSIMMON and PITLOCHRY were bought in England. Soon the first 5-master joined them, the swift POTOSI. The rapid increase in the firm's tonnage in so short a time brought much work for the man who, as inspector, bore the immediate responsibility to his shipowner for these vessels. Captain Opitz carried this responsibility through 3 decades, and never could any nautical official spot a lack in any of the vessels placed under his inspection. To be sure, that was in the first place due to the service of the captains concerned, but it spoke also of the understanding of the man who had helped determine the selection of these commanders. In the plans for the powerful PREUSSEN, the expert knowledge of Captain Opitz was tested to the utmost. A handsome visible acknowledgement of his services in regard to the successful vessel was the bestowal of the order of the crown. After he had taken an active part in the rebuilding of our merchant marine, the condition of his health compelled him to retire in 1922. To his great satisfaction, it was given him to live to see the restoration of his company. Then, in November, 1933, Captain Paul Opitz started on that great outward passage from which there is no returning.

Capt. J. Hermann Piening

As a still living member of the captains of sailing vessels for the firm of F. Laeisz, we may salute Captain Piening. In his memoirs, he tells how he as a sailor serving on various vessels heard everywhere of the fabulous achievements of the "nitrate clippers" of the firm of F. Laeisz, and how, after passing his mate's examination "with distinction", he succeeded, through Captain Opitz, in becoming Third Officer on the 4-masted barque, PETSCHILI. Also, he passed his test for captain with great success, became First Officer on the 4-masted barque, PINGUIN, had to give

(Capt. Robert K. MIETHE)

Twenty-Four Masters Of The 25 German Vessels Laid Up In Valparaiso, Chile, During World War I
(Read From Left To Right And From Bottom To Top)

	Master	Type	Vessel
Foremost:	P. Jacobsen	Ship	JOHN
	H. Kaiser	Barque	PELIKAN
File 1:	Robert K. Miethe	5m. Barque	POTOSI
	H. Loeser	S.S.	YORK
	- Langerhaus	S.S.	SANTA RITA
	- Nauss	S.S.	GOETTINGEN
	W. Olthaus	4m. Barque	J. C. VINNEN
	G. Ahlers	Barque	OBOTRITA
	Hans J. Ravn	4m. Barque	POMMERN
File 2:	- Von Zwirrlein	S.S.	WESTPHALEN
	K. Petersen	S.S.	TANIS
	J. Hoehs	S.S.	SAIS
	- Hillmann	S.S.	GOTHA
	A. Oetzmann	4m. Barque	PEKING
	Heinrich A. G. Oellerich	Ship	PINNAS
	C. Willenburg	4m. Barque	CHRISTEL VINNEN
	H. Merkens	4m. Barque	ISEBECK
File 3:	Alex Teschner	4m. Barque	PETSCHILI
	H. Oellerich	Ship	OLIVA
	Niklaus Bohn	S.S.	SANTA INES
	Ad. Wienecke	Ship	WOGLINDE
	- Kagelmacher	S.S.	NEGADA
	- Freese	S.S.	RIOL
	Martin Looks	Ship	ALBERTUS VINNEN

The Captain Of The 15th Sailing Vessel Laid Up In Valparaiso, H. Kähler Of The Ship CLAUS, Is Missing In The Photograph.

(F. LAEISZ)

Capt. J. Hermann PIENING
1888-
Master Of PEKING, PADUA, And PUMA Between 1926-1936

(F. LAEISZ)

Steel 4-Masted Barque PEKING, 3,100 Gross Tons

(1) (Dr. Charles A. MARSH)

Cape Horn

(2) (Capt. J. Ferrell COLTON)

Cape Horn Seas
PASSAT: 21, March, 1936
These Seas Measured 60 Feet By Sextant Angle, Were 1 1/4 Miles From Crest To Crest, And The Breaking Crests Were 12 Feet In Depth

up this position at the outbreak of the World War, and in this career got as far as Naval Lieutenant for the Reserves, advanced to a U-boat watch officer, and was cited with the E.K.2 and the E.K.1. After the lost war, there came for Germany, and particularly for the people of the sea, a comfortless time. Captain Piening had to manage in other ways for several years; in 1926, however, he was able to return to his old company and to merchant shipping. In 1930, he gave up "Christian seafaring" — that is, the command of a sailing vessel — and took over the command of the newly built Laeisz banana steamer, the PUMA. With this, we have already arrived at a post-war undertaking of the firm, the "African Fruit Company", of which we shall speak later in more detail. In 1936, Captain Piening was in the inspection department of the firm, and at the outbreak of the Second World War, was called as a reserve officer into the "Gray Steamship Company", as the war navy was known in Hamburg. Captain Fred Schmidt in his book, *Captains Report,* now in the press of Dietrich Reimer in Berlin, has included a lively description of the West Coast passage, which was written by Captain J. Hermann Piening. May we quote it in full?

Chapter Two: UNDER PYRAMIDS OF SAILS TO THE WEST COAST OF SOUTH AMERICA

Capt. Piening Describes A West Coast Passage Under Sail

"When a great sailer gets ready for its voyage, the whole harbor takes notice. It is an interesting picture. Singing, the crew hauls the silver-gray giant sausages in a long chain out of the sail locker, the treasure-chest of the windjammer. Singing, they draw through the gantlines by which the sails are to be hoisted. Like young martins, the seamen chatter in the rigging; orders ring out; the rhythmic, half-exulting, half-sobbing 'singing out' of the crew of a great sailer echoes far over the harbor. One mast competes with another, and in 2 days, the 33 various sails of our PEKING are sitting up there where they belong. And among them are some trifles nearly 98½ feet broad and 33 feet high, house walls of heaviest linen hemmed around with bolt-rope, bordered with steel wire, and further strengthened with leather and pieces of chain. But whoever finds no joy in laying hold, after all he does not belong on a sailer! And every important hand-hold is tested by experienced officers. For on the thoroughness with which a single piece of line is set, men's lives and the safety of the entire vessel may hang in the moment of danger.

"Among the lighters from which the last of the loading will be taken are long boats with provisions and materials for the passage. Thirty young fellows with good appetites need a mountain of flour and rice, beans and peas, potatoes, vegetables, and a hundred other edible things that would make a housewife's hair stand on end; and our PEKING, during such a voyage, has also all sorts of needs for her wardrobe. Dozens of rolls of new sailcloth come aboard, an endless series of bundles of cordage, barrels and metal containers of tar and petroleum, cement and red lead, paint and tallow. Hand tools are replaced. A water boat lies alongside with pounding pumps, and fills our freshwater tanks full for the passage.

"When everything in the rigging is complete, then, as usual, I make the inspection tour with my First. For Marienbad regular customers, this would be nothing, but our officers certainly have no need of a reducing treatment. Their service keeps them in 'fasson' (good shape). We investigate to the last detail, mast by mast, yard by yard, feel out shackles and grappling irons, shake the lines and riders. Many long years on such giant sailers have sharpened our eyes for quality of work and material. And when we return from this sky-tour to the deck again without having found anything wrong, then one can go out to sea under this rigging in full confidence! All is in order. Meanwhile, on deck, hatchways have been closed. Now the First sits down and writes in his log:

"'The cargo has been stacked by professional stackers according to nautical custom and under the oversight of the officers; all preparations for the safety of the cargo have been made, dunnage and matting laid wherever needed. The hatches are covered threefold with good tarpaulins, caulked and lashed down. The pumps and the conduits to tanks and bilges have been overhauled and found in order. Drinking water, provisions, and materials are on board in sufficient quantities for the coming passage. The medical stores have been checked, and what was lacking supplied according to the latest prescriptions. Compasses, barometers, and thermometers have been checked and certified. Lifeboats, life preservers, and pneumatic vests have been inspected and found in order. The living quarters have been inspected by the health authorities and found good.

The vessel is in good condition in all her parts, thoroughly equipped and manned, therefore in every respect seaworthy for the coming passage. The crew is all on board.'

"This entry must be made before the beginning of every passage. It is really of great importance, and, poetic as always, the mariner calls it 'the maiden's prayer'.

"PEKING is clear for the sea. The passage can begin.

"The pilot and the tug are here punctually; our lines and cable are freed from the bollards, the tug takes the hawser on his hook, and slowly the PEKING glides out of the basin of the sailers' harbor into the Elbe. Across from the St. Paul landing bridges, our Dutchmen give the Hamburger girls their 3 hurrahs. Here the SEEFALKE waits for us, the most powerful tug and life-steam-boat of Germany. Behind her smoking stacks, we steer out from the Elbe. A cloud of screaming gulls hangs over our wake.

"The entire crew is still busy on deck. The running gear is set in order, for, with the favorable southeast wind, I wish to raise the first sails as soon as the channel becomes a little broader. From all the passing steamers, comrades and pilots wave to us. A great 4-master has become a rare sight today, and they know that we have something more ahead of us than the crews of the 'smoke-ewers' who are heading out to sea with us!

"A sharp pfiff, followed by the command of the First: 'Every man to the forward deck!' The watches are to be assigned. From the great crowd, the First and Second now choose their men alternately. According to old tradition, the First commands the port watch. The men now rapidly settle their belongings and their bedding in the quarters that for at least 8 months will be their home. With the watch on board and the pilot, the natural subject of conversation on a sailing vessel has already made its appearance: the weather. Much derided theme for the embarrassed land-dweller, hundred-times mocked dance-hour conversation piece of tender youth,—here, under the towering pyramids of sails, it becomes the theme that rules all our thoughts, that must rule them. How are the clouds moving? What is the atmosphere bringing? What is the wind doing? No sort of steam pressure can help us. The necessary horse-power for our passage must be supplied by the wind and our strong arms. And the problem of the sailing vessel's commander lies in so laying his route that he shall always have wind — not too much, but also not too little, and always favorable.

"Centuries of experience by our predecessors and teachers come to the aid of the knowledge we have assembled in our own seafaring time. And today, modern technique also offers us help. We have the wireless on board and receive the weather news from the great meteorological institutions. But here an explanatory word may be needed.

"The weather maps and reports which are given out daily by the German Maritime Observatory and similar foreign institutions do, it is true, offer a reliable picture of temperatures, air pressures, and wind directions. At first glance it must be clear that the correctness of these news items must depend on the accuracy of the available observation material. In all civilized countries, observations are taken several times a day in many hundreds of weather stations. All these notices together give the central station an exact, comprehensive picture of pressures and wind directions over all the observed territory, so that it may draw from them corresponding conclusions. The probability of a weather forecast depends, as we see, in great measure on the density of the network of the observation stations.

"It is easy to realize from what has just been said what difficulties stand in the way of weather prophesying for the ocean. For the benefit of the much-traveled portions of the world-ocean, such as the North Atlantic and the Mediterranean, there are, in the officers of the numerous steamers to be found there, a little army of willing co-workers at the disposal of the meteorological institutions, whose conscientiousness has often been proved. But what about the portions of the ocean that are seldom traveled? Immeasurable stretches of our world-ocean lie even today in primitive solitude; weeks go be before a vessel passes there. If in these regions foul weather and storms are brewing, no notice from the weather stations warns of the approaching shift in weather. Therefore, it can happen that bad storms break on coasts whose inhabitants could become aware of the approaching storm only by the same means as their forefathers used centuries ago: from the appearance of the heavens, the dimming of the sunlight, the clouds and rising wind, and oftentimes too from the behavior of the animal kingdom. Thus the much prized achievements of modern technical science cannot always serve to warn us. If a storm comes out of a region in which there are no stations, no vessels, and therefore no observers, then against this storm the entire modern weather service is doomed to complete inefficiency.

"So long as we keep our vessel in much-traveled waters, we are in the position to make a right clear picture of the strength and direction of wind in the region ahead of us through the weather reports that come to us regularly over the wireless. Once outside of the net of the regular weather observation stations, we under our masts stand dependent on almost the same aids to weather-knowledge as Columbus and his time were dependent on. That is, in the main, an open eye, the gift of observing, a modest but sound human understanding, and — a good weather-trained nose.

"Steadily the SEEFALKE ploughs down the Elbe. Ever wider stretches the stream; the waving people ashore have become marionettes, their shouts no longer reach us. The wind has freshened; for 2 days it has blown unchangingly from the east. Here, we already have more space; the active traffic of vessels is no longer shut up in a narrow runway. Here we can venture to spread the first sails on our great seabird. My First has been waiting for the order; shrilly his whistle sweeps the deck: 'All lower topsails free!' Far over the river echoes the singing out of our men as they make the sheets taut. The heavy chains rattle against the steel masts until they roll out like temple drums.

"Now even the pilot seems to have got the taste of it. 'If you would like to spread the topsails too, Captain Piening, I will have nothing to say against it.' I know how you feel, you old sailor heart! Even if you have found fault with the old windjammers a hundred times, if a thousand times you have sung the praises of modern steamship travel, now, under the heaven-reaching tops of the PEKING, the memory of your youthful years grips you hard, and under your gray hair, you cannot let slip the opportunity of hearing once again the singing and whistling of the breeze in the wind-swollen sails above you, the music that none forgets who has ever been privileged to hear it. For who knows whether you will ever have the chance to hear it again! The great square-riggers, they have unfortunately grown so few.

"On seesaws of shrouds, the gymnasts climb upward. The topsails rustle in great folds from the yards. When, hoisted, they offer their house-high surfaces to the wind, our tow-rope to the SEEFALKE is no longer so tight, and the black smoke clouds from the towboat's chimney show that she has to get her steam up if she is to hold the line taut. I am keeping the towboat now only in case of unforeseen incidents in the narrow channel in order to have her assistance in case of the need for a sudden turn or evasion. But as Elbe I comes into sight ahead,

I order the signal given for letting go; soon after, the pilot climbs into the motorboat that calls for him from the lightship. With the last handshake, he gets also a bundle of letters, farewells to our folks at home. One more waving to this side and that; then the last bond is broken that tied us still to the homeland. The seabird draws out free into the unending space that is her home.

"Attentive study of the weather notices has shown that over southern England and the St. George Channel, the heart of a widespread deep-pressure zone has settled in solidly. In order to estimate the significance of this condition for a sailer, one must know that with us in the north latitudes, the wind blows in counter-clockwise spirals in a low-pressure area. This means that east wind is dominant north of the low; south of it, west wind. And whereas on the east of a low-pressure area, the wind blows from the south, one must reckon with north wind west of the low. Besides this, it is well to remember that in our latitudes, these low-pressure spirals mostly wander from the west toward the east Only very special circumstances can bring it about that such a low remains stationary for several days.

"It seemed as if I had the situation described ahead of me. Therefore if I sailed through the Channel as usual, I must be prepared to meet an opposing wind all the way. And for a great sailer, that is particularly unpleasant in that much-traveled narrow way. Yet west of Ireland, the reported pressure distribution must cause fresh northern winds; whereas in the North Sea, south to southeastern winds could be expected. For a sailer, the weather situation always decides the choice of routes. The detour around the north point of Scotland, senseless for a steamer, is often justified for a sailer. Two vessels have been known to leave the mouth of the Elbe at the same time, one of which took the route through the Channel, the other the detour around Scotland. Both were southbound, and it developed that the northward-starting sailer was already swimming far out on the Atlantic while her rival with unspeakable difficulty was still boxing a stiff west wind in the Channel.

"Deciding quickly, I gave orders to steer with square-braced yards for the course around the northern tip of Scotland. Under the pressure of her 30 sails, the PEKING rushed north at 12 knots.

"Yet a few hours later, I received reports which made it evident that the great England low seemed to have split up into several centers. That means that one can no longer reckon on the simple system of winds described above. Under these conditions, the winds blow unsettled until the ground-plan of a new steady weather condition has crystallized. Changeable winds — that may well mean it is blowing toward us now, yet one may just as likely count on favorable winds. And if one gets a bit of luck, then he will get much wind from aft and only a little from before—maybe even none at all. And a navigator who will not take a chance for once, he is hardly worth his salt.

"'Brace starboard! Brace to starboard!' Slowly swing the tower-high planes of our topsails; simultaneously I change the course to southward. Delicate dazzling white threads high in the air which are moving from north to south convince me that I am on the right track. And in fact — after an hour, the wind, until now from the east, begins to turn into the north. To be sure, we lie later for a few hours in the Hoofde, the southern part of the North Sea between Holland and England, in weak, changeable winds. But then it comes through, the longed-for northeast wind, which we need for a quick passage through the Channel.

"Nothing is more hideous to the deep-sea navigator that to made his way through the Lord's most traveled ditch without any wind, or perhaps even caught by a counter-wind. That means tacking every hour. And if it is stormy besides, it means wearing, which involves 3 times the work, not to mention a heavy loss of time on the much criss-crossed pathway. Here in the Channel, deep-sea sailers have had to tack against an opposing storm for weeks. Every mariner has memories of a peculiarly unpleasant kind connected with this highway. All the more agreeable is the surprise when, with a favorable wind, in clear air, one can slip through the narrows past Dover under full sail, as we did on this passage.

"We pass the sandy point of Dungeness. The high chalk-cliffs of Beachy Head fade out in the twilight of a winter evening. In rapid flight, we pass many a small, heavily laden steamer that steered west with us. Laughing, our crew toss rope-ends to the steaming competition. If they wish, they can hang on behind.

"But God does not let trees grow in the sky. Not half a day later, the wind had so far died down that we were creeping at scarcely 3 knots an hour toward the exit of the Channel. And along with that, Heaven sent us a program number especially welcome and dear to the navigator: it grew foggy. Far and near around us, buzzed the whistles of the steamers. — Now they were in luck; they did not have to worry about every troublesome wind.

"And more than that, we were obliged to hope, with beating hearts, that the giant grayhounds would make way for us in time. Not all nations train their ship's officers on sailers, as we do in Germany. On many a great mail steamer, there are men on the bridge who have never stepped foot on a sailing vessel. Naturally, they can have no idea of the swiftness or of the peculiarities of maneuvering of the sailer that crosses their path. Fatal collisions which cost the lives of many men can be traced back to this incompleteness of training of the officers of certain other lands. If, then, the position lights of a steamer appear suddenly before us and it is clear that in all probability she is going to ram us, then often there is only 1 means of warning left to us. We light blue flares, run to the forecastle with them and light up the high surfaces of the sails with the glaring magnesium lights. The suddenly flaming brilliant glare has in many cases in the last unwary second drawn the attention of the steamer's officers, ignorant of the ways of sailing vessels.

"Fortunately the next morning sees the PEKING already outside the main-traveled route of the steamers. The favorable east wind has set in again; the barometer begins to fall steadily. An old rule goes: — If you would find the center of a low-pressure area, place yourself with your back to the wind, and, in the north latitude, you have the low 6 points ahead to port, in the south latitude 6 points to starboard. Besides that, the obvious consideration holds: if the glass falls, then you are approaching the low or the low is approaching you; if the barometer rises, the reverse is true.

"The rules, applied to our case, meant that in all probability a low must lie west of Finisterre, the north tip of Spain. Therefore, if I bent too soon to the south, I must run head-on into a southeast and later into a southern wind. The only thing reasonable in this situation was to sail north around the low and then to use the northern wind west of the low to hold south.

"It was carried out as planned. And the fresh east wind and, farther west, a stiff north wind confirmed the correctness of my deliberations.

"The air became warmer. Already we had sighted the schools of dolphins and porpoises. The crew had not been idle. First they had got out of the way the sailor's greatest abomination. With water and sand, with scrubbers and brooms, the traces of dirt and rust accumulated during the stay in port were washed away. Painfully clean lay the decks; once more, all the brass plate shone bright in the sun. Now the First began a systematic check of the rigging. As on every vessel, he is responsible for the condition of our little floating world. Under his direction, the seamen on their watches carry out all the necessary repairs and renewals. New braces, new buntlines and clew lines are cut, shrouds, backstays, horses and riders are tested for their firmness. And whoever may believe that the crew of a sailer has nothing to do en route but to change the set of the sails according to the wind, he is fundamentally wrong. Hardly any other child of man is so busy at so many things as the deep-sea sailorman! In the early morning around 6, the watch on duty begins the washing of the deck. From that moment on, until 6 in the afternoon, whichever half of the crew is on watch is continually at work, which is interrupted only when wind and weather demand work in the rigging like the setting or furling of sails or the bracing of the yards. At night, nothing is done except to service the rigging. Before the first World War, it was customary that in the daytime the free watch, too, was called upon for 2 hours of work on deck. Every older seaman still remembers well enough what '10 and 3' means. But this custom was given up shortly before 1914. Now only in special circumstances is the free watch ordered to help the deck watch in tasks that require the entire crew, — for example, to take in the great sail or to draw the hawsers taut.

"Yet I can say one thing with a clear conscience concerning the admittedly hard work of the men on the great sailers: I have never in my long years of service, seen one that was injured by it. But many dozens of young men came aboard to me pale and thin who 2 or 3 years later went away broad-shouldered and tanned, the firm bones packed with muscles, like young athletes. And I am convinced that my comrades could tell of the same experiences.

"Certainly there have been accidents, bad accidents even. The number of fallen comrades is not small. They fell in sacrificial loyalty to a great and important task, and we hold their memory in honor. But to condemn the sailing business for this is unreasonable. Every calling requires its sacrifices, and how many men close their eyes in the course of a year whose life was spent solely in the service of an industry which perhaps served only luxury? Yet if one considers the many hundreds of young men who on our great sailers grew to sound, fearless manhood, to a view of life always ready for sacrifice, then he will justify me in saying that the sacrifices in the sailing profession have not been made in vain.

"The great oceans of our planet are the playgrounds of powerful wind-systems. Near the Equator, the air is intensely heated by the sun's rays. This girdle of heated, disturbed masses of air is marked by low air pressure. Just as people who live crowded thickly together throng to uninhabited places, so from the regions of higher air pressure north and south of the Line, the air-masses move in a far-spread broad front toward the equator, in order to equalize the differences in pressure in the atmosphere. Following eternal laws, these air currents are turned aside by the revolution of the earth, in northern latitudes to the right, in southern to the left. So it comes about that north of the Line, year in, year out, the northwest trade wind blows, and south of the Equator the southeast trade wind shows his mirrored image.

"Trade wind! Paradise of the sailing vessel. For weeks, the stem furrows a gently moving, deep blue sea. Mild the air and spicy as old wine. Over the deep blue heaven, sail snow-white cloud-puffs like the ships of a heavenly argonaut. Trade wind weather — too lovely to be caught in words! Scarce can even the mastery of a great marine painter give back this splendor.

"The passing over into this realm is celebrated on board with a special festival. Namely, all the sails are changed.

"You say, 'But that is work'? Yes, there have been vessels on which that was a task. Vessels on which ill temper and incompatibility ruled, and one could hardly say which side was to blame, the officers behind or the men before the mast. Probably both...

"But on a deep-sea sailer where the right spirit reigned, where, to be sure, no one talked about comradeship, but everyone lived in comradeship, there sail-shifting was a festival! A sports festival, if you will. It began very early. Instead of starting the day with buckets and brooms, the watch began by bringing up the gantlines, endlessly long manila ropes which were reeved through a block high up on the mast. Starting with the royals, sail after sail was exchanged. It is a kind of third-best costume which the vessel puts on. Faded, weathered old sails, often cobbled and patched, that is the Trade Wind costume, that is sufficient to carry the vessel through the ever-laughing fair-weather region. And in the gayest of moods was the vessel dressed in this costume by the regular sail crew. The whole day through, the shouting and singing echoed between the high canvas walls. Jests and ribbing flew back and forth. They would hardly have been fitting in a girls' boarding school, I fear. Perhaps they were not always fitting in those surroundings. But they showed that these young tanned sinewy fellows who were tumbling around on the yards and shrouds, looked upon their really hard and often dangerous task not as a task, but as a sport, even if they did not call it that. For many of them were hardly familiar with the word, 'sport'. For all that, they could have posed as models for a sports group for any sculptor.

"And often during this sail-changing, they cursed like Turks. But how they intended it was shown by the way their eyes danced whenever one watch in changing their sail on their topmast came within a nose length of striking the other. Ask any seaman what were the days which stand out for him as the essence of all the beauty and all the freedom of the sea. Like one man, they will all answer you: Those were the days in the trade winds.

"But, like everything beautiful, this time too must come to an end. Slowly, but steadily, the barometer level has gone down. The white puffs of the trade wind clouds have been growing larger for days, their dazzling white rims are faded, and great gray fields cover the blue of the heavens. Already scattered rain showers are moving over the ocean. The air is oppressively hot and sultry. It is noticeable that we are coming nearer to the belt of weak winds and calms which lies between the two regions of trade winds and which we call the doldrums.

"With the approach to the doldrums, the trade winds drop off more and more. The sky shows only a few remaining holes in the clouds, and rain falls frequently. You are not to think that we are dealing here with a domain of absolute lack of wind. That seldom exists, for even slight variations in pressure must always result in movements of air. But the wind is uncertain and faint here. And the navigator who is not continually ready to make use of even the lightest breath for the furthering of his passage can spend weeks in this uncomfortable hothouse. But I have yet to see the captain who in the doldrums does not go after every scrap of breeze like lively Satan after a poor soul! For the sailors, there is no rest. There are watches in which they hardly get off the shrouds for 10 minutes. And what these Johnny-Goodfellows have found here in the way of flowery, strong speech goes far beyond all that our pseudo-writers are capable of with their eternally stupid 'Oddzooks! Foresails and topgallant shrouds!'

"There is only one pleasant thing about this region: it rains frequently. Indeed, it rains as it can rain only in the tropics. In a compact mass, the water falls from the blue-gray sky. On those days everything aboard revels in soap and water, for the freshwater store of a sailer is limited and the duration of the passage highly uncertain. Especially when the first rainfalls come, madness seizes everyone. Clad only in a cake of soap, the whole crew leaps around on the deck and lets itself be washed clean by the luke-warm ablution. Filled with envy, the steersman looks at the laughing foam-snowmen into which his comrades have transformed themselves. After the bath, everyone pulls out whatever he can wash and lets the sea-salt get rinsed out thoroughly for once. The heavy lightning flashes in this region present a splendid show. All night, the heavens flame copper-red and sulphur-yellow, and hardly for a second is the vessel surrounded by complete darkness.

"Sailing through this region makes special demands on the skill of the navigator. To a high degree, it depends on his knowledge and his experience how long the passage will be delayed here. Like a wedge, the belt of calms lies diagonally across the Atlantic, the broad end on the African coast, growing narrower toward the west. Southward from here, one can look forward to the southeast trade wind, a steady wind which he uses gladly to get a good long stretch ahead. Now, naturally, a sailer can steer against the wind, 'sail by the wind', only up to a certain angle. If the yards are braced hard to starboard, then I can lie with my vessel so that the wind comes in from port perhaps 20-25 degrees more ahead than across. That is called veering to port. No one knows whether the southeast trade will blow more 'raum', that is more from behind, or more 'schral', more from ahead, from the south. The farther toward the east I penetrate the calm belt, the less the probability that a head-on southeast trade will force me against the Brazilian coast near Cape San Roque or even north of there.

"That is a skill born of experience, for a sailer caught in near the coast so far north must tack laboriously against the southeast trades, until she is able to hold south free of the land. Meanwhile a powerful ocean current makes her tacking difficult. This is the Guiana current, which, parallel to the coast of northern Brazil, sets to the northwest. On the other hand, the farther east I cross the doldrums, the longer I must sail with weak winds and calms, for here this disagreeable low-pressure belt is at its broadest. And besides all this, something more is added: the doldrums do not remain stationary. Seasonally, oscillating north and south, they vary continually their position and extent. You can see from this that a good portion of knowledge and experience is required to negotiate a successful navigation of the belt of calms. Also something of luck, of which the navigator can never have too much.

It is like coming out of a hothouse into mild, breezy summer air when one sails out of the sullen doldrums into the golden clear trades. When the rain-heavy zone is conquered and over the topmasts the thick cotton tufts of the trade-wind clouds are flying, everything breathes again. Navigation is easy in the southeast trade-winds. Braced to port, the topsails keep their position for days. And if, when noon comes, a navigator learns from his astronomical observations that he has made 200 or 250 nautical miles in a day, he feels at home and at peace with God and the world.

"Parallel to the coast of the South American mainland, PEKING ploughs toward the southwest. More often than before, the First Officer himself stands in the rigging. We are approaching the neighborhood of the mouth of La Plata. How long now before the first bad weather will be blowing about our ears? By that time, everything must be fast against wind and weather. If a man does the sort of work expected of him up there, then he must have a feeling of certainty that wherever his hand seeks a hold, it shall find a secure grip, and where his foot may need a support, all will prove firm and reliable.

"The days fly past. Soon the trade wind begins to blow less steadily. The time has come for the fair-weather sails to disappear again. Once more, sail after sail comes flapping down. But this time what the men are getting out of the sail lockers on the deck brings out heavy sweat on their foreheads. These are the best sails that the vessel has. Unyielding, the canvas, and heavy as leather; stiff and stubborn, the thick steel cables. None of them has been much used; some are nearly new. There is capital invested in these sails. And if now and then someone asserts that a sailer must make astonishing profits, since she requires neither coal nor oil and the Lord God lets the wind blow tax-free, this opinion rises from a lack of knowledge of facts. A complete set of sails for a vessel like our PEKING costs around 33,000 marks. And let no one believe that sails last forever, even when they are not torn to bits by the wind. It is the great, and correspondingly costly, sails that must suffer most in the worst weather. And if our old sailmaker looks with a certain pride on the treasure in his sail chest, where are stored about 3 complete sets of sails, he is completely justified. Under his protection is greater wealth than is to be found in many a branch bank.

"The region around the mouth of La Plata again presents the navigator with serious problems. In winter as in summer, storms can break here which burst suddenly and are feared because of their might. The contrast between the warm Brazilian air and the cold air-masses from the south, as well as the difference in level between the wide pampas and the Cordilleras, creates in the Argentinian plains low pressure spirals which rush eastward with irresistible force into the South Atlantic over the La Plata delta. They are called 'pamperos' from their origin. The only warning of their approach is often the appearance of a heavy bank of cloud. It looks like a giant sausage; the ends are thinner and hang down like a Mongolian's moustache. They come on in mad haste. Air and ocean take on a threatening appearance, yet only a faint breeze keeps blowing, and the sea is quiet. But woe to the vessel whose commander does not know this sign, who does not furl all upper sails and the heavy lower sails in time. At the instant in which the approaching cloud bank has covered half the sky, the storm breaks loose, often with unpredictable power. Even the first squall has cost many a vessel her life.

"While passing through this realm, the navigator observes with increased watchfulness and distrust all unfavorable weather signs. Nevertheless, once south of the mouth of La Plata, the peaceful life in the trade winds is over. A drafty region is this down below! For the most part the wind blows from western directions, a fresh wind, stiff to stormy breezes, letting one make good headway. But storms also are no rarity, and this is the more true, the farther south one pushes.

"The passing of the 50th degree of latitude, we Germans reckon as the entrance into the region of Cape Horn, in contradistinction to our English comrades, who count in all that lies south of 40°. Fifty degrees south latitude corresponds to the latitude of Mainz on the north half of our earth. But the southern hemisphere is land-poor. Immeasurably the world oceans stretch out, and at about 56 degrees southern latitude, one could sail around the earth without ever being stopped by land. This fact has an important result for shipping. The sea-swell, which in these latitudes is mostly built up by west winds, can roll unhindered to the east. Nothing impedes its course. Thus when one of the heavy storms breeds in the southern Pacific, it drives before it a sea such as can be found in no other part of our earth.

"Moreover, there often lies in the region of Cape Horn a realm of low air pressure. If one will picture in his mind what I said at the beginning of my discussion on the direction of wind in low pressure areas, he can easily understand why off Cape Horn one so often meets with western winds. For here in southern latitudes, the air spirals clockwise into the center of the low. The navigator must plot his course according to this and stand far out on the westward passage in order to take advantage of the easterly return wind south of the low.

"That sounds simple enough. Yet even today, low pressure whirlwinds unfortunately still have the unpleasant habit of behaving with mighty little regard to meteorological theorems and the dogmas of learned folios. Moreover, what I said about the value of weather reports is true in the highest degree here in this sea down under. Here we are in a section of our earth in which, throughout millions of square miles, we have not one miserable little weather station. So what should a weather prognosis have to go on here? In spite of our picturesque, fully modern coast wireless station, we stand before the weather processes of the southern ocean with the same weapons that Magellan was familiar with. Namely: keep your eyes as wide open as you can, and if you have a nose, a seaman's nose, you will smell the wind in time. If you cannot do this, then hands off! — you will never make a good Cape Horn circumnavigation. Then it can come to pass that you may never come back home again, and neither will those with you.

"The region down there by the last cape is unique. If a north wind is blowing, and all the signs of heaven point to its remaining steady, then one passes around Cape Horn through a special gateway, choosing the course through the straits of Le Maire. This is a 12-14 mile wide sound between the eastern tip of Tierra del Fuego and Staten Island. The passage is considered risky — and it is.

"Now you may ask in surprise: what can be risky about sailing through a strait 12 miles wide? Naturally, it sounds a bit ridiculous. One cannot really understand what a LeMaire passage actually means until he has sailed through it himself. Under full sail, we are holding before a stiff north wind toward the south. Like a small dark-blue cloud, something rises to starboard out of the gray sea. Whoever does not know how land looks from a distance would not recognize Cape San Diego until it had shoved itself up higher above the water. Then land comes into sight on the port side also. First it is a low blue streak, but an hour later one can recognize through the glass the most comfortless shore he can imagine. Steep cones of rock, naked to the mercy of God, rise from a cleft foreground. It looks as if a giant's child had shaken out his building blocks, so wildly do the blocks and squares tower above one another, the archetype of the island, Thule. Now, to the starboard, blue mountain ridges rise above the Cape. Before our prow, between the 2 land's-ends, the gateway opens through which we are to pass.

"From a study of the sailors' handbooks, one knows that the current in the straits has a speed of 2-6 knots. But what this current can do to the southward steering vessel, of that one first becomes aware on steering into the strait. This mighty swell of waters, which giant forces press through the gate between Tierra del Fuego and the island, this crowding together of millions and more millions of tons of water, creates a sharp piling up of backwater, and what the sailor calls a 'stronkabbelung' (water devouring the shore). As I said, one sails into the strait only under favoring winds, and this northerly wind obviously drives its own sea rollers ahead of it. In the narrows now flares up a conflict between the northward striving current and the opposite running swell, which at times has something uncanny about it. The sea is mightily stirred. But that is no ordinary ocean swell, rolling on and wandering, such as one is accustomed to see. These waves rush up perpendicularly, as if cast up by an invisible power, and fall to ruin again on the same spot.

"Simultaneously with the entrance into the narrows, one becomes aware of an uncanny seizure by the current. The rocking and heaving of the vessel in the billows, that gentlest of all rhythmic motions that are, ceases suddenly. The vessel no longer rolls, she does not pitch — but she moves nevertheless. Hard stand the sails before the north wind; full south we steer into the straits. But if we check the course of the vessel by the compass bearings, we soon realize how, seized by hidden forces, she is hauled now to one side, now backward. In a flash, the reports of the many strandings in this passage come before our eyes. To be sure, vessels have been stranded in every strait of the sea, but those who remained in these narrows are counted by many dozens. It is only 16 sea-miles that we must push on to the south, but the hours in the narrows lengthen themselves unnaturally. To be sure, the log on the afterdeck shows 10 knots an hour, yet after 3 hours one still sees land on both sides. No wonder that the old seamen gave to the southern doorpost on the Tierra del Fuego side the name, Cap Buen Successo, the Cape of Good Success. We take it with us on our way as a favorable omen for the circumnavigation of the Cape.

"As soon as the vessel has got out into free water, a large swell seizes her. It rolls up from the southwest, a sign that in the neighborhood of the Horn, this time too, the obliging north wind waits. Farther on toward the south plows the PEKING. Suddenly the north wind begins to turn into the west. Good that we are out of the narrows! With every hour that we press southward, the swell grows longer and higher. Like boxers, our 164-ft. masts swing back and forth. A glance at the barometer shows a rapid lowering of the air pressure. It would be better that I should furl the topsails now for the night. It does not look good in the southwest; also the steadily increasing swell gives me something to think about.

"Quick and threatening, night breaks. Before another hour has been lost to the furling of the lower topsails, I must have the free watch called back on deck. In this weather, both watches are needed, to take away 2 of the heavy upper topsails and to reef the great sails and the crossjacks. The night is growing heavy, but it is not in vain that the PEKING carries all-steel rigging from deck to flag to truck. Hard though it blows, the wind is favorable. Sailing is our job; we have a long way yet before us and must hold forward. Also something can confidently be expected of a vessel like this.

"A whole hellish concert roars in the rigging. Rushing come the seas over the port rail, strike the deck threateningly, wash in a fury around hatches and capstans, and run off gurgling through the wash ports. When the wind squalls hit, our vessel hauls farther over to leeward and buries our bulwarks deep under the waters that rush by, foaming. A broader stripe of spray shimmers blue-green in the inky darkness of the night. Then the storm again lets in a little air; the vessel rights herself and rushes on farther to the south. For 'down under to the south' must for a time be our watchword. Although it will be colder down there in the neighborhood of the eternal ice, nevertheless I must try to find, on the south side of the storm's center, the east wind that will then carry us to the west around the Cape of storms.

"When morning dawns, many of our ship's boys look a little anxious. In an endless procession, the glassy gray-blue mountains are marching from the west. From their summits blow flapping manes of blinding spray, which the storm tears to shreds. The black-gray clouds are balled deep. A universal roaring fills the air, that seems to stop the ears as if with sand. No one can make himself understood except by shouting full-strength into another's ear. When the squalls strike, a man must turn his head away in order to be able to breathe at all. The excessive pressure of the madly rushing air forces itself through mouth and nose into the body, blows up the lungs until they are no longer in condition to breathe out. At times rain and hail showers come down; then a strange hissing and singing mingles with the roaring of the storm. The air is gray with flying water and opaque as milk glass.

"Doubled up against a clew in the lee of the chart house stands the watch, or behind the awning of strong canvas which is attached to the weather side of the great mast. Most of them are young, hardly 20 or slightly over. Two 16-year-olds and a lubber of 15 are among them. And it is good that they are here. On this vessel, down here at the end of the world, here is the right school for them. Here they are learning that Greek vowels and history of literature, that boarding school polish and papa's bank account are not everything in the life of a man. Here they are learning that the Lord God gave man 2 hands to lay hold with and 2 legs to keep his place with. And here they are learning that he received along with these a skull so solid that it does not need to go to pieces with every buffet. And when they haul on the ropes and braces and when they lie shoulder to shoulder on the yards to tear a sail out of the teeth of a storm, then they learn the most important lesson that the young man has to learn, namely, that he is not all alone, that when worse comes to worst, the individual can put a thing through only when true comrades are standing by his side. And that even the apparently impossible can be accomplished if only a group of determined and fearless fellows set their firm wills to achieve it.

"Often when I see my boys on deck in oilskins and southwesters, I have to remember my own youthful years, the weeks and months that I had to live through here 'down under' as an apprentice seaman aboard the full-rigged ship, SUZANNE,[15] under Captain Jürgens. Fully 99 days we lay down here off the Cape. That is a length of time for circumnavigating the Cape somewhat overdone even for hardened spirits. I do not know whether or not it is the record. But I do not want that sort of passage twice.

"There were no brace-winches on the old SUZANNE, and also no halliard-winches. Everything was still operated according to the approved 'Armstrong patent'; that is, strong arms must take the place of all mechanical aids. The least loved job was to hold thoroughfoot in the setting of the upper topgallant sail. There one sat with the thick topgallant halliard runner in his fist under the watermark bridge in front of the capstan, around which the others were running like circus horses. If then Rasmus swept over the railing with a real breaker, they might all high-jump and actually reach the spot where the man sat who held the thoroughfoot. Like iron, one clung to the halliard. Ice-cold, the entire flood washed away over one; and he was happy if, half strangled, he could just stretch his head above the gurgling water in order to spit out the salty stuff from mouth and nose. And meanwhile one must hold fast to that coil of rope to prevent its being washed overboard through the scuppers and whipped away. And always the cold! The fingers benumbed, the oilskin leaking, the wrists and the skin of the neck rubbed raw by the constant chafing of the hard oilskin, the hands split at the knuckles in deep, bloody cracks. The many salt washes ate

[15] J. F. Colton, *Windjammers Significant* (Flagstaff: J. F. Colton & Co., 1954), p. 8.

the wounds deeper. Therefore, after the loosening of the sails, everyone seeks to get the jobs of overhauling the lines up on the masts. Even if the ice-cold storm bites through to the skin, still a man is not washed onto the scuppers and drenched every 3 minutes. Naturally, all this does not go on without injuries and bone-breaking. At that time, our Second Officer, Bansen, ruined forever what was his pride and joy, his Greek nose. One day I had started to take the coffee kettles to the caboose, just as the command, 'Clear for the hawsers' rang out. That time, the speed of so many comrades running aft nearly caught me off guard. I had just stepped out of the shelter of our deckhouse when an immense wave broke roaring leeward over the bulwarks. Before I could get hold of the life-line, the heaving mass washed me away from it with both my kettles. The giant strength of the mass of water lifted up one of the heavy spare spars which lay lashed by chains to the main deck on the starboard side. The raging water washed me across the deck with both legs stuck out in front and rammed me like a wedge under the spar. I lay helpless locked fast with a yard or two of foaming sea water above me. I twisted and tugged; then I felt the spar settling back throughout its length. A frantic pain burned through my legs. All I remember is that the thought flashed through me: now your good bones are done for forever. Then everything grew black before my eyes. Fortunately, Captain Jürgens had seen my accident from the poop. Otherwise, I should have been drowned under the spar. At once all hands rushed to me, my comrades, and worked themselves through the roaring water to where they knew I must be lying. Ignoring their own danger, they dived into the icy flood, seized me, and tried to pull me out. No use: the spar held me with an iron grip. They had to work all together to lift up the spar with great hand-spikes; then they pulled me out of my heavy leather boots. Whether it was still worth while, no one knew. I lay in the arms of my companions without a sign of life as they carried me to my berth.

"The next thing I was conscious of was lying on the deck in my lodging — alone. From out there came the roaring of heavy seas. The SUZANNE was rolling madly from side to side. I had been thrown out of my berth by it. My companions were still on deck at the lines. Overpowering joy flooded through me when I discovered that, even though every separate bone in my body hurt, my legs would still hold me up. Sailor's luck!

"Where are they now, the comrades of those days? — The valiant Third, Speckensnieder (whale-cutter) Schmüdsch, has for a long time been a Channel pilot. Willi Rehse, my cousin, and Hein Brüllau, whom the sailors called 'Nauke' (Slim?), have both become Elbe-pilots. Ferdinand is captain of a dredger. But life did not deal with all of them so gently. Poor Louis lost a leg at sea, Hans Boysen died at Iquique, and our Willi Östergaard had to share the fate of so many seamen: years ago, he was lost without a trace. And our old Jan Israel with his great beard, who could curse so fearfully and Chilean-fantastically when racked by the cramps due to the continual dampness of our quarters — probably he, like our old sailmaker, has long since 'gone west'.

"But all those who, like myself, can still rejoice that our hard trade has left us hale and sound, will think back again and again to those days off the Cape. When drinking water ran short, we had to eke out with snow and rain water. Both were indeed well mixed with salt water. And the way our coffee and tea tasted of that still makes me shudder today.

"We have it better this time with the PEKING. Before we have reached 58 degrees south latitude the wind turns south, and later southwest. Scarcely 10 days after passing of the Le Maire straits, we are able to pass latitude 50 on 'the other side', going north. Before the stiff southwest breeze, I hold north in a straight course. Now we get further aid from the powerful drive of the Humboldt current, which flows northward along the Patagonian coast.

"Early on the fourth day after passing 50 degrees, the mountains of the West Coast come into sight, the snowy crest of Monte Osorno overtopping them all. Then, between steep rock walls and wooded mountains, we enter the bay of Valdivia, and an hour later our anchors rattle down in the harbor of Corral. Today is the 64th day of our passage since leaving the English Channel. The PEKING is at her destination."

The PEKING, whose outward passage to the West Coast, Captain Piening has described to us here, was built in January, 1911. Her present brilliant passage was one of many. When in 1912 at the International Congress For Insurance Of Transportation, which met in Baden, the premium on saltpeter shipped by sailer was raised about 30%, many believed that only the French vessels with their high state gratuities could endure the additional burden of the tax. However, the sailers of the firm of Laeisz proved the opposite to be true, as far as the German merchant and sailing vessels were concerned. The ships, the crews, and the organization of the Laeisz line remained in the running.

PART IV

FATES OF THE "FLYING P" LINERS

PART IV

FATES OF THE "FLYING P" LINERS

Chapter One: EARLY LOSSES

A fleet of sailers that, from the beginning of the shipping firm's activity to the present, has numbered 81 vessels could not, in the course of three generations, avoid some losses. Whoever has any conception of ocean voyages in sailing vessels will understand this to be unavoidable. There is no longer in existence any exact record of the place, time and cause of the loss of vessels in the early days of the firm. Of the 391-ton (gross) PATRIA,[1] it is noted: stranded off Mazatian in Mexico; of the 402-ton CAROLINA[2] and the 625-ton capacity HENRIETTE BEHN,[3] the only report is: "stranded in harbor". In what harbor these two wrecks occurred is no longer to be learned. PACHA,[4] 432-ton gross, was recorded as lost in 1876 or 1877; PALADIN,[5] 547-ton gross, was stranded in Mexico. Concerning the fate of the crews of these vessels, no news is available. According to an uncertain tradition,[6] a small Laeisz sailer of the early days disappeared without any report. It could perhaps have been the PACHA.

Concerning the metal sailers of later times, let us recall the decisions of Professor Laas. The first to be lost was the full-rigged ship, POLYNESIA, of 985 gross tonnage, built 1874. She ran aground off Eastbourne on the Channel coast,[7] on a return passage from Iquique. In the following year, 1891, the firm suffered two losses: PLUTO, 1,135 tons, and POTSDAM, 1,411 tons gross. PLUTO[8] had grown very old, built in England in 1862. The last news of her comes on July 7, from Valparaiso. After that, there is no record in existence except the mention of her loss. Apparently, it occurred on the return passage from Valparaiso. POTSDAM, built 1889, went aground on January 18, 1891, during a norther in the harbor of Valparaiso. The same fate overtook the PETSCHILI, 3,087 gross tonnage, built in 1903 during the World War.[9] On July 12, 1919, before Valparaiso, she was hit by a heavy norther and torn from her anchor. With a number of other vessels of various flags,[10] she was thrown up on the coast. The crew were saved.

On the Chile-passage, there are two especially dangerous runs, that around Cape Horn and that through the English Channel. In the region around Cape Horn, as we have heard in the description by Captain Piening, and shall often hear in the following accounts, the wind conditions are for the most part unfavorable to sailing vessels coming from Europe, and the seas are dangerously high. In the Channel, on the other hand, the Laeisz vessels several times came

[1] [In error: Sold in 1884 to G. Kindler, Rostock, Germany - EDITOR]
[2] [1881: Mazatlan, Mexico - EDITOR]
[3] [1885: Mazatlan, Mexico - EDITOR]
[4] [1877: Sold Spanish owners - EDITOR]
[5] [1883: W. Coast - EDITOR]
[6] [1863: INDIA Stranded, total loss. 1865, Nov.: REPUBLIC missing China Sea. 1870, Jan.: PERU total loss, China Sea. 1883: PALADIN wrecked W. Coast of Mexico. 1883: PAVIAN missing - EDITOR]
[7] [24, April, 1890 - EDITOR]
[8] [Sold, after collision to W. Maack, Rostock, Germany - EDITOR]
[9] [Error - EDITOR]
[10] [All German: 1 ship and 2 steamers - EDITOR]

to grief as a result of their unusual swiftness under sail, since captains of steamers that crossed their path did not think of the danger of collision because of the experience they had had with other sailers. Actually, the vessels of the Laeisz line have had most of their ill fortune in the Channel and in the neighborhood of Cape Horn.

As concerns the material side of the losses, let it be said that the vessels of the firm of F. Laeisz were self-insured and that because of the swiftness of their passage, which allowed on the average two out-and-back voyages a year between Europe and the West Coast, the profit, during the time of the successful saltpeter trade, could carry relatively heavy losses.

Chapter Two: TRIALS AND TRIBULATIONS

The fate of the Laeisz sailers lost or injured on the high seas by stranding, collision, storm, or burning, unrolls before us a chapter not only of the dangers of seafaring, but also of the ability and heroic courage of the captains, officers, and crews of the Line, so arresting and gripping that we should like to give the events as much as possible in detail. In so doing, we can rely chiefly on the accounts supplied by the Laeisz captains themselves, which are contained in the two books published by Fred Schmidt, *Captains Report* ("Kapitäne Berichten"), and *New Captain's-Reports* ("Neue Kapitäns-Berichte"). Further material may be found in the book, also published by Fred Schmidt, *Ships and Destinies* ("Schiffe und Schicksale"), and in Lubbock's *Nitrate Clippers*.

The vessels whose destiny will concern us, before the mishaps which came to them, had given years of service and had made many fortunate voyages and some even famous for their speed. One of these vessels was sunk 4 years after her building, but the others had a life-span of from 10 to 25 years or more.

We shall begin with the fate of the barque PARSIFAL, built in 1882, and follow the story in *Ships and Destinies*.

FOUNDERING OF THE PARSIFAL

Fate of PARSIFAL

On February 15, 1886, the PARSIFAL, under Captain Hilgendorf, the patriarch of sail navigation, had left the English harbor of Shields with 1,500 hundred tons of coal bound for Chile. On May 2, the vessel lay with a south wind a hundred miles southward of LeMaire straits in severe weather. The heavy rolling had set the cargo into motion. All the men were in the hold to trim the coal cargo in order to assure the vessel her former equilibrium. At 4:30, a terrifying sea hit the vessel. By 6 o'clock the lower yards were 6 feet deep in water. It looked as if the PARSIFAL would capsize. With a roar, the entire cargo slid to one side; the coal had shifted. Only the quickest action could avert a catastrophe, and Captain Hilgendorf decided instantly to cut the masts. Now the vessel lay a helpless wreck surrendered to the heaving of the sea. Even the bottom no longer remained impermeable: the water began to rise in the hold. When the rigging of another vessel came in sight, they gave the distress signal. Simultaneously, they embarked in the boats. With all their might, the men pulled toward the strange sailer; but, without having noticed their signal, the stranger held on her course and disappeared. In disappointment, the boats toiled back to the PARSIFAL. With difficulty, a few men succeeded in getting on board again. That was important, for in their haste, the boats had been incompletely provisioned. More food and water were taken over, for who knew how long the boats must fight against this storm that blew from shore before they could reach land? But in a short time the movements of the wreck gave warning of danger. If they did not wish to be drawn into the whirlpool, they must get away. Hardly a quarter of an hour later, the vessel went down. Now without hesitation, they pulled in the direction of the land. At the coming of dark, they set off rockets. Fate meant well by them this time. By half-past 7, they sighted a flare, evidence that their signal had been understood. Two hours later found them all in good condition on the English barque, SARAKA, which landed them in Cork, Ireland, on July 31."

STRANDING OF PALMYRA

Fate of the PALMYRA

The next vessel of the firm to be overtaken by fate was the PALMYRA, built in 1889. In June 1908, she was on her way to Chile under Captain Lessel. Concerning her stranding and the ensuing boat voyage of the Captain and his First Officer, Gustave Thiel, the latter told the story himself in *New Captain's Reports*, during his activity with the German Coastguard.

The first part of his narrative, we give in brief. The report of the boat-journey is so rich in adventure content that the reader will thank us to report most of this word for word:

The passage through the Atlantic was relatively fast and good. The difficult Cape Horn had been rounded, and the course lay north along the thousand islands and cliffs bordering the west coast of Patagonia, which belongs politically to Chile. A severe storm broke. On the basis of his reckonings, the captain estimated his distance from land at more than 100 nautical miles. He did not suspect his error even on meeting a steamer, although his First Officer thought they must conclude that they were on the regular steamer route along the West Coast, consequently in dangerous proximity to land for a sailer. Then suddenly the men of the PALMYRA saw themselves among cliffs against which the breakers were roaring. With a crash, the prow hit hard ground so that all on board were tumbled together. The PALMYRA was aground, and heavy breakers began to wash roaring across the deck. Getting her off was not to be thought of. The sole hope of rescue was her boats. With difficulty, 2 boats, the large one and a small one, were got into the water, the one with 15 men, the other with 6 men. The Captain and the First Officer remained on board. Of all those who went into the boats, not one came out alive. The gig, the smallest boat, was still on deck. For the 2 men remaining on the vessel, there began a sorrowful night. The next morning, the wind and sea were somewhat quieter, but the vessel lay dangerously on her side and it was time to leave her. The captain showed little inclination to go. Not until his officer reminded him of his family did he say, after a long pause: "Yes, Thiel, I have still a mother and a sister; for their sakes, I must go back home. I will think of them."

With difficulty, they succeeded in getting the gig into the water. Food and hand tools were put in, an axe, saw, hammer, and nails. Also spun twine, two table cloths that were to be used as sails, a mattress, wool covers, a generous supply of tobacco in a watertight box, coffee, matches, and the ship's papers. For orienting, there were only an old English chart of the Patagonian coast, and two small hand compasses. Before the coming on of dusk, the two shipwrecked men reached the shore, and were sheltered from the present emergency. When they looked out the following morning, they saw that, during the night, the PALMYRA had disappeared into the depths.

Now the two men were faced with the almost hopeless appearing task of finding the way from the place where they were stranded, whence far and wide no human creature was to be seen (In fact, as they learned later, they had been continually watched by Indians.), through an unknown waste of waters full of islands and of cliffs, to some port of rescue. The PALMYRA had gone aground in the Gulf of Trinidad somewhat below the 50-degree latitude. Now in Thiel's report comes the story of the second part of the adventurous boat journey and the final rescue.

". . . On the morning of the *eighth* day, we reached the coast again. The rain had lessened, the air became clearer, the sea swell began to fall. Only a long, high roller ran in from the northwest. What more should that portend? But why think so far ahead? We sat apathetically on the thwarts and pulled among cliffs and reefs towards a small rocky island. We had not slept for 72 hours, not for a minute. We were as in a dream. How we made a fire and prepared our coffee, I do not know, but you may believe me, it tasted good to us in spite of the water being brackish. Then we each ate a piece of hardtack, finished our milky coffee, and lighted our pipes. Indescribable comfort! How would it have gone with us without tobacco and pipes?

"A quarter of an hour later, we sat again at the oars and pulled southward. Our short pipes were smoking. After our coffee, we were as if born again. All weariness was wiped out. Only — not to lose any of the favorable weather! On ahead! At mid-day, a northwest wind came up and we set our sail at once. Luxuriously we ran with wind and oars over the long rollers. Then we succeeded in rigging up a second mast. Under both tablecloths, the gig looked quite stately; also the boat steered far better. Then some sort of high land came into sight on the port. More and more clearly, the outlines of a steep mountain range stood out — according to the map, Cape George at the entrance to the Nelson straits. Until night, we kept hoping to find a quiet bay under its protection, for now we were becoming aware of a leaden weariness. Again, we were to be disappointed. Soon the sunset left nothing good to be expected. A giant, glowing, copper shield, so sank the sun in a bank of blue-black clouds. The wind freshened rapidly. At about 6 o'clock, it was already whistling through our 'rigging' so that we had to take it down in order not to lose it. It was high time that we reached the shelter of land, for pitch blackness came racing on behind us. And behind it, drove our old friend of the PALMYRA, the northwester. What our arms could do, we put into our rowing. The cape rose heavily above us, like a dark mighty wall. A favorable current seemed to help us. Soon we stood to the east of the cape and pulled with all our strength against both wind and sea. Even so, the storm was already there. A squall chased us howling from above. Rain and hail fell rattling down on us. Only don't give up! Another 10 strokes, now another 5 . . . now I went to the bow, reached for the painter, ready to jump out and make the boat fast to a stone, a bush. The shore was within reach. A stab of wind struck me like a blow from a board — I fell into the boat. Around us was a bellowing as of a thousand steers. Hail and rain shut us in so thick we had to close our eyes. One of the terrible williwams had us in its grip, drove our boat irresistibly out from shore into the sea, which was now one seething mass.

"How a man can live through a night like the one that followed, I do not know. Certainly a wonderful urge to live is at work in the human being which gives him strength which he never suspected he had, streams of power, the source of which perhaps lies outside ourselves . . . only, the need must be there, the final need. If I have ever experienced what is called a hurricane, it was in these days. Squall followed on squall; the air was a compact mass of rain, spray, and hail. We pulled for our lives. If one of us missed 3 strokes, the gig started to slant to the blows, and that would have meant immediate overturning. In spite of all, we managed to hold the boat afloat through the valleys.

"After an especially hard hailstorm, all at once, morning was with us. As the rustling rain veils were drawn off to leeward, we saw to our astonishment that it was growing lighter. The sea around us was a whitish gray plain. Looking around, I realized that the hurricane, in spite of continuous desperate rowing had driven us into the middle of the Nelson current, and there was no sign that could give hope of a letting up. With undiminished fury, the storm raged on, and now the rollers grew wilder, the farther we drove to the southeast out of the shelter of the cape – to the southeast, where bristling cliffs and heaven-high breakers awaited us. Hours went by. Visibly, the wall rose higher before us, and we could feel how our strength was ebbing. Was this the end of all troubles? The thought came to me: how if in the shore opposite us there should be a channel opening? We could run in before the wind and be saved!

"When the pauses between squalls allowed a bit of free air, I raised myself carefully and looked across at the steely coast. Almost it seemed to me that I could discern an inlet eastward from our position. Quick, the chart! Right! Just here is the sign for a channel inlet. Nothing certain, for this coast had never been surveyed. Nevertheless, here was a hope – perhaps our last! For our endurance was coming to an end. We could hardly get through another night. . .

"The storm was already over us again in full force. Now it depended on our gathering together whatever of the will to live and of courage was left in us. Throughout more hours, we worked with a numb obstinacy. The hailstorms were often so thick that we could not see 150 feet away. Then again, a free vista would open and we have to acknowledge that all our bitter, bitter effort had brought hardly any result. And again, the next squall would howl around us, and again our hands would cramp about the oars. . .

"Daylight was beginning to lessen when we gauged the opening in the rock wall as a little southeast. But if now, after all, it were no channel-inlet at all, but only a little shallow bay, in which the rollers dashed full force? Then we were lost! But we had to take the risk. There was no longer any other way out. Our strength would not reach any farther. When we now turned the boat in from the sea, the Captain sat himself on the middle thwart with his weight forward, held his arms side-wise so that the oilskin spread out a little; I laid in the heavy steering-oar – and the race with death began. The flats of our backs made sail enough for the hurricane: with at least 5 knots, the boat ran forward toward the steel wall. But it was at worst a great relief that the fearful strain of the rowing had ceased.

"Higher rose the coast. Already we could see behind us the shimmering streak of the first roller of a swell. Tensely we stared ahead at the dark spot which had to be the inlet to a channel if there were to remain any hope whatever of a rescue for us. And now it seemed as if truly the longed-for way were opening. After a quarter of an hour, we could see it clearly: actually, there before us a door gaped open into the rock. Whether it led to a channel or a fiord was now immaterial; at least, quiet water would await us in there, protection from the merciless rage of the hurricane. Now the first projecting cliffs came into sight. Those breakers! Terrifying and grand at the same time! Now we could realize for the first time how fast we were shooting in. Everything hung on the rudder. I clutched the oars and looked neither to left nor right, for there the spray dashed heavenward when the mighty rollers broke on the reefs. A single instant of carelessness, and we would turn. The rollers grew steeper: each one drove us forward with the speed of a fast train. Whenever we were riding high on the crest, the belt of surf looked like a giant snow wall. Now straight ahead was a hatchway – the door to rescue out of this witches' cauldron! Around us was a roaring like the end of the world. Already we stood close before the entrance. Now we were seized by a frightfully steep, steely sea. I could feel giant fists tearing at the helm, trying to throw the boat crosswise. Just don't lose nerve now! Keep cool now! The waves drew us on with a motion like flying. Nearer came the glassy wall, lifted the stern of our boat until the keel hung at an angle of 45 degrees. This is the end, flashed through me. Then the crest fell away close behind us, the water rushed together yapping. The wave lost its strength, ebbed away under the boat. Still 1, 2 more long breakers — and all at once it was as if we had been carried into a closed room. The sudden stillness seemed almost uncanny. The boat floated in quiet water. We were through, we had made the entrance. . .

"The high cliff walls already lay in a gray twilight when we picked up the oars again and rowed farther into the bay. Our limbs were like lead, and our eyes seemed coals of fire. When we got out on land, we stumbled like drunken men. Right where we stood, we sat down on the stones. It seemed as if the rocks were swaying under us. We fell asleep where we sat. . . An ice-cold, rattling rain made us jump up. Outside there, we could hear the storm still raging. When the gust had gone by, we hauled the gig up under a clump of thick, overhanging bushes and built ourselves a 'tent'. Then we poured the water out of our boots, wrung out our stockings, and put them back on again. Sleep? That is a mistake, friend! First of all, we lighted our pipes again. Then we squatted in our 'tent', drew our wet covers over us, and smoked away in silence. Anyway, it was too cold to sleep. It must have been midnight when we heard the rain stop. We stretched our stiff limbs, started a fire, and made us some coffee, which refreshed us marvelously.

"But with the new day, interest in food returned. Our provisions had shrunk so that we absolutely had to keep the remainder for the final stretch. Therefore, we must find us mussels. After 2 hours, fortune smiled on us. And at last it was a sunny smile! We found a little bay in which there were mussel banks such as we had never yet seen. With our coal-tin full of mussel meat, we ate it all at 1 sitting. Without salt or seasoning, simply stewed in water, the mess tasted to us like ambrosia. It was the first time since Kalau that we had really been able to eat our fill. And then came the great weariness and demanded its right. Two days we remained in this nook of Paradise. High above the channel walls, the storm tore on with unbroken violence. Up in the mountains, it snowed; in the valley, it rained and the hail drummed. We did not quarrel with all this. In the morning, we gathered mussels, a generous supply for the entire day. With these, we prepared ourselves 3 warm meals. In the meantime, we sat in our rain hut, smoked, and talked of whatever we were moved to. Only, the eternal dampness made itself felt gradually in pains and swollen joints. And the nights were not fair. . .every 2 hours, we had to bail out the water; otherwise, the gig would have sunk here in the 'harbor'. Then we would squat close together again with the covers over our heads and doze. The cold would not allow real sleep.

"At about 3 in the morning, it was over. The wind had swung around into the northwest. So we set sail, and steered our course south-southwest. Quietly and evenly, our true gig carried us southward. About 5 o'clock, a white, flashing light came into view, the lighthouse of the Evangelista. We sat and stared in speechless rapture at the little point of light that blazed up and disappeared, blazed up and went out in regular alternation. It seemed to me as if my breast would burst. When it grew light, the entire tower stood out sharp against the horizon. Gradually, then, the islands appeared in the circle of our vision. With renewed energy, we pulled toward the goal that now seemed so near. Then we saw how there on the tower the Chilean flag was going up. They had seen us! Here, now, we allowed ourselves the last short pause for rest, while we consumed the remnant of our victuals: the last piece of hardtack and the last can of milk. We still had need for strengthening. Unnoticeably, the swell had increased. A glance to the northwest made us grab the oars again, for already dark scraps of torn storm-clouds came flying up. Under the pressure of her sails, the gig lay far over and threw a foaming wake from her bows. The islands were coming nearer fast. Then we saw that we had got into a strong southwest current, which was driving us with increasing speed onto a group of cliffs. There before us the spray dashed up white. Now and again it allowed us for a second a glimpse of some giant stone lurking there like an ocean monster. Without stopping to question, I pulled out my knife. A couple of quick strokes and both sails flew off. Down with the masts and grab the oars, unless we want to be dashed to bits by the surf in sight of the rescuers! It took the utmost effort to tear the boat past the cliff at a short 15 feet distance. In spite of the cold, sweat poured down our foreheads. But that was to be our last testing.

"Rounding an uninhabited island, we came fortunately to the mainland, but here we sought a landing place in vain. Here was a smooth rock wall some 1,100 to 1,200 feet long and stretching perpendicularly up for about 100 feet, on the summit of which we discovered a crane. Here the landing place seemed to be. But we still had to shout for almost a quarter of an hour before a head stretched out over the edge above us. He stared at us puzzled, cried 'Spera pocuuiiito' (Wait half a minute!), and disappeared again. Later, we learned that the watchers had seen us disappear into the surf. They believed that we had been drowned on the cliffs. Immediately after this, the entire population of the Evangelista was assembled on the cliff — 4 men! Quickly, they threw us a line. We made our boat fast to it and turned upward to the island. We were saved! Now, however, the fearful nervous tension of the time past avenged itself. I had to sit down on the first stone, while the tears ran down into my rough beard. . .

"Four lonely pillars of rock, the Evangelists, reach defiantly almost 200 feet out of the wastes of the Cape Horn sea towards a heaven almost always gray and louring. At their feet, rage against the wolf-teeth of the cliffs the almighty surges of the open Pacific. On the main island stretches up the lighthouse tower, a blessing to the seamen. Four men guard its warning light, employees of the Chilean government. We were received in the most hospitable way. Our first questions concerned our companions. No, they had seen no one. Since the lighthouse had been standing, we were the first shipwrecked men who had arrived there! But they knew exactly what we needed, the fine fellows. In ten minutes, there was a meal set before us — princely! Our stomachs seemed to have forgotten that such things existed as white bread, butter, eggs, sausage. Now — I was ashamed of the monstrous quantity that I stowed away inside me, and still I had no feeling at all of being full. After that, we could bathe. . . Warm!. . . I cannot describe what satisfaction that was. I doubt if anyone can express in words a thing like that. But when we looked into a mirror, we were startled. Was that what we had become? Those deathshead masks? Lord God! Then it would not have taken much more before the sea and the cold had conquered us. Suddenly, I was aware of every bone in my body. The men had given over two small rooms to us; in each stood a heavenly bed of llama skins. I sank down in, and it was beautiful beyond reality. A bed — warm — soft — and dry. Dry!. . . and I could not go to sleep in it. Lay all night awake, stared with wide-open eyes into the darkness and listened to the storm out there rattling the windows. The storm which could not get at us any more now. Fourteen days I had to stay in bed, had a pretty high fever, and also a painful foot trouble resulting from the long dampness. The Captain too complained of severe rheumatic pains in the legs, but was otherwise well. The 4 watchmen were sympathetic.

We had lived on the island 4 weeks when one morning the lookout called from the tower, 'El Vapor viene!' (The steamer is coming). The communication steamer of the government was in sight. Our hosts were quite excited when the steamer arrived at the rock wall. Then followed the taking up of provisions, fuel and material by means of the crane. And now the moment had arrived for us when we must part from our friends. The farewell was hearty. Unfortunately, we could leave the men nothing as a parting gift except our brave little gig. When the commandant of the steamer heard that we had come here from Kalau in this boat, he said just one word, 'Impossible!' Only more detailed accounts could convince him. Two days later, we walked into the port official's office in Punta Arenas and there made a report. At last we came to the German consul to make the clearing that the laws of commerce demand.

"In a high-hearted way, the Chilean administration now put their steamer, JUANITA, at our disposal for the search after our comrades. We were received in the most amiable fashion by her commandant, a German Chilean. With this vessel, we now scoured the Patagonian archipelago from the Magellan straits to the Stosch channel (north of the place of the wreck). Here we experienced a great surprise. One morning we sighted a ship's boat that was approaching us. As 'First', a man acquires an eye for his own boats; one look through the glass, and I could have sworn that this was our smaller boat that had stood on the port deck and that 4 sailors had pulled away in. Our excitement is easy to understand. Every hope sprang to life again! But then we recognized that it was manned by natives. The side walls had been broken amidships; the fellows had repaired it sketchily with boards. On a stone platform, a small fire was burning, around which 12 persons squatted, men, women, and children. The young ones were starknaked in spite of the cold, and seemed to feel happy that way. But the grown ones were clad very differently from their usual custom. Immediately, we recognized the clothing of our men. The leader of the band, who stood abaft and steered, had put on 2 thick blue jackets 1 over the other, also 3 pairs of stockings, and leather shoes, and above this had knotted several handkershiefs around his neck. (So the bodies of the drowned men had been dashed up on the land.) When we heard the people, they related to us exactly the procedure of the wrecking, of our landing, and what we had done as far as the Gulf of Trinidad. So unseen eyes had been watching our every step the entire time. Otherwise they certainly could not have seen.

"From Kalau, the place of the wreck, the JUANITA then steamed south again through the inner channel. I can only say it was a passage of dream-like beauty. Rock walls and snow peaks, primitive forests and glaciers and waterfalls, an endlessly changing panorama of gripping beauty and timeless solitude. That is Patagonia. It affected me strangely when we stood again at all the places where we had encamped. What a contrast! Then, half-starved, frozen to the marrow, damp, worn out; now, with the blessed certainty of having a good vessel under us, warmly dressed, well-fed. Civilization can no longer realize how wide a cleft lies between those 2 worlds: sated and hungry. It is possible to understand that only when a man has himself gone hungry. After a 23-day cruise, the JUANITA again ran into Punta Arenas. Eight days later, we began the journey to Hamburg on a German freighter. Of the 17 who had gone onto the sea in the large boat, nothing more was ever seen. They were among the missing, as so many others that the blue water has summoned before."

That was the fate of the PALMYRA and her men, which, because of her tragedy and the final saving of the two men, deserved to be fully told.

EXPLOSION OF THE POSEN

Fate of the POSEN

The Laeisz-sailer, POSEN, a full-rigged ship that until 1902, the year of the building of a newer and greater PREUSSEN, carried the latter name, was known for her good records in the saltpeter traffic. She was built in 1891, and in the fall of the year, 1909, was once more on her way to Valparaiso with package cargo and gunpowder aboard. On October 14, fire broke out on the vessel which could not be put out. The dangerous nature of her cargo forced a quick abandoning. On the same day, the crew was picked up in the mid-Atlantic by the English steamer, EARL OF CARRICK, and taken to Pernambuco in Brazil. The vessel was destroyed by the powder-explosion.

LOSS OF THE MIGHTY PREUSSEN

Fate of the PREUSSEN

The circumstances which led to the loss of the five-masted, full-rigged vessel, PREUSSEN, we can best follow with the aid of the records of the marine office of Hamburg, which in the line of duty undertook a detailed investigation. On October 31, 1910, under the command of Captain H. Nissen, the vessel had begun her 14th outward passage, bound for Valparaiso with a full load of coal and general cargo.[11] Besides her full crew of 48 men, there were two guests aboard, an academic teacher[12] of the school of navigation, Rostock, who was to participate in a deep-sea passage for the purpose of gaining information, and the marine painter, Chr. Rave.

In the North Sea, a very unfavorable wind was blowing, and it gave no indication of veering. Therefore, Captain Nissen kept the great ocean tug, PRESIDENT LEEUW, with the vessel to tow her into the Channel. In the late afternoon of November 5, the strait between Dover and Cape Gris-Nez had been reached; at 10, they passed the Royal Sovereign Lightship, therefore were standing almost directly south off the famous English watering place of Hastings. Long since, the top sails had been set for the assistance of the tug, and since a fresh breeze had come up out of the NNW, the PREUSSEN was making something like 9 knots. Unfortunately, it seemed as if the wind had an inclination to die down, and the visibility was growing poorer. Although it was not yet necessary according to marine law and custom, yet because of the lively traffic in this region, Captain Nissen ordered the fog signals given. As expected, the wind began to slacken, and the PREUSSEN lost speed rapidly.

Shortly before midnight, the command to cast loose was given to the tug. No sooner had the steamer, with a last friendly greeting from her whistle, disappeared into the darkness of the autumn night than the watchman on the forecastle of the PREUSSEN reported a light to starboard. Captain Nissen, who, with the Second Officer and the boatswain, stood on the bridge, had already noticed the light. Soon after, they could make out a second white light and a red light, the white a trifle diagonally above the first, the red between and a little below it. The meaning of those lights was unmistakable: a steamer was coming whose course cut across that of the PREUSSEN and that would have to come dangerously close unless it changed its direction.

For the chance of a meeting between a sailer and a steamer under such conditions, marine ordinance prescribed that the steamer must unconditionally yield way. Moreover, it must, if at all possible, forbear to cross before the bows of the sailer, but must rather pass her astern. The sailer, on the other hand, has the duty of keeping course and speed unchanged. This is the clear reading of the legal regulations for avoidance of collisions of vessels at sea. They are, when the weather is not too thick and only 2 vessels are meeting,

[11] [Bagged cement, bulk furnace coke, and general merchandise - EDITOR]
[12] [Dr. Budzies - EDITOR]

relatively easy to carry out. One has only to keep his lamps in order and stay on the alert.

On the PREUSSEN, the situation had been immediately recognized. The officer on duty at once sent a sailor to make sure that the green side-lamp toward the foreign steamer was burning clearly. The man called back that everything was in order. Now one had only to hold his course calmly; nothing further could be done here toward the clearing-up of the situation. The men on the bridge of the PREUSSEN stared tensely at the 3 lights of the stranger. With surprise, they saw that the necessary change of course had not begun; otherwise, instead of the red light, a green one would have appeared. The steamer needed to do nothing more than to alter her course to port, to the left side. Then nothing untoward could happen. The situation contained absolutely nothing difficult, nothing unforeseen. The youngest ship's officer should have been able to deal with it easily.

How, under these circumstances, it could come to a collision, is a mystery. Basil Lubbock, who, in his before-mentioned book, gives an account of the end of the PREUSSEN, passes over the collision in a few lines, without trying to find an explanation. Now, as a landsman, the event as such may be sufficient for him! But the seaman, and with him every friend of good ships, is pained by a completely causeless destruction of one of the few absolute masterpieces of the shipbuilding art. Certainly, as long as man shall follow the sea, there will always be loss of vessels. There are situations at sea which, in spite of the greatest coolness and insight, cannot be resolved. Bad storms, overpowering currents, fogs, reefs – these things and many others may bring a vessel to distress from which there is no way out. But here, where the steamer had only to make at the right time her simple passing maneuver, by which everything would have gone well, as in a thousand similar movements of vessels incidental to every day, what could have led to a catastrophe here will remain forever incomprehensible.

Moreover, the sworn testimony of those concerned on the crew of the steamer, given before the Board of Trade – the proper English authority – offers no explanation. On the other hand, it makes everything even harder to understand. For this document testifies that on the bridge of the steamer no young, uncertain, and worried beginner held watch. No! There on watch was a Second Officer experienced in service at sea, and beside him stood the Commander of the vessel, Captain Hemmings, in person! To be sure, there is a contradiction in the testimony of the 2 men: although they put out fog signals and thereby made evident that they did not consider the visibility good, they gave command to tear ahead at 17 knots – and that, crosswise of the Channel, the most active waterway on earth!

At the same time, the PREUSSEN was making about 4 knots. What happened was what so often occurred when the swift Laeisz sailers met a steamer whose command was unable to estimate the maneuverability and the speed of sailing vessels. English ship's officers and ship's commanders are never required – in contrast to ours – to serve on sailing vessels before they are allowed to take their professional examinations the passing of which puts into their hands the power over sailing vessels. They have done service only on steamers; so how can one expect that they will be able to appraise with sufficient exactness the speed even a small sailer can make under a certain controlling force of wind and what speed a great sailer of the nature of the PREUSSEN can develop? Herein lies the reason for so many disastrous collisions, and especially the fast P-Liners have fallen sacrifices to the errors of these foreign ship's officers who have been merely steamer-trained.

Nearer rushed the steamer onto the single light before her bows. After all, it was "only" a sailer — why should that require any special caution! At shortest distance, the BRIGHTON tried that maneuver so often tried by steamers and against the simplest rules of marine circumspection: she changed her course somewhat to starboard in order to tear past with all speed *across* the bows of the sailer. So came the collision.

The strong bowsprit of the PREUSSEN sheared away one of the two smokestacks and one of the masts of the steamer. The sharp bow of the sailer, raking past the side wall of the BRIGHTON, did severe damage to the bulwarks, the boats, and the boat davits. Unfortunately, the PREUSSEN also suffered considerable injuries: her jib boom broke, and the plates tore off the bow back from the bar stem and opened a leak of perhaps $16\frac{1}{2}$ feet, which reached under the water line. Gurgling, the water poured into the flapping crack.

Close behind the bar stem of every vessel, however, and diagonally through the body, is built a waterproof wall, the so-called collision-bulkhead. Its function is, in case of injury to the bow, to prevent the entire hold of the vessel from filling up. Here, this precaution was once again to prove itself good. To be sure, ahead of the partition, the hold filled in a few minutes. But the partition itself remained uninjured, the vessel kept afloat and, in spite of her hurt, was in no immediate danger.

By a neat maneuver in the last second before the shock, Captain Nissen had appreciably lessened the force of the blow. As soon as both vessels were free of each other, all sails on the PREUSSEN up to the topsails were furled and braced back. The steamer also lay motionless, her engines stopped. According to marine practice, the names of the vessels were now exchanged, those of their captains, their ports of departure and of destination, and help offered on both sides. Each, however, refused the help of the other. Since the captain of the BRIGHTON announced that, because of his severe injuries, he must return to his port of departure, Newhaven, Captain Nissen asked him that he send him a strong tug from there. The other promised it, turned away, and steamed slowly toward the north. Now he had time to proceed carefully!

Now the men on the PREUSSEN went to work with determination to clear up the tangle of ropes and sails on the forecastle. Meanwhile, they also checked to see if any water were getting into the hold behind the partition. But the work of the Bremerhavn shipbuilders was to be trusted, the vessel held tight. After just 2 hours, the English tow-steamer, ALERT, arrived, and after a short discussion, declared herself ready to tow the PREUSSEN to a port of rescue.

Captain Nissen, after a discussion with his officers, had decided to go to Portsmouth with his vessel, in order to have her repaired there. The hawsers were given to the towboat, the English pilot, who had come with the ALERT, came aboard, and the passage began.

However, it was not long before there occurred the second in the series of unfortunate circumstances that were to seal the fate of this splendid sailer: the wind turned into the west, exactly opposite to the course of the PREUSSEN! It was soon evident that the ALERT was far too weak to oppose the force of the wind in that powerful rigging. Captain Nissen saw that he would have to renounce his purpose. After a short discussion, he gave the order to turn and head for Dover, which the pilot also recommended as the most likely haven. In the sad gray light of early morning, they passed the sky-reaching chalk cliffs of Beachy Head and through flag signals gave the station on top the commission to notify the shipping firm by telegraph of what had happened. With difficulty, the ALERT rolled on toward the east with the wounded giant in tow. It was still 48 nautical miles to Dover.

Again the weather cut through the reckoning. It grew rough quickly. Out of thick rain-shrouds, whistling squalls were driving in from the west a rapidly rising sea, in which the PREUSSEN began to pitch heavily. The jib boom is an extremely important fulcrum of the entire rigging of a sailer. When it is destroyed with all its means of gravitation, one dares not urge on the vessel too much for fear of endangering the masts. A glance at the barometer and at the western sky showed plainly threatening symptoms. Therefore, after careful reflection, Captain Nissen decided to anchor the vessel at some suitable spot and wait for better weather. He did not want to risk those still sound masts.

Some 18 miles west of Dover, there projects from the English coast a sandy tongue of land, the promontory of Dungeness. Here many sailers had already found shelter from western storms; here Captain Nissen decided to anchor his vessel until the weather should grow quieter. But again his purpose was denied. When they had reached a suitable anchoring place and the heavy chains were rumbling through the hawsers, a squall struck, attacking the high rigging until the network of standing and running gear roared like a giant organ. The powerful blow tore the first chain over the capstan like lightning — A ringing jerk! The end, bolted down deep below in the vessel had torn loose, and clattering, chain and anchor chased away into the foaming water of the Channel. Freed from this fetter, the mighty force that was bearing down on the vessel and the rigging tore at the second chain. Even the best brakes could not now hold back capstan and chain. Faster and faster, the chain ran out until it too — tearing loose from its fastenings with a tremendous jerk — disappeared overboard. Without any restraint, the PREUSSEN drove east before the raging wind. Now there was only 1 way out: to run into the nearest port of refuge. That was Dover.

In the times of the great sailing-ship commerce, there always lay, at various points along the Channel, a series of tow-steamers and waited for the great seabirds who might need help in the narrows. And when the wind was high, then the higher-powered rescue tugs especially held themselves ready, which are appointed to bring aid to vessels in need. So in the neighborhood of the PREUSSEN, towing boats were at hand, ready to hook on, and since ALERT could not possibly bring the great, hard-to-handle vessel into port alone, Captain Nissen took on also the tugs, ALBATROSS and JOHN BULL. Two steamers ahead, the third fast to her starboard side, the 5-master drew towards Dover. Standing off in a wide curve, they steered for the east entrance of the harbor. In a few minutes, they would have been inside, in quiet water, in security. The foremost tug was already between the breakwaters, when once more the malice of the storm struck disastrously. A squall of great violence broke, and it was soon evident that the combined strength of the 3 steamers was not sufficient. The PREUSSEN'S rigging had a windsail for which they were no match. First inchwise, then faster and faster, the PREUSSEN drove along with the 3 tugs, sidewise toward land. Suddenly, the towline of the JOHN BULL broke with a snap. This seemed to rob the pilot of the last remnants of his calmness and presence of mind. He went wild in a series of senseless commands. Captain Nissen saw that he would have to interfere if he wanted to save his vessel.

At his orders, the German seamen sprang to work. A couple of lightning strokes, and the PREUSSEN floated free from the restricting towlines of the other 2 tugs. More quick commands like trumpet notes above the roaring of the rain and the whistling of the squall — With amazement, the English saw a line of giant sails unfolding. Already the yards flew about, the 3 after-topsails came square, and what those watching would never have thought possible happened before their eyes: the great sailer began to glide back away from the dangerous narrows into deeper, freer water! Another minute, and the PREUSSEN would have been saved. Again the malicious Fate which this master seaman carried on his vessel entered the lists. A hidden buried reef caught the forward part of the vessel and held it fast. A rock over which the sound PREUSSEN could perhaps have escaped! But now when the water in the forward hold made the fore part of the vessel draw deeper, the lurking block had been able to reach the bottom of the vessel. It was enough to hinder her course. Meanwhile the storm forced about the long body with the towering rigging above it, and only a little later, the PREUSSEN settled firmly onto the reefs of Crab Bay. It was 4:30 in the afternoon.

By 8:30 in the evening, there were already 20 inches of water in the hold; in the high surf, the vessel had sprung a leak. In the pouring rain, the crew worked at the bilge pumps with all their might, warding off further incursion of the water. To the rhythmic gulping and sucking of the pumps, the beautiful old coast chanties rang out across to where freezing reporters shook their heads in amazement. Again that night, when it was high water, the attempt was made by 2 tugs to get the vessel free. In vain! About 3 o'clock, the towlines were cast off. About 4 in the early dawn of November 7, the carpenter determined the depth of water in the hold at 12 feet. But still Captain Nissen would not give up his vessel.

In the morning, the storm let up somewhat. At once, the Captain went ashore and engaged 2 strong pump-steamers, by the help of which he hoped at next high tide to get the PREUSSEN afloat. But all of the weather-devils seemed to have sworn enmity against the intrepid man: 1 hour before noon, a new southwester came roaring in against the coast, which drove the surf in high cascades over the defenseless vessel. Under such conditions, not even the most foolhardy rescuer could have had hope for the PREUSSEN.

The attempts of the English lifeboat crews of Dover to bring help to the PREUSSEN'S crew deserve recognition. But what they could not understand was that the German seamen were fully determined not to accept aid. Obviously, they trusted more to the plates of their surf-bound vessel than to the most modern salvage vessels. Also the men of the St. Margaret and Dover life-saving stations made the most comradely attempts on behalf of the stranded men. But in this, too, the PREUSSEN'S crew had no interest. They remained stubbornly on board, took a hearty lunch now and then, and went on working undiscouraged at the saving of their vessel.

In Hamburg, the news of the threatening loss of the PREUSSEN drove to consternation all the friends of seafaring. In detailed news items, the great dailies, even far inland, expressed a concern over what had happened that went far beyond the measure normal in Germany, a sign that the fame of the Flying-P had spread far beyond professional circles. A telegram from the Kaiser came to the Laeisz home:

> "Deeply moved by the news of the mishap to the five-master, PREUSSEN, I wish to express my warmest sympathy to the shipowners. I should be glad to receive direct news of the outcome of the catastrophe, especially concerning the fate of the gallant crew, which disturbs me greatly."

With this evidence of the sympathy in the homeland, 'Mr. Erich Laeisz came aboard with 3 associates, the firm's inspector, Captain Opitz, and 2 of the most experienced of the insurance agents. When the dispatch from the Kaiser was read to the assembled crew by their shipowner, the roaring hurrahs with which the seamen gave thanks for the interest shown by the leader of their country demonstrated by the color and strength of their shouting that every worry in *that* direction would be happily resolved.

But in regard to the vessel, unfortunately, the worst fears were to be justified. It soon had to be recognized that the PREUSSEN was lost beyond saving. Now with decision and clear vision, Captain Nissen went at the salvaging of the equipment and the cargo entrusted to her. The largest part of the piece goods lading from between decks was lowered onto lighters and tugs. Piles of boxes, filled with every conceivable object of use in daily life, huge rolls of packing paper, thick rolls of cloth and carpet, enamel and glassware, — then more than a hundred pianos — all was set uninjured on the land. A new storm interrupted the salvaging. Then winter set in and made all further work impossible.

Not until spring could the work be resumed, but up to the time of the war of 1914, a significant part of the valuable rigging as well as of the deck planks was recovered. During the war, a portion of the wreck broke off and disappeared. The first German steamers to pass Dover saw not the 5 formerly proud masts of the PREUSSEN reaching for the sky, but only the stump of 1. A few years later, the last remains of the greatest square-rigger of all time had disappeared. The surges had carried them away.

In the process over the collision, the shipping firm had had to lay the entire blame in plain terms to the BRIGHTON by reason of the action of her command. Therewith went the blame for the stranding that followed. A complete legal satisfaction — but that could not bring back the PREUSSEN alive on deep water. She had gone as a sacrifice to stubborn ignoring of duty and to narrowmindedness.

PISAGUA-OCEANA COLLISION

Fate of the PISAGUA

A second collision took place in the English Channel on March 16, 1912, between the Laeisz sailer, PISAGUA, homeward bound from Chile with a load of saltpeter, and the English P and O Steamer, OCEANA, outward bound to Bombay. The collision occurred at 4:30 in the morning; the PISAGUA ran into the side of the steamer and made 2 great holes in her forward part. At the first alarm, the crew of Lascars on the OCEANA seemed to go into a panic, but the officers and the white portion of the crew soon got order again, the life-savers were given out and the boats lowered quickly. Unfortunately, the first boat overturned, and 7 passengers and several of the crew were drowned.

Soon after the collision, the mail steamer, SUSSEX, from Newhaven, came past and took on 27 passengers and the greater part of the crew. The rest were brought to land by lifeboats from Newhaven and Eastbourne. The captain, the pilot, and 16 of the officers and crew remained on board while the OCEANA herself was towed by a tug and another steamer. The idea was to get the vessel to land, but from the first, it became clear that she might go down at any moment, so that the captain and his men had to go aboard the towboat. All efforts to bring the OCEANA into shallow water before she sank were in vain. About 10 o' clock in the morning, she went down in 12 fathoms of water 6 nautical miles from the coast. In the meantime, the PISAGUA continued on her way eastward, her fore part full of water, seriously injured in the foremast and rigging. Fortunately, the Channel water remained smooth, and with the help of two towboats she reached an anchorage in the harbor of Dover still in the afternoon of the 16th of March.

Investigation showed extensive injuries to the PISAGUA, and the vessel would have sunk like stone if the forward bulkhead had given way. The injury was closed off, and the precaution also taken of keeping the towboats at hand. On the 23rd of March, the steamer MAGDALENA BLUMENTAL came alongside and took off 2,150 tons of saltpeter. Then the vessel was grounded in the tidal reservoir so that she lay dry in low tide. The prow was provisionally repaired, and on April 3, the PISAGUA left Dover, towed by the two tugs, ROLAND and SIMSON, in the direction of Hamburg. She reached there on April 6, and was sold by the firm[13] in her damaged condition as a wreck. By the marine court, the OCEANA was declared at fault for the collision, and her owners had to pay for the damage to the PISAGUA.

The OCEANA had among her cargo a quantity of silver bars and minted gold. The salvaging of this treasure by diving lasted from March 18 until July 5. After that, the wreck was broken up as a danger to shipping.

PANGANI RUN DOWN

Fate of the PANGANI

Only 10 months after the collision of the PISAGUA, on January 28, 1913, the PANGANI, built in 1902, outward bound for Chile, was run into at night off Cape La Hague in the English Channel by the French steamer PHRYNE. She sank so rapidly that there was not even time to get 1 boat out. Of her 34-man crew, only the First Officer and 3 seamen were saved. The investigation assigned the sole blame to the PHRYNE, but because of the beginning of the World War, the trial before the marine court was never carried out, and in 1920, it was annulled by the French government. All 3 collisions, of the PREUSSEN, the PISAGUA, and the PANGANI, took place, in the course of only 3 years, in the English Channel, which is the most thickly traveled piece of ocean in the world. In no case did the fault lie with the German sailer.

BURNING OF THE POTOSI

Burning of the POTOSI

A peculiar fate awaited the mighty POTOSI, built in 1895. She too was caught by the outbreak of the World War, in Valparaiso. In 1920, she was sold to the shipping firm of Vinnen in Bremen, but on the basis of the Versaille terms had to be surrendered to France. During her internment in order to make her unseaworthy, the vessel was seriously injured by her own crew, since it was feared that the English would pay no heed to the Chilean neutrality, but would take away the German vessels. The entire steering machinery and most of the standing and running gear had to be renewed, which the French would have nothing to do with. Since they also had no sailors to man her, they let the vessel lie there, and she was finally taken over by the Chilean firm of shipowners, Gonzales, Sofia, and Company in Valparaiso, repaired, and renamed FLORA. The Chileans used her at first for passages between various ports on the West Coast of South America, but in 1925, they decided to send her to Europe with a saltpeter loading.

On March 30, 1925, for the first time in more than 10 years, the POTOSI ran into Hamburg again. It was justly said, however, that by the war-time injuries she had been made a "lame bird", for whereas earlier her complete passages from Chile to Hamburg took only around 80 days, this time she had required 110 days to get as far as the English Channel. For the return passage, she took on

[13] [To S. L. Christensen, Sandefjord, Norway - EDITOR]

(1) (NAUTICAL PHOTO AGENCY)

Steel Ship PINNAS, 1,946 Gross Tons

(2) (NAUTICAL PHOTO AGENCY)

Steel Ship PINNAS
27, April, 1929
Boat From The Chilean S. S. ALFONSO On Its Way To Take Off The Crew
25 Miles Southwest Of Diego Rameriez

(F. LAEISZ)

PREUSSEN (1)
After Collision In English Channel

5,800 tons of coal and coke at Cardiff and went out to sea on July 13 of that year, bound for the Mejillones off Iquique.

After that, she was not heard of for months until the owners of the freight received a cable message from Buenos Aires that an Argentine steamer had met the vessel on fire and with her course set for land, on September 16, at 45 degrees south and 66 west in the Atlantic Ocean not far off the coast of Patagonia. In this condition, the POTOSI went to anchor on September 18, in the Gulf of St. George off Comodoro Rivadavia the Argentine petroleum port. Pumps from the government oil-fields were brought under the vessel in haste, and it was hoped that the fire could be put out or at least brought under control by blowing steam into the hold. In spite of desperate work with the steam pumps, the fire spread more and more. On October 1, there came 2 explosions of coal gas, the mainmast fell over, and it was now clear to the captain that further efforts were useless. He tried to land the vessel on the beach, but this plan had to be given up because the fire was becoming so hot that no one could endure to stay on board any longer. The rudderless vessel drove out to sea again, and somewhat later was met 25 nautical miles south of Comodoro Rivadavia driving along half burned up. Since in this condition it was a danger to shipping at night, it was sunk by shellfire from an Argentine battleship.

PINNAS ABANDONED

Fate of the PINNAS

The sinking of the full-rigged ship, PINNAS, in the Cape Horn Sea on April 26, 1929, is thus described in *Ships And Destinies*. The PINNAS set out on January 21 from Hamburg for Chile with a cargo of coke and cement. After 73 days, she had passed the Le Maire straits. "Then on April 12, a severe storm came up. From day to day, the weather grew worse and the sea higher. But on the 18th morning at 8:30, it let up suddenly – in a few minutes, the hurricane-like wind fell off to a light breeze. That is the most alarming thing that a sailer can run into. Whereas, before, the vessel kept a balance of wind in her sails, now she was driven here and there by the sea without support. Imagine iron masts 164 feet high, with tons of weight of yards and sails swinging back and forth 50 degrees or more to either side! No rigging can stand that. After 10 minutes, the foremast and the mainmast broke shortly above the deck, unluckily fell astern and shattered the main pumps. Soon after, the cross bars broke close under the topsail yards. As a miracle, no one on the deck was killed. But now the wind started up again. A few minutes after the catastrophe, the first hurricane squall was howling over the wreck, a rattling hailstorm darkened the day. The violence of the storm kept rising. Before the following day, the barometer had fallen to 718 mm. On a deck continually washed over by breakers, the crew worked like madmen to protect the hatchways against the sea by lashing timbers across them. No one now remained uninjured. With bleeding hands, bruised limbs, and battered bodies, they worked night and day with the expending of all their strength. Each one knew it was a question of bare life. If the hatchways did not hold, then in that weather everything would be over in minutes! Two of the brave ship-boys were so beaten by the sea that they had to be carried into the cabin. The others went on fighting tirelessly. At last, on the 23rd, the storm became somewhat less. With fresh courage, they rigged up an emergency lateen yard and set a sail on the stump of the mizzen mast so that the wreck should lie somewhat steadier in the sea. Out through the air went the seamen's call for help, SOS, Save Our Souls! But not until the following evening came back the answer, friendly and comforting. The 5,000-ton

Chilean passenger steamer, ALFONSO, which was landing its passengers in the Magellans, promised to come to their aid. At the same time came the message of the English steamer, SCOTTISH STRATH, which was steering toward the place of the accident.

"Already at midnight, the lights of the Chilean were sighted. On the next morning the Englishman was to make the attempt to take the wreck in tow. Yet it was to come out otherwise. That same night, the wind rose again. By morning, it was full hurricane strength. The deck seams of the PINNAS began to open. The crew worked constantly at caulking the vessel. In spite of this, the water rose steadily in the hold. Now the SCOTTISH STRATH sent word that she could not make steam ahead into these waters. She would pass on word of the position of the PINNAS to the English steamer, BRITISH PEER, whose arrival was awaited for the evening of the 27th. To wait 2 more days — on a rudderless and leaking wreck — in this storm? They accepted it like men and undiscouraged toiled on at the leaky deck seams.

"On the 26th, the hurricane raged on with undiminished force. On the morning of the 27th, it looked bad for the PINNAS. The quantity of water in her hold had pressed her deep into the sea. Breaker after breaker dashed foaming over the wreck, and no notice had been received from the BRITISH PEER. In yet another way, the situation had grown more drastic — in the east toward the north, at perhaps 25 nautical miles distance, the needle-sharp ridges of the rock island, Diego Ramirez, were clearly visible behind the foam-wall of sky-high surf. Storm and sea were driving the wreck inevitably toward those reefs. In the face of this desperate situation, the ship's command decided to give up the hope of salvage and to desert the wreck. After hours of sacrificial labor in constant danger of death, one boat of the ALFONSO made her way twice through the maddened sea. (The steamer had held herself nearby ready for help of this sort for 36 hours.) From the jib boom, the German sailors let themselves fall into the boat of the brave Chileans or leaped into the waves. All 25 men of the crew were saved. The PINNAS disappeared into the gray veil of a hailstorm and was never sighted again."

RECAPITULATION

In the years between 1886 and 1929 (PARSIFAL was lost in a storm in 1886 and PINNAS in 1929), the Laeisz sailers had made some *thousands of passages*. This makes 3 collisions, 2 losses through storms on the high seas, 3 groundings, and 1 burning.[14] The burning of the POTOSI took place under a foreign flag, and the grounding of the PETSCHILI off Valparaiso was occasioned by the overlong compulsory lying at anchor during the war. However, painful is the loss of a brave sailor and of a good vessel, the comparison shows that, in relation to the total number of passages, the losses were kept within comparatively narrow limits. Only 2 crews,[15] that of the PALMYRA on the West Coast of South

[14] [Three collisions, 2 storm losses, 11 strandings, 1 burning, and 3 missing, a total of 20 losses making something less than 25% of the total fleet - EDITOR
Besides these, the following were also lost: In December, 1896, POTRIMPOS stranded at Ilwaco, Columbia River, Washington. PERGAMON has been missing since May, 1891. On 28, November, 1913, PITLOCHRY was sunk by the S.S. BOULAMA in the Channel. On 16, March, 1923, PEIHO stranded near Cape San Diego, Straits of Le Maire.]

[15] [Five crews. Nothing was ever heard from those on board REPUBLIC, PAVIAN, or PERGAMON - EDITOR]
Note: There were other channel Collisions: PREUSSEN ex POSEN was 1. PASSAT, Capt. E. Muller, was run into by the French S.S. DAPHNE off Dungeness on 25, August, 1928, and again, when commended by Capt. Hans J. Rowher, of the English S.S. BRITISH GOVERNOR near the Royal Sovereign Light Vessel on 25, June, 1929. Both times she was able to make port.

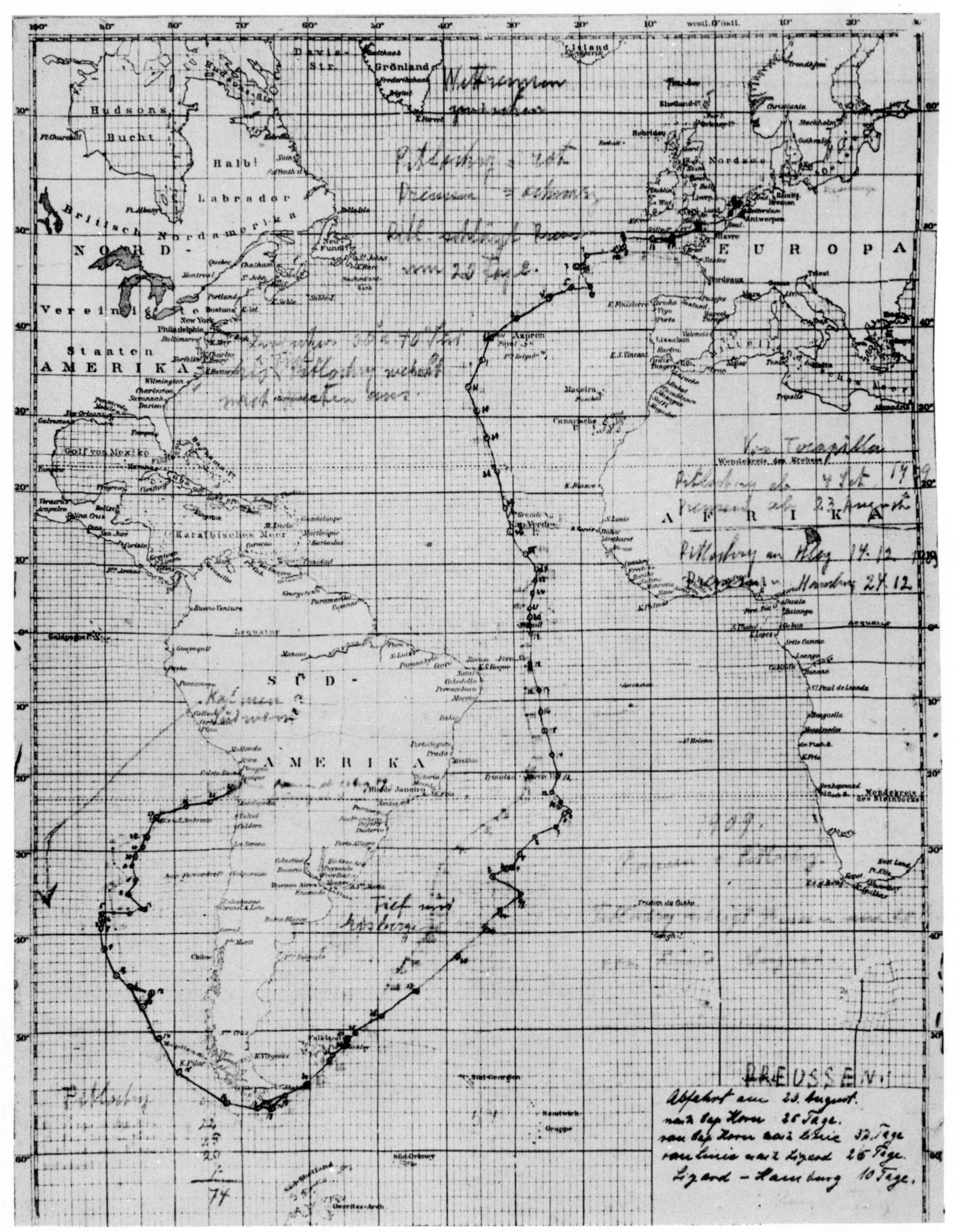

(Capt. Robert K. MIETHE)

Race Between PITLOCHRY (74 Days) And PREUSSEN (94 Days)
Topocilla - Hamburg In 1909

(1) (F. LAEISZ)

Hamburg

(2) (F. LAEISZ)

Musikhalle

(1) (F. LAEISZ)

St. Pauli Landing Stage

(2) (F. LAEISZ)

Deutsche Werft Reihersteig

(F. LAEISZ

Hamburg Sailing Ship Harbor
1906

America and that of the PANGANI in the English Channel found (except for a few rescued) death in the waves.

It is refreshing, in these days when individual iniative is rare, when free enterprise is no longer understood, and when businesses spring up around us almost overnight and fade out as soon, to hark back to those far-off days of the 19th Century and to reflect that with a small hat factory in Hamburg, Germany, started by a carpenter's grandson, the foundations of the virile and enterprising House of Laeisz were laid. It is, also, a pleasing reflection and a source of inspiration that, while time works many changes, in all these 131 years it has not stopped this undertaking nor altered its personal character. Through such examples we may maintain our faith in the future of mankind.

EDITOR

— End —

A LIST OF THE MASTERS OF LAEISZ SAILING VESSELS 1839 TO 1941

COMPILED BY THE EDITOR FROM PARTICULARS SUPPLIED BY THE FIRM, FROM VESSEL LOGS, FROM INFORMATION GIVEN BY MASTERS, AND FROM OTHER SOURCES

Master	Vessel	Notes	Date
Ahrns			
	PARCHIM		1903-1909
Allwardt, M.			
	PERA		1906
	POMMERN		1906-1911
Bahlke, C.			
	POLYNESIA		1882-1885
	POTRIMPOS		1887-1890
	POSEN		1901-1902
	PISAGUA		1902-1903
Bannau, J. H.			
	PAPA		1880-1882
Becker, Gustav A. H. H.			
	PAMELIA		1909
	PARCHIM		1910
	PAMIR		1912-1914
Benecke, H. T.			
	ADOLPH		1860-1862
	PACIFIC		1862-1863
Betzendahl, A.			
	PELIKAN		1912
Blöse, C. F.			
	PAPA		1870-1880
	PLUTO		1886-1889
	POTSDAM	1891: Stranded at Valparaiso, Chile, during a Norther	
Boysen, A. T.			
	PANDUR		1880-1889
	PIRAT		1893-1894
	PAPOSO		1894-1896
Brockhöft, Carl M.			
	PIRNA		1914
	PRIWALL		1921-1924
	PASSAT		1924-1925
	PAMIR		1926-1928
	PARMA		1929-1931
Buchwitz-Schachtel			
	HENRIETTE BEHN		1875-1879
Burgdorff, P. C.			
	PANAMA (2)		1874-1876
	PARADOX		1878-1886

Master	Vessel	Notes	Date
Christiansen, C. F.			
	INDIA		1860-1862
	PERLE		1864-1879
Clauss, Robert			
	PAMIR		1929-1930
	PADUA		1930-1932
			1935-1938
	PRIWALL		1932-1934
Dahm, R.			
	PAMELIA		1907-1908
	PISAGUA		1909-1911
Dehnhardt, H. A.			
	PAMELIA		1891-1898
	PERSIMMON		1899-1902
	PISAGUA		1903-1908
Diederichsen, H. J.			
	ROSA Y ISABEL		1867-1869
	PYRMONT		1869-1879
Diederichsen, V. B.			
	RICARDO		1867-1870
Dumneicher, Th. M.			
	PRINCESS		1873-1874
Dunseicher, E. Th. M.			
	HENRIQUE THEODORE		1864-1880
Eck, J. H.			
	PINNAS		1909-1911
	PENANG		1911
	PEIHO		1912-1913
Eckhardt, C.			
	PONAPE	1914: Captured by H.M.S. MAJESTIC	1914
Ehlert, L. H. C.			
	PATRIA		1863-1868
Ehlert, Wilhelm Johann			
	PIRNA		1913
	PAMIR		1913
	PINGUIN		1914
Elverts, C.			
	REPUBLIC		1862-1864
Feddersen, F.			
	ADOLPH		1857-1858
	PACIFIC		1860-1862
Feddersen, Thom.			
	PERSIA		1862-1869
	DON JULIO	1870, 30, Nov.: Seized by French.	1869-1870

Master	Vessel	Notes	Date
Frömcke, C.			
	PAMELIA		1904-1905
	PERA		1905-1906
	PEIHO		1906-1908
	PISAGUA		1908
	POTOSI		1909-1911
	POMMERN	Became insane	1912-1913
Früdden, J.			
	PARNASS		1888-1889
	PARCHIM		1889-1891
	PISAGUA		1892-1893
Gerke			
	PENANG		1914
Grapow, C. J. M.			
	PUCK		1883-1888
Grapow, M.			
	PONCHO		1891-1892
	PARCHIM		1892-1893 1902-1903
	PROMPT		1893-1901
Hahler, F.			
	PLUTO		1886-1890
Hamm, H.			
	PEIHO		1914-1921
Hamm, J.			
	PAMPA		1908-1910
	PONAPE		1911-1913
Hans, Albert B. W.			
	PINNAS		1920
Hansen, G. L.			
	PAQUITA		1881-1887
Hass, Fr. A.			
	MERCEDES		1869-1881
Hauth			
	PRIWALL		1937-1941
Heinrichsen, J.			
	NEPTUN		1862-1863
Hellwege, E. H.			
	PONCHO		1887-1889
	PAMELIA		1889-1890
	PERA		1890-1893
	POTRIMPOS	1896, Dec.: Stranded, Wash., U.S.A.	1895-1896
Hellwege, H. E.			
	PATAGONIA		1879-1886
Hildebrandt, C.			
	PERA		1907-1910

Master	Vessel	Notes	Date
Hilgendorfl, Robert			
	PARNASS		1883-1884
	PARSIFAL	1886: Foundered off Cape Horn.	1884-1886
	PROFESSOR		1887
	PIRAT		1888
	PERGAMMON		1888
	PALMYRA		1889-1893
	PLACILLA		1893-1894
	PITLOCHRY		1895
	POTOSI		1895-1901
Hirsch, F.			
	PIRAT		1895-1897
			1898-1901
Holst			
	PARMA		1926-1928
Holtzmann, A.			
	PERIM		1912
Hörmann, C.			
	LOS HERMANOS		1864-1866
Horn, Heinrich			
	PAPOSO		1898-1902
	PESTALOZZI		1902-1903
	PERSIMMON		1903-1908
	PAMIR		1908-1911
	PITLOCHRY	1913, 28, Nov.: Run down by Br. S.S.BOULAMA in Channel and sunk. All hands saved.	1911-1913
Hoyer, Ferd.			
	DON JULIO		1867-1869
Jacobsen, Th. H.			
	HENRIQUE THEODORE		1867-1869
	COSTA RICA		1869-1870
	PRINCESS		1870-1872
	PACHA	1876: Lost	1872-1876
Jäger, E.			
	PAPOSO		1894
	PARCHIM		1894-1895
Jakobs, J.			
	PARCHIM		1895-1899
Jansen, A.			
	PRINCESS		1870-1869
	PATRIA		1870-1873
	PANDUR		1877-1880
Jensen, J. E.			
	PESTALOZZI		1892-1896
	PLUS		1897-1898
	PAMPA		1898-1899

Master	Vessel	Notes	Date
Jessen, C. V.			
	PALMYRA		1897-1902
	PITLOCHRY		1903-1906
Jörgensen, N. P.			
	PALADIN	1883: Wrecked W. Coast Of Mexico	1880-1882
Junge, F.			
	PROMPT		1902-1906
	PETSCHILI		1908-1909
	PANGANI	1913, 28, Jan.: Run down off Cape De La Hogue by Fr. S.S. PHYRNE. Master and 29 men lost. Chief Officer and 3 hands saved.	1909-1913
Jürss, Max Jürgen Heinrich			
	PAMPA		1911-1913
	PIRNA		1913
	PAMIR		1914-1920
	PRIWALL		1920-1922
			1925-1928
			1935-1936
	PINNAS		1922-1925
	PEKING		1928-1931
	PASSAT		1931
	PADUA		1933-1935
			1938
Kähler, F.			
	PLUTO		1890
	PLUS		1892-1896
Kaiser, H.			
	PELIKAN		1914
Kayser, H.			
	PERGAMMON	1891, May: Missing with 21 hands all told.	1890-1891
Keppler, W.			
	PIRAT		1902
Kleist, P.			
	PEIHO	1923, 16, Mar.: Stranded near Cape San Diego, Straits Of Le Maire.	1922-1923
Klyhn, C.			
	PERLE		1879-1881
Kolcklöser, T.			
	PUDEL		1860-1870

Master	Vessel	Notes	Date
Lehmann			
	PINNAS	1929, 27, April: Dismasted and abandoned off Cape Horn.	1928-1929
Lessel, G.			
	PROMPT		1906-1907
	PALMYRA	1908, 2, July: Stranded on Wellington Is. Capt. Lessel and Mate saved, 20 drowned.	1907-1908
Lottge, N.			
	REPUBLIC	1865, Nov.: Missing in China Sea.	1864-1865
Lütjens, J. T. A.			
	PATRIA		1868-1870
	PARNASS		1878-1880
Mathiesen, F. E.			
	PROFESSOR		1869-1871
Miethe, Robert Karl			
	PROMPT		1905-1906
	PAMPA		1906-1907
	PITLOCHRY		1908-1911
	PAMIR		1911-1912
	POTOSI		1912-1920
Müller, Eilert			
	PASSAT		1926-1928
	PEKING		
Neumann, G.			
	PROFESSOR		1886-1888
	PAPOSO		1890-1893
	PERA		1894-1897
Nielsen, A.			
	PANAMA (2)		1870-1874
Nielsen, H.			
	PACIFIC		1863-1864
Neimeyer, R.			
	PATAGONIA		1873-1879
Niemeyer, R.			
	ROSA Y ISABEL		1870-1880
Niemeyer, R.			
	PANAMA (2)		1876-1880
Nissen, C. A. H.			
	MERCEDES		1867-1869

Master	Vessel	Notes	Date
Nissen, J. Hinrich H.			
	PARCHIM		1898-1901
	PITLOCHRY		1902
	POTOSI		1903-1908
	PREUSSEN	1910, 7, Nov.: Stranded after collision with Br. S.S. BRIGHTON in Channel and lost on N. Foreland, England.	1909-1910
	PEKING		1911-1914 1925-1926
	PERKEO	1914, 8, Aug.: Captured by H.M.S. Cruiser off Dover, England.	1914
	PARMA		1921-1923
	PAMIR		1924-1925
Nissen, H. W. B.			
	HENRIQUE THEODORE		1867-1870
Oellerich, Heinrich A. G.			
	PINNAS		1914-1920
	PEKING		1921- 1923-1925
	PEIHO		1921-1922
	PAMIR		1925
Oetzmann, A.			
	PARCHIM		1909-1910 1910-1911
	PERSIMMON		1911-1912
	PENANG		1912-1913
	PINNAS		1913-1914
	PEKING		1914-1921
Ohlsen, P.			
	PROFESSOR		1880-1886
Ohlsen, P. F.			
	PONCHO		1881-1887
Opitz, F.			
	PESTALOZZI		1884-1889
Opitz, Paul E.			
	PARADOX		1886-1889
Paulsen, E.			
	PALMYRA		1903-1906
	POSEN	1909, 14, Oct.: Exploded and sank in the S. Atlantic. All hands saved.	1906-1909

Master	Vessel	Notes	Date
Petersen, Boye R.			
	PESTALOZZI		1896-1897
	POSEN		1897-1901
	PREUSSEN		1902-1909
	PINGUIN		1913-1914
Petersen, Detl.			
	PROFESSOR		1872-1880
Petersen, P.			
	PLUS		1902-1904
	PALMYRA		1906-1907
	PEIHO		1908-1909
Petersen, W. H.			
	PERSIA		1864-1870
Piening, J.			
	PAPA		1865-1870
	PERSIA		1875-1877
	HENRIETTE BEHN	1885, Nov.: Stranded Mazatlan, Mexico. All hands saved.	1879-1885
Piening, J. Hermann			
	PEKING		1926-1928
	PADUA		1928-1930
Piper, Otto P. J.			
	PEIHO		1913-1914
	PASSAT		1914-1921
			1922
Poetcher, H.			
	PLUS		1906-1908
Pohlig, W.			
	PENANG		1913-1914
Prützmann, C. M. E.			
	PAPOSO		1897-1899
	PAMPA		1899-1902
	PETSCHILI		1902-1905
	PAMIR		1905
Radfan, W.			
	PINNAS		1912-1913
Ravn, Hans J.			
	POMMERN		1914-1921
	PASSAT		1922-1925
Reimer, W.			
	PESTALOZZI		1903-1904
Reimers, H.			
	PITLOCHRY		1907
Reimers, W.			
	PAMELIA		1906-1907

Master	Vessel	Notes	Date
Reitmann, J. N. A.			
	PATRIA		1880-1882
	POLYNESIA		1887-1890
Rohwer, Hans J.			
	PINNAS		1925-1928
	PARMA		1928-1929
	PASSAT		1929-1931
	PEKING		1931
Saltzkorn, E.			
	SCHILLER		1858-1859
Schacht, H. J.			
	PLUTO		1881-1886
Schaer, Walter			
	PAMIR		1930-1931
Schimper, H. O.			
	PESTALOZZI		1898-1899
	PARCHIM		1899-1901
	PISAGUA		1902
Schlepp, F.			
	PIRAT		1901
Schlüter, G.			
	PANAMA (1)		1864-1868
Schlüter, G. H.			
	ROSA Y ISABEL		1882-1884
	PROMPT		1887-1889
	PALMYRA		1892-1894
	PITLOCHRY		1895-1902
	POTOSI		1901-1903
Schmidt, H.			
	POSEN		1894-1897
Schmidt, J.			
	PAMELIA		1899-1903
	PANGANI		1903-1905
Schmidt, O.			
	PARNASS		1888-1890
	POTRIMPOS		1891-1894
	PLACILLA		1894-1901
Schommartz, O.			
	PADUA		1940
Schröder, H. F. M.			
	PYRMONT		1879-1882
	PAVIAN	1883: Missing	1882-1883
Schröder, W.			
	PLUS		1898-1900
	PAMPA		1902-1905
Schwaner, J. H.			
	POLYNESIA		1877-1879

Master	Vessel	Notes	Date
Schuberg, C.			
	PADUA		1926-1928
	PRIWALL		1928
Schultz, C. W.			
	PATRIA		1873-1880
Schütt, A.			
	POSEN		1903-1905
Seemann, J. H. M. C.			
	REPUBLIC		1861-1862
	LOUIS KNIFFLER		1863-1868
Seemann, J. H. W.			
	INDIA	1863: Stranded. Total loss.	1863
Siemer, H. A.			
	PIRNA		1910-1911
	PENANG		1911-1912
Shepp, J. F.			
	PAPOSO		1902-1903
Spliedt,			
	HENRIQUE THEODORE		1880-1882
Steineck, J.			
	PAMPA		1892-1897
Steinicke, C. J.			
	PROFESSOR		1880-1881
	PLUS		1885-1890
Sternberg, A. W.			
	PERSIA		1875-1877
Teschner, Alex.			
	PIRAT		1894-1895
	PALMYRA		1895-1896
	PERA		1897-1904
	PETSCHILI	1919, 12, July: Stranded and lost in a Valparaiso Norther.	1906-1907 1909-1919
Thedens, J.			
	ROSA Y ISABEL		1880-1882
	PIRAT		1883-1886
Thedens, J. P. M.			
	POLYNESIA		1879-1881
	PARSIFAL		1881-1884
Thomsen, P. M.			
	CAROLINA	1881: Stranded during a hurricane at Mazatlan, Mexico.	1867-1881

Master	Vessel	Notes	Date
Töepper, H.			
	PARMA		1923-1926
	PRIWALL		1930-1931
Truelsen, T.			
	PERU	1870, Jan.: Lost in China Sea.	1862-1870
Visser, J. J.			
	CARL		1840-1847
Von Hacht, C. J.			
	PUDEL		1856-1860
Wendler, Johannes Th.			
	PIRNA		1907-1910
	PASSAT		1911-1914
Wendt, H. Richard			
	PADUA		1938-1940
Wenzel, F.			
	SOPHIE & FRIEDERICKE		1857-1860
	PANAMA (1)		1862-1864
Wienefeld, F. C. H.			
	PONCHO		1893-
Winter, L. H.			
	COSTA RICA		1860-1868
Wist, A.			
	PEIHO		1909-1912
	PELIKAN		1913
	PARMA		1914
	PELLWORM		1924-1925
Wolf, Fritz			
	PIRNA		1911-1912
	PARMA		1912-1914
Wunderlich,			
	PROFESSOR		1871-1872
Wunderlich, J. W. G. V.			
	COSTA RICA		1868-1869
	PANAMA (2)		1870-1887

DR. PAUL ALBERT ROHRBACH

Dr. Paul Albert Rohrbach, Ph. D. and Theol. D., was born 29, June 1869, in Irgen, Livonia, Russia. After majoring in geography, history, and theology at Tartu University, Dorpat, Russia, he emigrated from the Balkan States to Berlin, Germany. From 1897 onwards he traveled widely, visiting most of the areas of the Earth with, perhaps, the single exception of Australia. From 1903 to 1906 he was Commissioner of Immigration in Southwest Africa. He is distinguished by a large number of writings on theology and World politics and was active in bringing his books up to date until his death in the summer of 1956.

Married in 1897, his wife was his life-companion, co-worker, and secretary to the end. Their eldest son is Ministerial Councilor in the Bund's Ministry Of Nutrition in Bonn. A second son is Professor of mathematics in Mainz. Of two daughters, one lives in Munich and the other, Mrs. Willi Ganssauge, resides in Hamburg.

CAPTAIN J. HERMANN PIENING

Captain J. Hermann Piening was born 3, July, 1888, in Hamburg, Germany, and, at the age of 16, went to sea. After serving in various German, English, Norwegian, Australian, and American sailing vessels he passed as Mate. Then, through Captain Opitz, then Marine Superintendent of Reederei F. Laeisz, he obtained a berth as 3d Officer of that Company's PETSCHILI. Later, he passed his Master's examination with high honors and followed as Chief Officer in PARCHIM, PONAPE, PINGUIN, and PRIWALL. During World War I, he served as a Lieutenant in the Naval Reserve. As a U-Boat watch officer he was cited with the E. K. 2 and the E. K. 1, and finished the War as Executive Officer of the U91.

Following the War, between 1926 and 1930, Captain Piening commanded the 4-masted barques PEKING and PADUA with distinction and then, in succession, had the S.S. PUMA and motor vessels PIONIER, PELIKAN, PONTOS, PYTHON, PALIME, and POMONA. In 1936 he was called into the marine inspection department of the firm.

Once more he was caught in the toils of War where he was badly wounded while serving as a Commander, Naval Reserve, in Crete. Nor was that all, for World War II, cost the Pienings both sons, one with the Infantry in Russia and the other while serving in the Luftwaffe.

CAPTAIN A. E. (FRED) SCHMIDT

Captain A. E. Schmidt, Master Mariner and free lance writer, sailed in F L and other craft of various nationalities including AMY TURNER, CITY OF BOSTON, CROWLIN, and OMAHA. Sometime after passing his tickets with high honors, he became ill and, thus, spent the World War II period as instructor in nautical schools for the merchant marine. He has been at sea since 1955.

Captain Schmidt ranks as one of Germany's foremost marine historians, having written numerous articles, more than 8 books, and translated others. Among his books are "Alle Mann An Deck", "Brauche Der Seeleute", Kapitansberichte", "Neue Kapitansberichte", "Peter Ramien" (Novel), "Schiffe Und Schicksale", and "Sklavenschiffe".

THE TRANSLATOR

DR. ANTOINETTE GREENE SMITH

Dr. Antoinette Greene Smith, Ph. D., was born in New Haven, Connecticut, U. S. A. She is a graduate of the Troy, New York, High School, received her A. B. at Cornell University, Ithaca, New York, in 1906, her A. M. in 1907, and her Ph. D. in 1910. She majored in English and German and was a member of French and German clubs. During 1907-1908 she was an instructor at Wells College, Aurora-On-Cayuga, New York; from 1910-1920 was Associate Professor at Elmira College, Elmira, New York; and followed this experience with 14 years as Professor and Head of the English Department at Olivet College, Olivet, Michigan, teaching German occasionally.

For Dr. Smith, the years of teaching were interrupted by marriage to Dr. Charles Cecil Smith, pastor of the Olivet Congregational Church, St. Paul, Minnesota. Following his death in December, 1940, she became head of a department at Schauffler College, Cleveland, Ohio. From 1943 to 1947, she served as Instructor at the University Of Minnesota after which she became Assistant Professor at Arizona State College at Flagstaff, Arizona, during the years 1947-1951.

Dr. Smith's academic career has been interspersed with experience in other walks of life such as that of book salesman, real estate, and ventures into retail fields. In addition, she organized the Southwest Workshop And Conference in the summer of 1950 and was its Director in 1950, 1951, 1952, and co-director in 1953. She has been Assistant Editor and Editor of J.F. Colton & Co. since 1955.

INDEX

A

B

C

D

E

F

G

H

M

N

O

P

Q

R

T

U

V

W

HAMBURG

180° West Länge 170°
160°
150°
140°
130°
120°
110°
100°
90°
BRITISCH AMERI
VEREINIGTE STAATEN
VON
AMERIKA
San Francisco
Portland
Victoria
Seattle
Olympia
C. Mendocino
Wilmington
San Diego
Guaymas
Mazatlan
Acapulco
New Orleans
Mobile
Charleston
Galveston
GOLF VON MEXICO
Galapagos I.
Sandwich Ins.
Honolulu
Hawaii
Fanning I.
Christmas I.
Malden I.
Starbuck I.
Marquesas I.
Samoa Ins.
Tuamotu od. Niedrige Ins.
Gesellschafts Ins.
Cook I.
Tongatabu
Mangareva I.
Pitcairn
Oster I.
Sala y Gomez
Kermadec I.
Chatham I.
Letzte Reise „Potosi"
unter deutscher Flagge.
DEUTSCHES SCHIFF „Potosi"
aus Hamburg
von „ „
am 4/7 14
nach „Valparaiso"
angekommen 23/9 14.
13/9. Signal mit „Adolf Vinnen"
von Hamburg nach Santa Rosalia
84 Tage in See. Alles wohl.
180° West Länge 170°